Drive Ireland

Dreoilín
PUBLICATIONS

Drive Ireland

DRIVE IRELAND is published by Dreoilín Specialist Publications Limited, Tankardstown, Garristown, County Meath, Ireland.
Telephone: +353 1 8354481   e-Mail: info@dreoilin.ie

Trade enquiries to Butler Sims Limited. Tel: +353 1 406 3639
Distributed by Gill. Tel: +353 1 500 9500

First published in March 2017

ISBN 978-1-902773-31-5

A CIP record is available for this title from the British Library.

Design by Alan Pepper Design.
Set in Helvetica Neue Light by Alan Pepper Design and printed by IVS, Galway.

See us on Facebook

Contents

INTRODUCTION

A personal journey through the best of Ireland

Welcome to Ireland! You have arrived in a very special place and my aim is to share with you some of the many places that have delighted and inspired me in many years of exploring this ancient island. This is not a guide book detailing every tourist attraction you might ever want to see. Rather it is my own personal journey, my own likes and preferences, the places I would like to share with my friends, and hopefully, having experienced them with me, you will want to share them with your friends in the future.

Included are trips in all corners of Ireland for this is an incredibly varied island with a range of experiences to be enjoyed, unmatched, I believe, anywhere else. As well as my favourite places you'll also find details on many unexpected detours and suggestions for some great things to do that will make your time in Ireland doubly memorable.

So let's get started by my telling you what you need to know about Ireland's past to help you understand the places, the landscape and most of all, the people you will encounter.

Bob Montgomery

A BRIEF HISTORY OF IRELAND

The Tara Brooch is a Celtic brooch made between 650 and 750 AD. It was found in 1850 near the seashore at Bettystown, County Meath.

In Ireland history is everywhere and even the most limited knowledge of this island's history will increase your enjoyment of the places that you will come across in your explorations. It's for this reason that I've included this brief history with a view to making sure that you get the maximum enjoyment out of your travels in Ireland. And don't worry if the thought of a history lesson turns you off – Hopefully it will entertain and inform, and certainly not bore you.

You'll also notice several 'history' pages spread throughout the pages of this guide. Where they appear they are relevant to the places being described, weather it be about Ireland's first aviator (Harry Ferguson) or the pirate queen (Grace O'Malley) who controlled shipping along Ireland's west coast throughout her lifetime and went 'face-to-face' with Queen Elizabeth I, these pages are intended to increase your enjoyment of the places associated with them.

IN EARLIEST TIMES

Its estimated that humans first arrived in Ireland around 10,000 years ago, relatively late in European terms. Farming was certainly carried out here around 4,000 BC marking the beginning of the Stone Age. It was not until around 300 BC that the Iron Age warriors known as the Celts made their first appearance in Ireland from mainland Europe. Their arrival marked the beginning of a period that helped shape the subsequent history of Ireland and the Irish language and many of Ireland's great myths and legends originate from this time.

CHRISTIAN IRELAND

In the mid-5th century, following the arrival in Ireland of St. Patrick and other Christian missionaries, Christianity began to take root and supplanted the previous pagan religions. By around the year 600 AD Ireland had become a land 'of saints and scholars' where Latin, Greek and Christian theology was studied in the many monastries established throughout Ireland. This golden age produced many of the finest metalwork's, carved stone crosses (High Cross) and most of all, the fabulous illuminated manuscripts such as the famous Book of Kells and the Book of Durrow that are today world-famous. The Book of Kells and the Book of Durrow can today be seen in Trinity College Library, Dublin, and the many golden objects of the period can be viewed in the National Museum of Ireland. Neither should be missed on any visit to Ireland.

THE VIKING KINGDOM

This golden age began to suffer raids in the late 8th century and into the 9th century from the Scandinavian warriors known as Vikings. They founded several settlements including Ireland's first city at Waterford and also the city of Dublin in 988 AD. One thing that I have learned in my travels though out Ireland is that their influence was far wider than I had imagined and spread though out the entire country. In time, the Irish chieftens organized against the invaders and following the Battle of

Clontarf in 1014 AD, Viking influence faded gradually from the island leaving many reminders of their presence here.

THE NORMANS ARRIVE
The arrival of the Normans in the 12th century was perhaps the key event in Ireland's history and led to 800 years domination by Anglo-Norman influences.

The Normans consolidated their presence in Ireland by building walled towns, castles and churches, while at the same time also increasing agriculture and commerce in Ireland.

After King Henry VIII declared himself head of the Church in England in 1534 AD the Irish Parliament declared him King of Ireland in 1541 AD. From that time until the late 17th century, an official English policy of 'plantation' led to the arrival of thousands of English and Scottish Protestant settlers. The most successful plantation occurred in Ulster, and from then onwards, sectarian conflict became the common theme in Irish history.

The Penal laws introduced in the 17th century disempowered Catholics, denying them the right to take leases or to own land above a certain value, and outlawing Catholic clergy, forbidding higher education and entry to the professions, and imposing oaths of conformity to the state church, the Church of Ireland. During the 18th century the Penal Laws were eased but by 1778 Catholics held only about 5% of the land in Ireland.

THE 1798 REBELLION
In 1791, inspired by the French Revolution, an organisation called the United Irishmen was formed with the ideal of bringing Irish people of all religions together to reform and reduce Britain's power in Ireland. The United Irishmen were the inspiration for the armed rebellion of 1798. Despite attempts at help from the French the rebellion was brutally put down and in 1801 the Act of Union was passed politically uniting Ireland with Britain and forming the United Kingdom.

In the year 1829, one of Ireland's greatest leaders Daniel O'Connell, known as 'the great liberator' was instrumental in getting the Act of Catholic Emancipation passed in the British Parliament in London. He succeeded in getting the total ban on voting by Catholics lifted and they could now also become Members of the Parliament in London. O'Connell then attempted to overthrow the Act of Union and re-establish an Irish parliament in Dublin. O'Connell's non-violent approach to this task was not supported by all, and in any case, his efforts were soon overshadowed by the worst disaster and greatest tragedy in Irish history – the Great Famine.

THE GREAT FAMINE
When blight (a form of plant disease) struck potato crops nationwide in 1845, 1846 and 1847 disaster followed. Potatoes were the staple food of a grow-

Below: The Scandinavian warriors known as the Vikings founded several settlements in Ireland including Waterford and Dublin.

The statue of Daniel O'Connell, 'The Liberator', looks down on the destruction of central Dublin in the Easter Rising of 1916.

ing population at the time, and the blighted potatoes were inedible with the result that with no alternative food, people began to starve to death. The response of the British government also contributed to the disaster - while hundreds of thousands of people were suffering from extreme hunger, Ireland was forced to export abundant harvests of wheat and dairy products to Britain and further overseas. Between 1845 and 1851 some two million people died or were forced to emigrate from Ireland. The population of Ireland pre-famine of approximately 8 million has never been approached since. It was this tragic event that began Ireland's long history of emigration with the majority of Irish emigrants going to the United States of America.

CHARLES STEWART PARNELL

Charles Stewart Parnell (1846-91) was the next politician to offer an effective challenge to Britain's rule in Ireland.. At the age of 31 he became leader of the Irish Home Rule Party, which became the Irish Parliamentary Party in 1882.

While Parnell did not achieve Home Rule (or self-government), his efforts and widely recognised skills in the House of Commons earned him the title of 'the uncrowned king of Ireland'. Brought down by a divorce scandal, Parnell represents one of the great 'what if's' of Irish history.

In Ulster in the north of Ireland the majority of people were Protestants. They were concerned about the prospect of Home Rule being granted as they would be a Protestant minority in an independent Ireland with a Catholic majority. They

favoured the union with Britain.

A Home Rule Bill was passed in 1912 but crucially it was not brought into law. In Northern Ireland the majority of the population were Protestant and they favoured the continuance of the Union with Britain. The Unionist Party, lead by Sir Edward Carson, threatened an armed struggle for a separate Northern Ireland if independence was granted to Ireland. The Home Rule Act was suspended at the outbreak of World War One in 1914. Many Irish nationalists believed that Home Rule would be granted after the war if they supported the British war effort. John Redmond the leader of the Irish Parliamentary Party encouraged people to join the British forces and many did so, however, a minority of nationalists did not trust the British government and this was to lead to one of the most pivotal events in Irish history, the Easter Rising.

THE EASTER RISING

On April 24th (Easter Monday) 1916, armed rebels, seized key locations in Dublin. Outside the GPO (General Post Office) in Dublin city centre, Padraig Pearse read the Proclamation of the Republic that declared an Irish Republic independent of Britain. Battles ensued with casualties on both sides and among the civilian population, as well as the destruction of the city centre due to British shelling. The Easter Rising ended on April 30th with the surrender of the rebels.

While the majority of the public was actually opposed to the Rising, public opinion soon turned when the British administration responded by executing many of the leaders and participants in the Rising. All seven signatories to the proclamation were executed including Pearse and Connolly. Two of the key figures that were involved in the rising and who avoided execution included Éamon de Valera and Michael Collins. In the December 1918 elections the Sinn Féin party led by Éamon de Valera won a majority of the Irish based seats of the House of Commons. On the 21st of January 1919 the Sinn Féin members of the House of Commons gathered in Dublin to form an Irish Republic parliament called Dáil Éireann, and unilaterally declared power over the entire island.

THE WAR OF INDEPENDENCE

What followed is known as the 'War of Independence' when the Irish Republican Army – the army of the newly declared Irish Republic – waged a guerilla war against British forces from 1919 to 1921. One of the key leaders of this war was Michael Collins and in December 1921 he was one of the signatories of a treaty agreed by the Irish and British authorities. But the details of the Treaty were to split Irish public and political opinion. One of the bitterest sources of division was that Ireland should be divided into Northern Ireland (6 counties) and the Irish Free State (26 counties) established in 1922.

CIVIL WAR

The result was a bitter Civil War from 1922 to 1923 between pro and anti treaty forces, with Collins (pro-treaty) and de Valera (anti-treaty) on opposing sides. The consequences of the Civil war can be seen to this day where the two largest political parties in Ireland have their roots in the opposing sides of the civil war – Fine Gael (pro-treaty) and Fianna Fáil (anti-treaty). Collins was to die in an ambush during the Civil War and after it came to an end a period of relative political stability followed.

NORTHERN IRELAND

Under the Government of Ireland Act of 1920 that created the Irish Free State, the Parliament of Northern Ireland was created. The Parliament consisted of a majority of Protestants and while there was relative stability for decades this was to come to an end in the late 1960s due to systematic discrimination against Catholics.

1968 saw the beginning of Catholic civil rights marches in Northern Ireland which led to violent reactions from some Protestant loyalists and from the police force. In 1969 British troops were sent to Derry and Belfast to maintain order and to protect the Catholic minority. However, the army soon came to be seen as a tool of the Protestant majority by the minority Catholic community. This was reinforced by events such as Bloody Sunday in 1972 when British forces opened fire on a Catholic civil rights march in Derry killing 13 people. An escalation of paramilitary violence followed with many atrocities committed by both sides. The period of 'the Troubles' came to an end with the Belfast (or Good Friday) Agreement of April 10th 1998. It is estimated that between 1969 and 1998 well over 3,000 people were killed by paramilitary groups on opposing sides of the conflict.

Since 1998 considerable stability and peace has come to Northern Ireland. In 2007 former bitterly opposing parties the Democratic Unionist Party (DUP) and Sinn Féin began to co-operate in government together in Northern Ireland.

Signs of our history are to be found wherever you go in Ireland, hopefully, the foregoing will lead you to a better understanding of them and their place in the Irish landscape.

Members of the Irish republican Army moving up Dublin's Grafton Street during the Irish Civil War.

A WORD ABOUT MAPS

"A map says to you, 'Read me carefully, ollow me closely; doubt me not,' It says, 'I am the earth in the palm of your hand. Without me, you are alone and lost.'

And indeed you are. Were all the maps in this world destroyed and vanished under the direction of some malevolent hand, each man would be blind again, each city be made a stranger to the next, each landmark become a meaningless sign-post pointing to nothing"

WEST WITH THE NIGHT
by Beryl Markham

In this day of GPS navigation, when even your smartphone can act as a map to guide you, what relevance, you may ask, have old fashioned maps? Actually, I think they have more revelance than ever. Personally, I have a great love of maps and many of the places detailed in this Guide were first discoiverd by my studying the relevant maps with great care. Maps have always been part of my life. My father was a keen private aviator and there was always a stock of maps kept in his 'flying' briefcase. Those maps fascinated me and with a childish curiosity that I would later recognise in the paintings of NC Wyeth I would examine them for hours, imagining what the landscapes were like and what places hid behind the strange-sounding names.

That curiosity led me through rally navigation when I acquired a more of less complete selection of the Ordnance Survey half inch maps essential to that sport at the time. As the years passed my map collection grew and it was to this collection that I first turned when I was asked by MichaelMcAleer of the *Irish Times* to contribute a series about 'Great Drives' to the Motoring section of the paper.

For the next nine years, maps and their study were an integral part of my searches for 'Great Drives' in all corners of this island. The plan was simple, at a time when motoring was becoming highly regulated, to find roads that could bring a smile to a motorist's face, either through the beauty of the landscape through which they passed or the associated history or better still, through both. The same plan has been followed in the selection of places in this Guide. I've tried to include the places that I especially love either for their inherant beauty or their history or some interesting connection they might have.

In writing the guide, there are a number of maps I would like to recommend. The first is a useful general map of the entire country. This is the Ordnance Survey Ireland Driving map and can be the only map you need. But if you really want to know the country then you need the Ordnance

Survey Discovery Series. There are 89 of these maps covering the entire country and I'm certainly not recommending that you need the lot of them. But if you're going to spend your time in, shall we say, County Kerry, then the purchase of sheets 70, 71, 83, 78 and 84 would certtainly add enormously to the places that you might discover during your stay.

Finally, something different. There are a series of hand painted maps called The Fir Tree Series of Aerial Maps of Ireland. They have been created by Cartographer and Artist Richard Chandler. They offer a true birds-eye view of the landscape and give a wonderful idea of the landscape and what to expect.

All of the above with the exception of the Fir Tree Series are available from Eason's stores throughout the country. For the Fir Tree Series see **www.themapcentre.com**.

MAKING THE MOST OF THE GUIDE

This Guide will prove useful to motorists who want to visit places that are interesting, or just plain beautiful, or historic, or maybe all three! What it will do is arm you with pertinent facts about the places you visit and hopefully direct you to the things and places that I've found it worthwhile to visit on my travels through this fascinating island.

Use it to plan your trips but remember this is Ireland, and the greatest joy is in the diversions and discoveries you make for yourself along the way. The best holidays in Ireland begin by setting out with a plan to go to somewhere or to see something but then to let yourself be diverted along the way by the things you come across that take your fancy. So allow plenty of time and do interact with the locals. We're a friendly race and our traditions welcome the traveller. I'll be surprised if, when the memories of the places you've visited have all but faded, the memory of the people you encountered along the way will be strongest in your memory.

The bulk of the Guide is taken up with 33 areas I recommend visiting. Virtually any of these places could occupy you for your entire holiday but probably you'll visit several of them. I strongly suggest you buy one or two of the maps we've recommended in the section 'A Word about Maps'. Using any of these maps will make your holiday so much more complete.

In some cases you'll notice that the section on a particular place or attraction is foillowed by a recommendation. There are three 'levels' of recommendation:

Recommended
Highly recommended
Very highly recommended

These are self-explanatory but don't be put off if an entry in the Guide has no recommendation. They're in the Guide because I found them interesting and worthy of a visit. It's the exceptional ones that merit one of the levels of recommendation.

For motoring enthusiasts we've included a selection of suggestions regarding places and events you might find interesting and the '50 Places you must visit' really is just that – every one of them is special.

Finally, we'd love to hear about the places you discover on our Facebook page and have your comments and photographs of them.

THE WILD ATLANTIC WAY AND IRELAND'S ANCIENT EAST

Perhaps you've already heard of Ireland's Wild Atlantic Way? It's a coastal driving route that extends all the way from the pretty town of Kinsale in the south of the island to Muff on the Inishowen Peninsula in the far north. Along the way it travels the entire south-western, western and north-western seaboard coastal roads of Ireland.

The Wild Atlantic Way is a great idea and it has quickly established itself as one of the world's great coastal driving routes. Each year it brings many visitors to Ireland to explore and discover the beauties of what is the western seaboard of Europe. Generally, its divided into six sections ranging from:

The south-west coast
The Kerry Peninsulas
Loop Head, Moher and the Burren
Connemara and South Mayo
North Mayo and Sligo
Donegal

Many visitors are content to pick one or two of these sections of the route and explore it thoroughly while others seek to drive the entire route. Either way, the entire woute is well signposted and there is numerous excellent literature to be found free in local Tourist Offices along the route. In particular there are three Discover Ireland bookets covering the North-West, the West and the South-West that cover everything you could possibly want to enjoy the Wild Atlantic Way. Together with an excellent map these are available free of charge and are highly recommended.

Ireland's Ancient East is designed to open up the rich heritage of Ireland's eastern region to the visitor. Unlike the Wild Atlantic Way, it's not a single route but rather a collection of places with a common thread – the part they played in Ireland's rich history. Like the Wild Atlantic Way, Ireland's Ancient East is to be highly recommended. The sites are well signposted and once again, there is plenty of litersture available from local tourist offices. Enjoy.

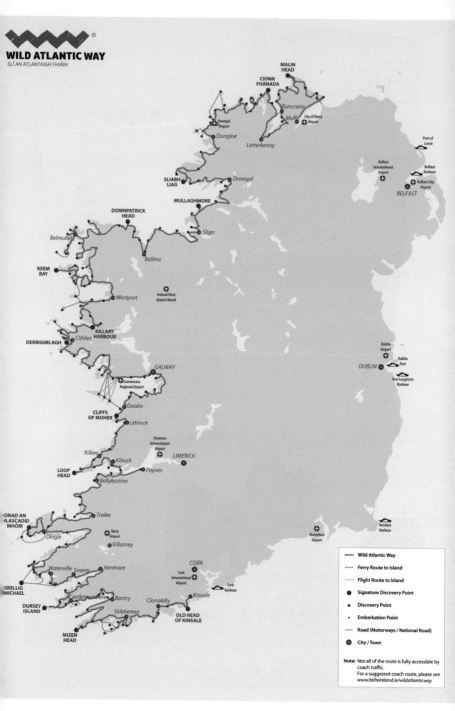

WILD ATLANTIC WAY
SLÍ AN ATLANTAIGH FHIÁIN

Wild Atlantic Way
Ferry Route to Island
Flight Route to Island
Signature Discovery Point
Discovery Point
Embarkation Point
Road (Motorways / National Road)
City / Town

Note: Not all of the route is fully accessible by coach traffic.
For a suggested coach route, please see
www.failteireland.ie/wildatlanticway

Castleroche, in Ireland's Ancient East.

DRIVING IN IRELAND

If you're planning on driving in Ireland, here are the essential things you need to know about driving laws, tolls and parking. If you plan to travel around Ireland by road, it is essential to be prepared. The information that follows provides a broad background to road laws in both the Republic of Ireland and Northern Ireland (the island of Ireland).

Roads in Ireland are generally of a high standard. One thing to be mindful of are terminology differences between, for example, the USA. and both the Republic of Ireland and Northern Ireland. Major driving routes, which would be comparable to highways or parkways in the US, are referred to as motorways, national roads and primary roads.

In the Republic of Ireland, motorways are designated with an 'M' prefix (for example the M50). National roads are prefixed with an 'N'"(for example the N21) and can be either national primary or national secondary roads. National primary roads usually consist of several driving lanes in each direction while national secondary roads will also include those with two-way traffic. Distances on road signs are shown in kilometers and speed limits are given in kilometers per hour (km/h) Roads in Northern Ireland are prefixed with an 'M' for motorway; an 'A' and a 'B' for primary and non-primary roads. In Northern Ireland, distances are provided in miles and speed limits are in miles per hour (mph).

Toll Roads

There are no tolled roads in Northern Ireland but you'll find tolls on a number of roads in the Republic of Ireland (Disabled drivers are not charged tolls on roads in the Republic of Ireland). Generally tolls are paid at the barrier of the toll booth, however, there is one exception – the M50 eFlow Barrier System on the ring road around Dublin. Instead of paying your toll at a toll-booth, the system records your trip by photographing your vehicle's licence plate number. You are required to pay your toll before 8pm the next day, either online, in branded Payzone outlets or by LoCall 1890 501050.

Driving in Ireland is on the left hand side of the road and all passengers are required to wear seat belts at all times in both the front and back of the vehicle. For those riding motorcycles, both motorcyclists and their passengers must wear helmets. Ireland's laws on drink driving are strict. Those drivers found to be contravening the laws will be heavily penalised. Use of mobile while driving is strictly prohibited.

License and insurance

You will need either a valid, full national driving licence or an international driving permit to drive in Ireland. In the Republic of Ireland, you must carry your driver's licence at all times. You must also have motor insurance either in your own name or as a named driver on another's policy. If you are renting a car, the Car Rental

Tips for North American Drivers

Driving styles and regulations differ in every country and Ireland is quite different to North America. It usually takes between a few hours and a day to get used to a new driving environment, particularly if you have not driven in the country before.

The following are some tips to help you adjust:

- If you normally drive an automatic, ensure that you specify auto matic when making your reservation
- When you drive the car for the first time, drive around at the airport a few times to get familiar with the controls and driving on the left-hand side of the road
- Try to stay on M and N rated roads (avoiding R roads) for the first day or so until you are familiar with your car and the driving envi ronment
- Ensure you have a good map or GPS and ideally have someone other than the driver to navigate
- Take your time - drive slowly at first until you gain confidence. Watch the signs carefully!
- If you cross the road to park or to visit a gas station, be sure to return to a driving position on the left-hand side when you return to road!

Council of Ireland advises on the various insurances, waivers and options appropriate to your needs.

The Speed Limits in operation on roads in the Irish Republic are:

50 kph / 30 mph in built-up urban areas

80 kph / 50 mph on single non-national open roads

120 kph / 74.5 mph on motorways

Parking
You will need to pay for parking in many cases in Ireland. Look for street signs showing parking information for guidance. You can pay for parking using:

1. Coins in the Pay and Display machine on the street.

2. www.parkbytext.ie (Republic of Ireland) and www.parkbytext.co.uk (Northern Ireland).

ft: Take time to become accustomed to
and's back roads.

Barberstown Castle, 1288

The Ideal base to Explore 5,000 years of history in Ireland's Ancient East

Straffan, County Kildare

www.barberstowncastle.ie

IRELAND'S ANCIENT EAST®

Wander Through Time

50 Places
you must
not miss!

1 **Skellig Michael**
Unrivaled monastic outpost off Kerry

2 The Book of Kells at Trinity College -
The greatest illuminated book in existence, and an awe-inspiring library!

3 Glendalough
Peaceful perfection in a beautiful valley.

4 The Giant's Causeway
The stuff of legends!

5 The Guinness Store House
Impressive home of the Black Stuff!

6   **Titanic Belfast**
The story of the tragic ship that Belfast built.

7   **The Rock of Cashel**
Breath-taking! Ireland's most impressive monument.

8 Cliffs of Moher
Awe-inspiring Atlantic coastline.

9 Brú na Bóinne (Newgrange)
Older than the Pyramids, one of the World's treasures.

10 Ring of Kerry
Ireland's most popular visitor trail.

11   Trim Castle
Mighty Norman fortress.

12   The Great Telescope of Birr
Where galaxies were first viewed.

13 **Titanic Experience Cobh**
The stories of the 123 passengers who boarded
the RMS Titanic at Cobh.

14 Kilkenny Castle's Great Hall
Monumental Great Hall that brings the past to life in spectacular fashion.

15 Howth
Beautiful peninsula full of varied attractions on Dublin's doorstep.

16 Ballaghabeama Pass
Ireland's wildest place.

17 Dun Aengus
Utterly unique ancient fortress.

18 Dublin's famous Zoo
Simply one of the World's greatest Zoos.

19 The Burren
A unique and other-worldly limestone landscape.

20 Gap of Dunloe
The heart of wild Kerry.

21 **National Museum of Ireland**
Housing a breath-taking golden history.

22 **Slea Head on the Dingle Peninsula**
Perhaps Ireland's most spectacular drive.

23 Fota Island Wildlife Park
Wonderful setting, wonderful Wildlife Park.

24 Dalkey Castle
The perfect visitor attraction.

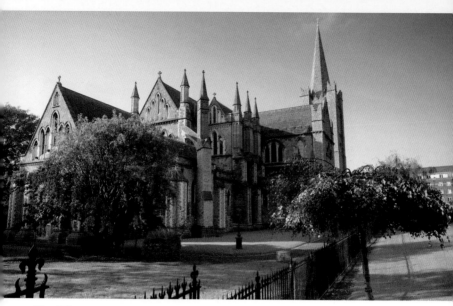

25   St. Patrick's Cathedral
Ireland's greatest and most historic cathedral.

26   Achill Island
Island of beauty and wonder.

27 National Gallery of Ireland
Award-winning treasury of Art.

28 Slieve League, Donegal
Spectacular sea cliffs among the highest in Europe.

29 Drumcliffe, the burial place of William Butler Yeats
Where Ireland's National Poet rests in his beloved Sligo.

30 Céide Fields, Mayo
Where the landscape tells a remarkable story.

31 Dunluce Castle
Spectacular setting for a castle of legend.

32 Glens of Antrim
The gentle, beautiful Glens of Antrim.

33 The Marino Casino
The most remarkable building in Ireland.

34 King John's Castle, Limerick
Impressive centre of Norman power in Limerick

35 **The English Market, Cork**
One of the World's great food markets.

36 Thomond Park Museum and Stadium, Limerick
The very heart of Irish rugby!

37 Killarney National Park
Discover the beauty of Kerry.

38 The South Pole Inn, Annascaul
Where the bravery of the remarkable Tom Crean,
Antarctic explorer, is remembered.

39 Dog's Bay, Roundstone
The perfect beach.

40 **Chester Beatty Library, Dublin**
One of the World's great Libraries and Museums.

41 Malahide Castle
A great place to visit on Dublin's doorstep.

42 Carrick-a-Rede Rope Bridge
Spectacular rope bridge for the brave.

43 The Tim Healey Pass
Is this Ireland's Stelvio Pass?

44 Dunbrody Famine Ship, New Ross
Brings home the realities of 19th century immigration to America.

45 Glenveagh National Park and Castle, Donegal
Tranquil beauty in the very heart of Donegal.

46 Oldbridge House, Drogheda
Where Ireland's greatest land battle is remembered.

47 Little Dublin Museum
Quirky and different – the history of Dublin city.

48 Dublin's Phoenix Park
Europe's largest walled park and much, much more.

49 Westport
The jewel among towns in Ireland's west.

50 Dublinia
Imaginative re-telling of Dublin's Viking and Medieval history.

PLACES AND EVENTS OF MOTORING INTEREST

Ireland has a wonderful history of motoring and motorsport events and there are reminders of this rich past all ove rthe country. We've included in this section of the guide a selection of some of the most interesting you might want to seek out.

The Lotus of EP Gill makes its way through Dunboyne village during the 1961 Dunboyne Trophy race.

Dunboyne Motor Races

The Dunboyne Circuit in County Meath based on the village of the same name was the 'last hurrah' of street racing in Ireland before the opening of Ireland's first permanent motor racing circuit at Mondello. In 1967. The races were held from 1958 to 1967 and attracted the cream of Irish drivers and a large overseas entry each year. The outright lap record of 101.24 mph was set in 1965 and the races are remembered by the Dunboyne Motor Club's Festival of Speed in September - a great event to watch.

A plaque in the village recalls the racing held there.

The plaque in the village commemorating the races held there.

The Gordon Bennett Trail

Probably the most important and influential motor sport event ever held in Ireland was the 1903 Gordon Bennett Race held on a figure eight course based on the town of Athy. This was the true start of international motor racing and is commemorated by a monument at the extrodinary Moate of Ardscull and in the Athy Heritage Museum. The Gordon Bennett Trail is detailed elsewhere in this guide and is a signp[osted route around the original ciruit used for the race.

The 1903 is race is recalled by the monument at the Mote of Ardscull, just north of Athy.

Harry Ferguson photographed outside the premises in May Street, Belfast, where he established Harry Ferguson Motors.

The Harry Ferguson Trail

The Harry Ferguson Trail is a self-guided tour that follows in the footsteps of the remarkable engineer and inventor Harry Ferguson. A Booklet and map is available from the Lisburn Tourist Information Centre. The Trail includes places associated with Harry's aviation achievements, the Ferguson Homestead, the Ulster Aviation Collection at the Maze/Long Kesh regeneration site, the Ulster Folk & Transport Museum and several other sites associated with Harry Ferguson. Also included in the tour is the homestead of Rex McCandless, another man from the Lagan Valley who achieved fame in the field of engineering and technology.

Motoring Memories Heritage Museum

Now this Museum of motoring memorabilia is something special! Located in Ballygowan in County Down, it's one man's collection accumulated over a lifetime. And what a collectio! Everything uyou could ever imagine associated with motoring is to be found here. For information about opening hours and direction phone 028 9752 8166 or 07714 345 355 or e-mail:raymondwallssnr@gmail.com. Very highly recommended.

Inside the Motoring Memories Heritage Museum is an Aladdin's Cave of motoring treasures.

Museum of Transport, Clonmel

Located in Gurtnafleur Business Park on the outskirts of Clonmel, Michael Lavins Museum is a treasure house of Irish County Motoring. Its not just the cars that fascinate but the items associated with motoring in times gone past. Telephone first (088 832 2471) to ascertain opening hours and don't forget to pause for a coffee and cake in the adjoining café. Recommended.

The RIAC Pioneer Run

The premier event for early cars in Ireland, this is your opportunity to see cars at least 100 years old travelling over a route of around 55/60 miles. The cars are fantastic and expect there to be several cars dating back to the late 1890s. Based in North Dublin and Kildare the event takes place on the last weekend of May each year. See the cars at the start or at the mid-way break usually at visitor attraction. Consult the website of the Royal Irish Automobile Club for details. Recommended.

Some of the participants in a recent RIAC Pioneer Run.

Time for an ices cream during a break in the RIAC Pioneer Run.

RIAC National Classic Car Show

The RIAC National Classic Car Show, held every second year (the next Show is 2018) in the prestigous Royal Dublin Society Simmonscourt Hall is Ireland's major Classic Car Show. The Show provides an opportunity to see everything from examples of the earliest cars to the very latest supercars. The cars on display are of very high quality and one of the features of the Show is that the cars dispalyed are claimbed by the organisers to be 99% different from Show to Show. Highly recommended..

Enjoying the cars at the RIAC National Classic Car show.

Kilgarvan Motor Museum

Follow the signs from Kilgarvan to this motor museum. Its different, its quirky and well worth a visit. The Museum is located along the River Slaheny just five minutes from Kilgarvan town in County Kerry.

The Statham-Ford Special

The Statham-Ford Special was a famous home-built Irish 'Special' racing car that competed in the big events of the 1930s. It was built in the workshops of Stathams in Kilkenny who were Ford dealers. Stathams is long gone but the hotel – the Pembroke – now on the site of the garage has very cleaverly themed the hotel based on the Statham-Ford Special. And they also have the car itself on display. All of which together with secure parking makes this a great stop-over for motor clubs touring in Ireland. The hotoel is on Patrick Street, Kilkenny, just around the corner from Kilkenny's famous Castle.

The Statham-Ford Special in the Bray races of 1935

The plaque on the wall of the Pembroke Hotel commemorating the Statham-Ford Special.

The plaque commemorating the site where the Statham-Ford Special was built in Kilkenny.

Terenure Show

Known universally as the 'Terenure Show' this the largest outdoor car show is organised by the Irish Jaguar and Daimler Club in the grounds of Terenure College every July. Over one thousand vehicles are claimed to take part and it's a great day out with autojumbles as well as club and feature displays. Recommended.

Motorcycles form several of the displays at the Terenure Show.

A wide variety of cars of all ages are to be found at the Terenure Show.

Ulster Folk & Transport Museum

The Ulster Folk & Transport Museum at Cultra just outside belfast is Ireland's premier transport musum. There are displays of trains, cars, motorcycles and aircraft as well as the nearby Folk Museum on the other side of the Belfast to Bangor road. The trains in particular are magnificent and the aviation section very interesting but I have to record a slight disappointment at the motoring displays. Nevertheless highly recommended and certainly not to be missed.

Trains, cars and aeroplanes feature in the Ulster Folk & Transport Museum.

Useful web addresses

GORDON BENNTT TRAIL	www.gordonbennettroute.com
SPIRIT OF DUNBOYNE FESTIVAL	www.dunboynemotorclub.com
HARRY FERGUSON TRAIL	www.visitlisburn.com
KILGARVAN MOTOR MUSEUM	www.kilgarvanmotormuseum.com
RIAC PIONEER RUN	www.riac.ie
THE STATHAM-FORD SPECIAL	www.pembrokekilkenny.com
THE TERENURE SHOW	www.irishjagclub.ie/terenure-car-show/
ULSTER FOLK & TRANSPORT MUSEUM	www.nmni.com/uftm

ROUTE CONTENTS

Trinity College, Dublin.

The Palace Bar, like many Dublin pubs, has many literary associations.

DUBLIN - A MODERN CITY STEEPED IN HISTORY

Dublin is one of the great cities of the world to visit, and while it may not be as large as some other such cities, what it lacks in size it makes up for in character. Dublin is vibrant, full of interesting things to do and see and with a plentiful choice of restaurants and cafes to satisfy your every need.

More than that, Dubliners are friendly and down-to-eartht and its no coincidence that we Irish have a saying 'A stranger is a friend you haven't met yet'. So do use every opportunity to interact with native Dubliners; you'll generally find them helpful to a fault and always keen to tell you about their city of which they are so proud.

The name Dublin comes from the Gaelic *dubh linn* or 'black pool' - where the Poddle stream met the River Liffey to form a deep pool at Dublin Castle. The city's modern name - *Baile Áth Cliath* – means the 'town of the ford of the hurdles'. Ireland's four principal routes converged at a crossing place made of hurdles of interwoven saplings straddling the Liffey. In 837 AD, sixty Viking longships attacked churches along the Poddle and Liffey estuary, and the invaders made a permanent settlement in 841 AD. By 917 AD Dublin was the Viking world's largest city and traded from Iceland to Constantinople. Dublin became the centre of English rule in Ireland when the Norman warrior Richard Fitzgilbert de Clare (Strongbow) seized Dublin and so it was to remain until after the signing of the Anglo-Irish Treaty in 1921. In more recent years Dublin has seen an influx of foreign nationals helping to give the city a welcome cosmopolitian feel.

The Long Room of Trinity College Library is nothing short of breathtaking and houses the world-famous Book of Kells.

TRINITY COLLEGE

Trinity College in the heart of Dublin is a must-see! Founded in 1592 and modelled after the universities of Oxford and Cambridge, it is Ireland's oldest university and one of the seven ancient universities of Britain and Ireland. Located on College Green, opposite the former Irish Houses of Parliament that now house the Bank of Ireland. The Library of Trinity College is a Legal Deposit Library for Ireland and the United Kingdom, containing over 4.5 million printed books as well as significant quantities of manuscripts, maps and music.

The most significant manuscript in the Trinity Library is the magnificent Book of Kells that is believed to have been written around 800 AD. It contains the four gospels and is written on vellum (prepared calfskin), lavishly decorated with quite stunning artistry. It is probable that the monastry on Iona, an island off Mull in Western Scotland, founded around 561 AD by St. Colum Cille, was abandoned by the monks following Viking raids and the community moved to Kells where the book was most probably produced.

The Book of Kells is Ireland's greatest cultural treasure and the world's most famous medieval manuscript and attracts thousands of visitors to the Trinity Library each year. There is a permanent exhibition that is open seven days a week. Tickets can be booked online or at the ticket office. The Book of Kells should not be missed and the Library in which it is contained is nothing short of breathtaking. Highly recommended. Trinity College itself is like an 18th century oasis in the heart of Dublin and is well worth taking the time to explore.

DUBLIN CASTLE

Just across College Green and at the head of Dame Street is Dublin Castle, the centre of British power in Ireland for eight hundred years until the signing of the Anglo-Irish Treaty in December 1921 when it was handed over to the newly formed Provisional Government.

Since its foundation in 1204, Dublin Castle has been at the heart of the history and evolution of the city. Today, spanning an area of over 44,000 square meters (11 acres), the site contains two museums, two cafés, an international conference centre, two gardens, Government Buildings and the State Apartments which are the most important state rooms in the country.

The grounds of the site are free to explore, as is the Chester Beatty Library and the Revenue Museum. Access to the State Apartments is by guided tour only and tickets may be purchased from the Apartments in the Upper Castle Yard. An exploration of Dublin Castle is a walk through Irish history and worth spending a half day over.

Special mention must be made of the Chester Beatty Library within the grounds of Dublin Castle. With free admission and described by the *Lonely Planet* as not just the best museum in Dublin, but one of the best in Europe, the Chester Beatty Library is a must-see on any Dublin visitor's itinerary. It is the only museum in Ireland to win 'European Museum of the Year' and is rated consistently in the top 5 of *TripAdvisor's* list of 'Top things to do in Dublin', the library's rich collections from countries across Asia, the Middle East, North Africa and Europe open a window on the artistic treasures of the great cultures and religions of the world.

The Chapel Royal at Dublin Castle.

St. Patrick's Cathedral.

ST. PATRICK'S AND CHRISTCHURCH CATHEDRALS

Saint Patrick's Cathedral was founded in 1191 AD, and is the National Cathedral of the Church of Ireland. With its 43-metre (141 ft) spire, St. Patrick's is the tallest church in Ireland and also the largest. Nearby Christ Church Cathedral, also a Church of Ireland Cathedral, is the local Cathedral of the diocese of Dublin and Glendalough.

St. Patrick's is the location for a number of public national ceremonies, and its carol service (the Service of Nine Lessons and Carols), celebrated twice in December, including every 24 December, is a colourful feature of Dublin life.

The funerals of two Irish presidents, Douglas Hyde and Erskine Childers, took place there in 1949 and 1974 respectively. At President Hyde's funeral, the entire Irish government and opposition, with the exception of Noel Browne and Erskine Childers, stayed in the foyer of the church. This was because, at the time of the funeral, the Holy See forbade Roman Catholics from entering the churches of other Christian traditions. Because President Erskine Childers died in office in 1974, his state funeral was a major state occasion and the attendance included foreign dignitaries King Baudouin of the Belgians, the Vice-President of the United States (Spiro T. Agnew representing President Nixon), Earl Mountbatten of Burma (representing Queen Elizabeth), British Prime Minister Harold Wilson and former British prime minister Edward Heath.

The Cathedral is open to worshipers and visitors seven days a week. It is important to check the Cathedral website to avoid

Christchurch Cathedral.

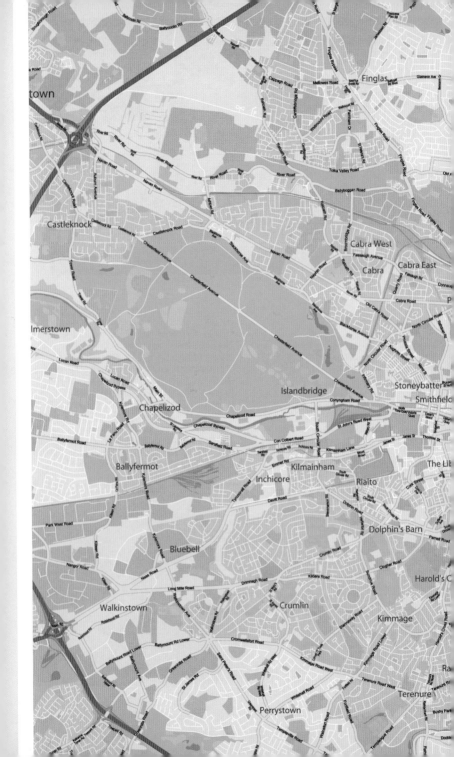

The iconic Halfpenny Bridge spanning the River Liffey was so named because of the toll charged for using it when it was built.

events that may be taking place there. Christchurch Cathedral was a major pilgrimage site in the medieval period and was founded c.1028 AD, it's origins thus being earlier than St. Patrick's Cathedral. As in St. Patrick's Cathedral, visitors are welcomed. Tours are available and the greatest interest is probably in the Medieval crypt beneath the building. Included in the crypt are 'the cat and the rat', the Treasury, an audio visual presentation, the cathedral shop and café as well as a number of fascinating memorials.

Perhaps the most popular attraction in the crypt are the mummified remains of 'the cat and the rat'. Mentioned by James Joyce in *Finnegans Wake,* they are also, perhaps not surprisingly, known as 'Tom & Jerry'.

The choir of the Cathedral is world-famous and took part in the first performance of Handel's Messiah in 1742. As with St. Patrick's Cathedral it is wisest to consult the Cathedral website to ascertain visitor information.

TEMPLE BAR

Located on the south bank of the River Liffey and bounded by Dame Street to the south, Temple Bar is Dublin's cultural quarter. It's a maze of narrow streets with bustling bars, restaurants and cafes and has a lively nightlife that is popular with visitors to Dublin.

There are a number of significant cultural institutions located in Temple Bar, including The National Photographic Archive, The Ark Children's Cultural Centre, the Irish Film Institute, the Arthouse Multimedia Centre and the Project Arts Centre. Meetinghouse Square is used for outdoor film screenings during the summer months.

Temple Bar and its nightlife are popular with visitors to Dublin.

The spectacular Gravity Bar at the Guinness Storehouse - Dublin's top attraction.

BUBLINIA

Dublinia, located at St. Michael's Hill adjacent to Christchurch Cathedral is to my mind, something quite unique and special. It's a trip back to Viking times through an exhibition that allows you to experience the sights, sounds and smells of the busy Medieval city that was Viking Dublin. You can experience what life was like aboard a Viking longship and the skills it took to become a Viking warrior. This is a history lesson like no other and one you won't easily forget. In addition there are spectacular views over Dublin city to be enjoyed from the recently restored St. Michael's Tower (but do be aware there are 96 steps to the top). Dublinia is open all year round and will be a highlight of your visit to Dublin.

THE GUINNESS STOREHOUSE

It's hard to beilieve but since the Guinness Storehouse opened in 2000 it has received over 4 million visitors! That's a quarter of a million visitors each year. Can 4 million visitors be wrong? I don't think so and a visit to the iconic brewery is probably high on your list of things to do in Dublin.

The Guinness Storehouse covers no less than seven floors surrounding a glass atrium shaped in the form of a pint of Guinness On the ground floor visitors are introduced to the beer's four ingredients (water, barley, hops and yeast), and the brewery's founder, Arthur Guinness. On other floors, visitors learn about the history of Guinness advertising and there is an interactive exhibit on responsible drinking. The seventh floor houses the spectacular Gravity Bar with views over Dublin and where visitors may drink a pint of Guinness (included in the price of admission), if they wish. At the base of the atrium a copy of the 9,000 year lease signed by Arthur Guinness for the brewery site can be viewed, while visitors also have the opportunity to 'pull a pint' and to sample Irish cuisine, all using Guinness as one of the ingredients. In 2011, Queen Elizabeth II and Prince Philip visited the Guiness Storehouse as part of their state visit to Ireland.

What more can I say? Go and see it for yourself and learn why it's Dublin's number one visitor attraction.

THE PHOENIX PARK

Dubliners are fortunate to have one of the world's great parks on the doorstep of the city. At 707 hectares (1752 acres) it is one of the largest enclosed recreational spaces within any European capital city. The 'Park', as it has been referred to by generations of Dubliners, was established in 1662 by one of Ireland's viceroys, James Butler, Duke of Ormond, on behalf of King Charles II. Conceived as a Royal deer park, it originally included the demesne of Kilmainham Priory south of the River Liffey, but with the building of the Royal Hospital at Kilmainham, which commenced in 1680, the Park was reduced to its present size, all of which is now north of the river. Shortly after the Park's acquisition it was enclosed within a stone wall, which was initially poorly constructed. Subsequent wall repair and new build were necessary as the Park's size and boundaries were adjusted and realigned.

About one third of the Phoenix Park is covered by trees, including oak, ash, lime, beech, sycamore and horse chestnut, and a herd of Fallow Deer has lived in the Park since the 1660's when they were introduced by the Duke of Ormond. The Phoenix Park is a sanctuary for many mammals and birds and a wide range of wildlife habitats are to be found in the park, particularly in the Furry Glen, which is managed as a conservation area.

Áras an Uachtaráin, the residence of the President of Ireland dates from 1750 and is located in the centre of the park adjacent to the United States Ambassador's residence, which was built in 1774. Many other historic buildings and monuments are located in the Park, the most noteworthy of which is the Wellington Monument, which dominates the skyline of the Park and its surroundings

The Victorian People's Flower Gardens were initially established in 1840 as the Promenade Grounds. They provide an opportunity to display Victorian horticulture at its best. Ornamental lakes, a children's playground, picnic area and Victorian bedding schemes are just some of the attractions of the gardens that are open from 8.00 am until dusk every day.

Just off the Phoenix roundabout on Chesterfield Avenue, the main road that bisects the Park, is Ashtown Castle and the Phoenix Park Visitor Centre. Adjacent to the Visitor Centre there is also a two and a half acre Victorian Kitchen Walled Garden and the Phoenix Café. No visit to Phoenix Park is complete without a visit to the Visitor Centre where the history and uniqueness of the Park is explained through a series of exhibitions and a fine audio-visual presentation. Refreshments can also be had at the Victorian Tea Rooms that serve teas and lunches with an outdoor picnic area and is situated between the Band Hollow and Dublin Zoo.

The Wellington Monument celebrates the career of the Irish-born Duke of Wellington, victor at Waterloo.

Tiger cub at Dublin's famous Zoo.

DUBLIN ZOO

Also located in Phoenix Park on a 28 hectares (69 acres) site is Dublin's famous Zoo, The Zoo is the largest in Ireland, and one of Dublin's most popular visitor attractions. Opened in 1831, the Zoo describes its role as conservation, study, and education. Its stated mission is to 'work in partnership with zoos worldwide to make a significant contribution to the conservation of the endangered species on Earth', something it does superbly.

The Zoo is divided into areas named Asian Forests, Orangutan Forest, The Kaziranga Forest Trail, Fringes of the Arctic, Sea Lion Cove, African Plains, Roberts House, House of Reptiles, City Farm and South American House. In recent times the Zoo has been the subject of the very popular RTÉ documentary TV series *The Zoo* produced by Moondance Productions and filmed almost entirely on location at Dublin Zoo,

A visit to Dublin Zoo is highly recommended. There is so much to see so if you can, allow a full day for your visit.

IRISH MUSEUM OF MODERN ART

The Irish Museum of Modern Art, housed in the magnificent former Royal Hospital, Kilmanham, across the Liffey from the park is home to the National Collection of modern and contemporary art, with over 3,500 artworks by Irish and International artists.

The Collection is rooted in the present and important new works are added to the Collection each year, with a particular emphasis on work from the 1940s onwards.

ROYAL HOSPITAL KILMAINHAM

The Royal Hospital Kilmainham was built in 1680 by royal command and predates its sister, the Royal Hospital Chelsea, by just two years. This is the oldest classical building in Ireland and was based on *Les Invalides* in Paris.

When built, the hospital housed just 20 people although it was designed for 400. In 1690 the care of army pensioners from the Battle pf The Boyne was undertaken there. In 1922 the building was handed over to the Irish Free State and five years later the last pensioner was moved to Chelsea.
Between 1930 and 1950 it served as Garda Headquarters but fell into a state of disrepair.

In 1980 Taoiseach Charles Haughey approved plans to renovate it at a cost of IR£3 million. The restoration took four years – the same length of time as it took to originally build it three centuries before. In 1991, the Royal Hospital Kilmainham became home to the Irish Museum of Modern Art (IMMA) as evidenced by the many stunning sculptures you'll see around the hospital's 48 acres grounds.

The Royal Hospital at Kilmainham houses the Irish Museum of Modern Art.

LITTLE MUSEUM OF DUBLIN

Different, and described by *The Irish Times* as 'Dublin's best museum experience', and by *TripAdvisor* as the number one museum in Ireland, the Little Museum of Dublin is a gem.
Its collection was created by public donation. Entry to the museum is by guided tour, and most tours fill up quickly, so to avoid

Drivers speed along the main straight (Chesterfield Avenue) of the Phoenix Park circuit during the 1929 Irish International Grand Prix.

WHEN MOTOR RACINGS' STARS RACED IN THE PHOENIX PARK

It may surprise visitors to Dublin to learn that the stately Phoenix Park has an association with motor racing dating back to July 1903 when Speed Trials were held along Chesterfield Avenue two days after the famous Gordon Bennett race. The 1903 Speed Trials brought motor sport to Dubliners for the first time and the association has continued until as recently as 2012 when motor races were last held on the Phoenix Park Oldtown Circuit.

The highlight of racing in the Park was without any doubt the three Irish International Grand Prix organised by the Royal Irish Automobile Club and held there between 1929 and 1931. Each of these events comprised two races – one for cars up to 1500cc in capacity and one for cars over 1500cc. The winner of the Grand Prix was the driver who completed either race in the fastest possible time. In 1929 this was the White Russian Prince Ivanowsky who drove an Alfa Romeo to victory. The organisation of the race and the track received great praise after the 1929 race and the 1930 running attracted the cream of Europe's drivers. On this

occasion it was the German driver Rudolf Caracciola who was victorious in a Mercedes SSK. Caracciola won despite the race being partly run in a thunderstorm that made conditions for high speed driving particularly hazardous.

The final Grand Prix was run in 1931 and clashed with the Le Mans 24 Hour race limiting the entry of top drivers. On this occasion the race was won by Norman Black driving an MG.

When the Grand Prix series ended, national motor sport took over and races were held successfully up until the outbreak of World War 2. Soon after the end of the conflict, motor racing returned to the Phoenix Park and between the 1950s and 1990s attracted huge crowds to the 'greatest free show in Dublin' and brought many top drivers to Ireland to compete in the Park. Recession and its effects made the races impractical in recent years but it is hoped that they will return in the near future to carry on their unique association with Phoenix Park.

Kilmainham Gaol was associated with the leaders of the many risings throughout Irish history.

disappointment book your tickets online This award-winning museum tells the story of the Irish capital, and the museums guided tours reveal the history of a city that has undergone remarkable changes in the last 100 years, from the visit of Queen Victoria to the global success of U2. Not to be missed, the museum is located on the north side of St. Stephen's Green close to the junction with Dawson Street.

KILMAINHAM GAOL

When built in 1796, Kilmainham Gaol was the new County Gaol for Dublin. Although it held many criminals for a broad range of crimes, it is for its association with political prisoners from the rebellion of 1798 to the Irish Civil War of 1922-23 that it is most interesting today. Leaders of the rebellions of 1798, 1803, 1848,1867 and 1916 were detained and in many cases executed here. Many members of the Irish Republican movement during the Anglo-Irish War (1919-21) were also detained in Kilmainham Gaol. Famous names from Irish history such as Henry Joy McCracken, Robert Emmet, Anne Devlin, Charles Stewart Parnell and the leaders of 1916 will forever be associated with the building.

Kilmanham Gaol is open all year round and is a fascinating place to visit. In recent years it has become a very popular attraction. Why not combine a visit to the Gaol with a visit to the Irish Museum of Modern Art in the adjacent Royal Hospital. Recommended.

NATIONAL GALLERY OF ART

In June 1852 William Dargan, the father of the Irish rail network, underwrote a spectacular exhibition on Leinster Lawn in Dublin, the then home of the Royal Dublin Society. Dargan wished to imitate the great exhibition that had taken place at Crystal Palace in London the previous year. Just eleven months later the exhibition was opened in a series of pavilions for which the architect, John Benson, received a knighthood. Such was the interest in the exhibition it was decided to establish a permanent public collection that would also be a fitting tribute to the generosity of Dargan

On Saturday, 30th of January 1864, the Earl of Carlisle officially opened the National Gallery of Ireland to the public. The collection comprised just one hundred

69

and twelve pictures, including thirty-nine purchased in Rome in 1856 and thirty which were on loan from the National Gallery of London and elsewhere.

In 1901 the Countess of Milltown gifted over 200 pictures to the gallery from her house at Russborough as well as a collection of silver, furniture and books from her library. The gift was so substantial that a new extension was constructed to accommodate it.

In 1968 the gallery was extended again with designs by Frank DuBerry, senior architect with the Office of Public Works. This new extension is today named the Beit Wing in acknowledgement of the exceptional generosity of Sir Alfred and Lady Beit who gifted seventeen outstanding old master pictures to the institution in 1987. Some six years later in 1993 the Gallery became the focus of international attention when Caravaggio's, 'The Taking of Christ', a painting recorded in contemporary biographies on the artist and known through copies but long believed to have

The National Gallery of Ireland is a must for art lovers visiting the capital city.

been lost or destroyed, was discovered in a Jesuit house of studies in Dublin. The picture remains in the gallery on indefinite loan from the Jesuit fathers.

The most recent addition to the Gallery complex was the Millennium Wing opened in January 2002. Designed by London based architects Benson & Forsyth and located on sites purchased by the Gallery in 1990 and 1996, the new wing introduced a new, second public entrance to the gallery from the busy thoroughfare of Clare Street. As part of this extension a superb bookshop was included in the new facilities.

The collection of the National Gallery of Art is quite superb and if you have any interest at all in art, then it must be on your list of places to visit in Dublin. Very highly recommended.

NATIONAL MUSEUM OF IRELAND

Prior to 1877, the Museum's collections were divided between Leinster House, originally the headquarters of the Royal Dublin Society, and the Natural History Museum in Merrion Street, built as an extension to Leinster House in 1856-1857. To consolidate them in a single location, the government purchased the museum buildings and collections. To provide storage and display space for the Leinster House collections, the government quickly implemented plans to construct a new, custom-built museum on Kildare Street and on 29 August 1890, the new museum opened its doors to the public.

The original museum building was designed by Cork architects, Thomas Newenham Deane and his son Thomas Manly Deane. Located on Kildare Street, it is today the home of the archaeological collections and is itself an architectural landmark. Built in the Victorian Palladian style it has been compared with the Altes Museum in Berlin, designed by Karl Schinkel in the 1820s. Neo-classical influences can be seen in the colonnaded entrance and the domed rotunda, which rises to a height of 20 metres, and is modelled on the Pantheon in Rome. Here are all the great relics of early Irish history including the many gold objects that have survived. The exhibitions are simply breathtaking and fill one with an awe of the rich past of this island and its peoples
The museum also operates in Dublin at

Collins Barracks where Decoretive Arts and History are based and at Merrion Square where the Natural History collection is displayed. Very highly recommended.

GPO

Forever associated with the 1916 Rising and the events that led to the creation of an independent Irish state, the striking General Post Office (GPO) building on O'Connell Street is one of Ireland's most iconic structures. During the course of its history, the GPO has witnessed much more than the dramatic events of Easter Week. Its foundation stone was laid by Lord Whitworth on the 12th August 1814 when the grand sum of £60 was spent on entertainment for the occasion. The architect was Francis Johnston whose considerable abilities place him in the first rank of Irish architects. In its GPO Dublin gained a building that was, in the words of a contemporary, 'commodious, well arranged and highly ornamental to the city..

The novelist, Anthony Trollope, branded 'worthless' by Post Office officials in London, was sent to Ireland in 1841 where he quickly built a reputation as a highly capable employee! As the century progressed, the GPO presided over an organisation that – through mail, financial services, telegraphs and telephones –

touched the lives of countless people every day. It became the centre of communications in Ireland and, for some few people, an unacceptable symbol of British influence in Ireland. Its occupation on Easter Monday 1916, therefore, had both a practical and a symbolic purpose.

Reconstruction and extension of the building after it was destroyed in the Rising was undertaken by an Office of Public Works team led by TJ Byrne who introduced the GPO Arcade, studios for Radio Éireann on the Henry Street wing and the Central Telegraph Office in the Prince's Street block. The enlarged Public Office, formally reopened by WT Cosgrave in 1929, retained elements of Johnston's design whilst also introducing some attractive art deco features. The grandeur and airy spaciousness of the office, combined with some fine craftsmanship, produced what remains an impressive and rather beautiful interior.

A more recent addition to the GPO is the Witness History exhibition – a self-guided tour taking about an hour that seeks to put you among the events and personalities of the Easter 1916 Rising.

THE WRITER'S MUSEUM

Given our literary history, it would indeed be strange if our famous writers that included four Nobel Prize winners were not

The iconic General Post Office on O'Connell Street was the focal point of the 1916 Rising.

THE RISING OF 1916

The destruction in the heart of Dublin was centered on the GPO where the rebels had proclaimed an Irish Republic.

The Easter Rising, also known as the Easter Rebellion, was an armed insurrection during Easter Week, April 1916. The Rising was launched by Irish republicans to end British rule in Ireland and establish an independent Irish Republic while the United Kingdom was heavily engaged in the First World War.

The Rising began on Easter Monday, 24th April 1916, and lasted for six days. Members of the Irish Volunteers — led by schoolmaster and Irish language activist Patrick Pearse, joined by the smaller Irish Citizen Army of James Connolly and 200 women of *Cumann na mBan* — seized the GPO and other key locations in Dublin and proclaimed an Irish Republic. The British Army brought in thousands of reinforcements as well as artillery and a gunboat, which together destroyed the centre of the city.

With much greater numbers and heavier weapons, the British Army soon suppressed the Rising and Pearse agreed to an unconditional surrender on Saturday 29th April, although sporadic fighting continued until Sunday. About 3,500 people were taken prisoner by the British, many of whom had played no part in the Rising, and 1,800 of them were sent to internment camps or prisons in Britain. Most of the leaders of the Rising were swiftly executed following courts-martial.

Almost 500 people were killed in the Easter Rising. About 54% were civilians, 30% were British military and police, and 16% were Irish rebels. More than 2,600 were wounded. Many of the civilians were killed as a result of the British using artillery and heavy machine guns, or mistaking civilians for rebels. Others were caught in the crossfire in a crowded city. The shelling and the fires it caused left the center of inner city Dublin in ruins.

celebrated in Ireland's capital city. Thus it was that the Dublin Writers Museum was opened in 1991 to house a history and celebration of literary Dublin.

The museum is housed in an 18th century building in the north city centre adjacent to Parnell Square and features, amongst many others, Swift and Sheridan, Shaw and Wilde, Yeats, Joyce and Beckett. The museum features exhibitions, lunchtime theatre and readings and even has a special room celebrating children's literature.

NATIONAL BOTANIC GARDENS OF IRELAND

Located just 3 km from Dublin city centre, the National Botanic Gardens at Glasnevin are an oasis of calm and beauty, and entry is free. A premier scientific institution, the gardens also contain the National Herbarium and several historic wrought iron glasshouses. It's a delightfully relaxing place to just stroll or to marvel at the collections housed in the amazing glasshouses.
Recommended.

CROKE PARK

Croke Park is the headquarters of the Gaelic Athletic Association (GAA). It is the third largest stadium in Europe with a capacity of 82,300. Croke Park has UEFA and FIFA approved certification and has hosted numerous high-profile international sporting, cultural and music events outside of Gaelic games. The Croke Park campus features the Croke Park Meetings and Events Centre, the GAA Museum, Stadium Tour and Etihad Skyline Tour.

The Eihad Skyline Tour is an experience not to be missed and provides a different and dramatic view of the skyline of Dublin.

GLASNEVIN CEMETARY AND MUSEUM

Since the opening of its museum a number of years ago, Glasnevin Cemetery has become one of Dublin's top visitor attractions. It's a fascinating place where over 1.5 million people lie in rest. The stories of many of the more famous are told in the museum and on the guided tours. Here also are the final resting places of Daniel O'Connell, marked by an Irish Round Tower that serves as a landmark for the

The National Botanic Gardens at Glasnevin contain the National Herbarium and several historic wrough iron glasshouses.

The fine museum building at historic Glasnevin cemetery.

cemetery, and also for many of those involved in the War of Independence and the subsequent Civil War.

A visit is highly recommended, but be sure to give yourself plenty of time as there is lots that is fascinating to be explored.

DUN LAOGHAIRE

To the south of Dublin city there are three locations along the coast that I want to mention. The first of these is Dun Laoghaire, situated 10 km outside Dublin City, Dún Laoghaire is a vibrant and attractive cultural hub that is a pleasing alternative to the city. It has a full range of attractions and features a harbour and promenade that are its focal point. Ireland's National Maritime Museum is housed in Dun Laoghaire's 180-year-old

Mariners Church, directly opposite the new Lexicon library. The museum's greatest artifact is probably the building itself as it is one of a few custom-built places of worship for seafarers remaining intact in the world to-day.

In the museum you will discover maritime history, exploration, navigation, radio, deep-sea cable technology, nature, wildlife and view art inspired by the sea. See the 10-tonne revolving Baily Optic, or try the electrified steam engine and perhaps pause to reflect at the Titanic exhibit, the re-created radio room, the Royal Navy prisoners docks and the war memorial. You can try sailor's knots and learn how they safely lifted heavy weights. The museum is a gem, don't miss it. Recommended.

Dun Laoghaire is a vibrant and attractive culture hub and has a harbour and promenade as its focal point.

Dalkey Castle on the main street of this very attractive village.

DALKEY

Further south is the village of Dalkey. Founded by the Vikings it was an important port in the Middle Ages. In more recent times it has been the home of many writers and celebrities including Enya, Maeve Binchy, Hugh Leonard, Van Morrison and Bono of U2 fame.

There are bars and restaurants in Dalkey to suit all tastes and pockets, and there is Dalkey Castle. This is a small castle almost opposite the church on the main street. Small the castle may be but the enthusiastic guides and actors who will take you through the buiding and the adjacent early Christian church and graveyard get across the story of the castle in excellent fashion. A wonderful place to visit and a great place to bring young people to awaken their interest in history. Very highly recommended.

Street art by the artist known as 'Solus', spotted just off the main street in Dalkey.

Dublin Bay looking towards the Sugarloaf Mountain.

KILLINEY HILL

Killiney Hill is the southernmost of the two hills which form the southern boundary of Dublin Bay (the other being Dalkey Hill). On its top sits an obelisk. My reason for mentioning it here is that the hill is 153 metres high and offers magnificent views over the surrounding areas: Dublin to the northwest; the Irish Sea and – on a clear day - the mountains of Wales to the east and southeast; and Bray Head and the Wicklow Mountains to the south.

The hill is crossed by various walking paths, and with its spectacular views in all directions, is a popular destination for walkers and hikers from the surrounding areas.

There are spectacular views from the top of Killiney Hill in all directions.

The Grand Canel passes through the very heart of Dublin.

Johnny Foxes pub on the slopes of the Dublin Mountains is a popular destination for Dubliners and visitors seeking a traditional Irish pub.

Useful web addresses

TRINITY COLLEGE & THE BOOK OF KELLS   www.tcd.ie/visitors/book-of-kells/

DUBLIN CASTLE   www.dublincastle.ie

DUBLINIA
www.heritageisland.com/attractions/dublinia-experience-viking-and-medieval-dublin/

ST. PATRICK'S CATHEDRAL   www.stpatrickscathedral.ie

CHRISTCHURCH CATHEDRAL   www.christchurchcathedral.ie/visit-us/

THE GUINNESS STOREHOUSE   www.guinness-storehouse.com/

THE PHOENIX PARK   www.phoenixpark.ie

DUBLIN ZOO   www.dublinzoo.ie

ROYAL HOSPITAL, KILMANHAM   www.rhk.ie

IRISH MUSEUM OF MODERN ART   www.imma.ie

KILMANHAM GAOL   www.kilmanhamgaolmuseum.ie

THE LITTLE MUSEUM OF DUBLIN   www.littlemuseum.ie

NATIONAL GALLERY OF ART   www.nationalgallery.ie

NATIONAL MUSEUM OF IRELAND   www.museum.ie

THE GPO   www.gpowitnesshistory.ie

DUBLIN WRITERS MUSEUM   www.writersmuseum.com

CROKE PARK   www.crokepark.ie

NATIONAL BOTANIC GARDENS OF IRELAND   www.botanic gardens.ie

GLASNEVIN CEMETERY AND MUSEUM   www.glasnevintrust.ie

NATIONAL MARITIME MUSEUM OF IRELAND   www.mariner.ie

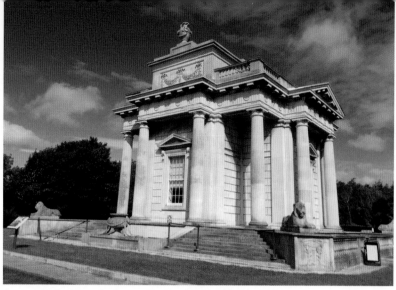

A very special building – the Casino at Marino – built as a pleasure house for James Caufield, the first Earl of Charlemont.

NORTH DUBLIN COASTAL ROUTE - HISTORY, VARIETY AND SURPRISES AT EVERY TURN

Dubliners constantly argue the merits of the North-side and the South-side. I have to admit to a certain bias being a life-long Dublin North-sider, but in truth, I also have to admit both sides of the city have their own particular attractions. Today, however, I want to take you on a journey along the North Dublin Coastal Route, and to some of the places close to the city that are very special to me.

THE CASINO AT MARINO
Our starting point is quite unique and is simply my favourite building anywhere I have travelled. The building is the Casino at Marino, just a short distance up the Malahide Road from Fairview and just three miles from the city centre and at the start of the road to Howth. So what makes this building so special? Time for a little bit of history.
The Casino was designed by Sir William Chambers (architect of Somerset House in London) as a pleasure house for James Caulfield, the 1st Earl of Charlemont. It is regarded as one of the very finest 18th

century neo-classical buildings in Europe. The name 'Casino', means 'a small house' but what appears to be a relatively modest-sized house at first sight contains no less than sixteen finely decorated rooms each of which is incredibly rich in subtely and design.
Take the guided tour of the Casino – you won't be disappointed and once you have done so you will know that you have had a unique experience in a unique building.

After leaving the Casino travel back down the Malahide Road the short distance to the coast. Just before joining the coast road again there is a short crescent shaped row of houses on your left, one of which was the home of Bram Stoker, creator of the immortal Dracula. As you travel along the road towards Howth, on your left side is historic Clontarf, where Ireland's Ard Rí (High King), Brian Ború met his end after winning a famous victory in 1014 AD that ended Viking power forever in Ireland.

Brian Boru's Well is said to mark the spot where, in his moment of victory over the Danes in the Battle of Clontarf in 1014 AD, the High King was cut down.

NORTH BULL ISLAND

Before long you will see on the sea side a wooden bridge to the North Bull Island. 'Bull Island' as it is known to Dubliners or 'Dollymount' after its 5 km strand, is a remarkable place and well worth a detour if you have the time. It's history is particularly interesting. It seems that in times gone by, Dublin Bay had a serious problem with silting at the mouth of the River Liffey. Various remedies were tried including building the Great South Wall that was completed in 1730. When this was found not to be the complete remedy a North Wall was contemplated and Captain William Bligh – yes, he of *Bounty* fame – was comissioned to make a study of Dublin Bay. Bligh's survey highlighted the potential of the North Bull sandbank and how the development of a North Bull Wall

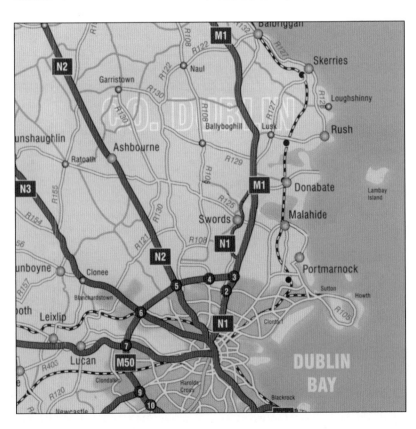

St. Anne's Park, Clontarf.

could keep the river mouth open by venturi effect.

This Wall was completed by 1825 and over the next 50 years the tidal effect so created deepened the mouth of the Liffey and what is now known as North Bull Island was formed from the redirection of the sandy deposits that had previously silted up the river entrance. Today, the island is an important nature reserve and was designated as a UNESCO Biosphere Reserve in 1981. Uniquely, it is the only Biosphere Reserve entirely in a capital city anywhere in the world. As well as the wooden bridge that links the island to the mainland there is a causeway constructed in more recent times near Raheny. When you are passing the causeway, do watch out on your left side for a fabulous tree carving.

This tree sculpture beside the road where St.Anne's meets the Bull Island causeway gloriously celebrates the wildlife of the area

ST. ANNE'S PARK

Just past the wooden bridge to Bull Island is a 240 acre park – the second largest in Dublin after the Bull Island. This is St. Anne's Park and although there are many entrances around its periferary it is best reached from Mount Prospect Avenue, a short distance up from the seafront where one first meets the park grounds.

St. Anne's was originally assembled as a 500 acre estate by descendants of Arthur Guinness, the founder of the famous

Dublin brewery. Within its boundaries are a very fine collection of over 1,000 trees, a pond, several intriguing follies, a playgound and a prize-winning rose garden.

I first discovered the charms of St.Anne's growing up in Clontarf and it retains a magical quality for me. Walk through some of it's shady paths, particularly down by the Naniken River, and you too will be transported to a special place.

The house that was the centerpiece of St. Anne's , 'The Mansion', was destroyed by fire in 1943 and its ruins were demolished

The Baily has been the site of a lighthouse since as early as 1667, the current building being completed in 1814.

One of the most interesting castles in the whole of Ireland, Howth Castle has had a structure on this site since the late 1100's. Parts of the current castle date back to the mid-fifteenth century. The castle was renovated by Sir Edwin Lutyens in 1911.

in 1968. The other significant building in the park is the Tudor red brick Ardilaun stables, developed in the 1990s and known today as the 'Red Stables' and housing a café as well as facilities for artists residences and an exhibition centre. The development of the Red Stables has won several international architecture awards.

HOWTH PENINSULA

Having left St. Anne's one again travels down to the sea and heads east towards the peninsula of Howth. Beloved of generations of Dubliners, Howth sits at the end of a gently curving shore-line. It's highest point is the Ben of Howth (560ft.) on which stands an ancient cairn and there are spectacular views in every direction including as far north as the Mountains of Mourne, a view that the writer, HG Wells, called 'the most beautiful view in the world'. Howth has something to delight every visitor. From spectacular cliff walks to sandy beaches, the Baily Lighthouse, an ancient castle and most of all, the charming village and harbour of Howth. And if you enjoy seafood then you will surely enjoy Howth's restaraunts and bars. Be sure to sample the Abbey Tavern on Howth village's main street, famous for it's part in the revival of Irish folk music in the 1950s and 60s.

It's worth saying that Howth, which was originally an island, was inhabited as long ago as 3250 BC and in the fine rhododendron gardens in the grounds of

Howth Castle, stands the Howth Dolmen, a Neolithic portal tomb built around 2000 BC. The rhododendron gardens are spectacular and were first planted in 1850. Today, they contain around 1,000 species and hybrids and the total number of varieties is almost 2,000.

Howth Castle is situated just a short dis-

The poet WB Yeats lived in Balscadden House, beside Howth village for a number of years.

tance from Howth Village as you head towards Sutton Cross, the narrow strip of land that today joins Howth to the mainland. To my mind, Howth Castle is one of the most interesting castles in the whole of Ireland. The castle has its origins in Medieval times. The First Lord of Howth, Almeric, came to Howth in 1177 AD with John de Courcey and legend has it that he gained possession of the peninsula of Howth by a victory on the feast day of St. Lawrence. In gratitude for this victory, he took the name St. Lawrence as his family name and built the original wooden castle above the harbour, however by 1235 AD a new stone castle had been built on the current site. The earliest parts of the present castle date from the mid-fifteenth century. The castle was extended and renovated several times, most notably by Sir Edwin Lutyens in 1911. Today, the descendants of Almeric, the Gaisford-St. Lawrence family, still live in the castle.

Also in the grounds of Howth Castle is The Irish Transport Museum. Let me state straight away that the title is a misnomer. If you travel there hoping to see examples of motor, rail and aviation transport you will be disappointed. What you will find is an impressive collection of public service- and commercial vehicles.

The Transport Museum in the grounds of Howth Castle has a varied and interesting collection of public service and commercial road vehicles.

The collection includes examples of the famous Howth trams that once journeyed from Sutton to the Summit and on into Howth village. Passanger, Commercial, Fire and Emergency, Military and Utility vehicles are all represented.

THE BAILEY LIGHTHOUSE
The Baily Lighthouse is located on a rocky outcrop facing Dublin Bay. Legend claims that it was to here that the Norse Vikings fled as they regrouped after their defeat at the Battle of Clontarf in 1014 AD. The battle broke the power of the Vikings in Ireland forever and when the Norman invasion reached Dublin, it was from here in 1177 AD that they left Ireland for the last time in their long boats. The first light signal on this site was established in 1667 and the current lighthouse was built in 1814. In modern times it was the last Irish lighthouse to go automatic when the last of the keepers left in 1997. Before leaving Howth, let me mention a beach of which most visitors to Howth will be unaware. As you leave Howth Castle grounds and begin to head towards Sutton Cross, there is a narrow bridge (Corr Bridge) over the railway line on your right-hand side. Cross over this bridge and turn left on to a quiet residential road seperated from the main road by the railway line. At intervals along this road are laneways that lead to Claremont Beach. It's small, it's not well-known and at low tide can be walked as far as the edge of Howth Harbour, all the while enjoying fine views of the two largest islands off Ireland's east coast, Ireland's Eye and Lambay Island. And as previously mentioned on a clear day you can even see as far as the Mountains of Mourne in Northern Ireland. I love it!

PORTMARNOCK
Portmarnock is the next place of interest along our coastal route. It lies between Baldoyle and Malahide and here is the stretch of sand known as the 'Velvet

The DH Puss Moth of Jim Mollison being readied for take-off from The Velvet Strand at the start of his solo east-west crossing of the Atlantic in August 1932.

Malahide Castle is one of the most popular attractions on Dublin's northside. The tour of the Castle is very worthwhile and there are also gardens, shops, a museum, walks and a children's playground.

Strand', the scene of several epic flights in the history of aviation. In the 1930s the Portmarnock sands were the starting point of two successful flights that used their expanse as a take-off point. On 23rd June 1930 the great Australian flyer, Charles Kingsford Smith and his crew took off in their Fokker Tri-motor The *Southern Cross*. Their flight took them to Newfoundland and then on to Oakland, California, thus completing a circumnavigation of the world. The navigator on that occasion was an Irishman, Paddy Saul. Before the flight, there were concerns that the Southern Cross might be too heavy to take off and some weight-saving began. One of the items to go was the second cronometer used as a back-up by the navigator. Saul gave this cronometer to a young friend of his.

Two years later, the newly married Jim Mollison and his bride, the avitrix Amy Johnson, arrived in Ireland from where Mollison planed to make the first solo east to west crossing of the Atlantic starting from The Velvet Strand. But the weather was unsettled and a period of waiting began. During this time they were entertained by a Dublin publisher, where Amy discovered that her host's son, Wilford, had the middle name of Jason – the same name as her famous De Havilland

biplane. As a result she took the young man, the same young man to whom Paddy Saul had given the cronometer from *The Southern Cross*, for a flight, his first, in *'Jason'*. Wilford Fitzsimmons, know to all as 'Wilf' went on to have a distingushed career in Irish motorsport with the cronometer of the *Southern Cross* fixed to the dashboard of each of his competition cars.

Today, a monument at the entrance to Portmarnock Strand commemorates the many aviators who departed from the Velvet Strand.

MALAHIDE

A little further along the coast is Malahide. This bustling town is one of the northside's jewels and is an excellent place to stop for a coffee or a meal in one of the many excellent restaraunts. Originally a Viking settlement, since 1180 AD the area has been part of the history of the Talbot family who were granted extensive lands in the surrounding area. In the early 1800s, the village had a population of just over 1,000 and by 1831 this had grown to 1,223. In recent times this figure has risen to above 16,000 and today Malahide has a higher percentage of professionals living in it than any other town in Ireland.

Close by is Malahide Castle, parts of which date back to the 12th century. The castle was home to the Talbot family for 791 years from 1185 AD until 1976 except for a short period during the Cromwellian Wars. The Castle has seen a lot of history and one story concerns the Battle of the Boyne when the family were on the losing side. It is said that on the day of the battle, fourteen members of the Talbot family sat down to breakfast in the great Hall and by nightfall all were dead.

In 1975, the estate was sold to the Irish State and has been operating as a tourist attraction since then. The Castle can be visited on a guided tour for a fee and there are also the Tadpolt Botanic Gardens behind the castle, a visitor centre and an excellent retail shop and café operated by Avoca Handweavers plus a museum shop and cycling and outdoor shops in the old courtyard of the Castle. For me, however, it is the grounds of Malahide Castle that are the real stars including woodland walks, a fine children's playground and a cricket facility where international cricket matches are played.

The monument at the entrance to The Velvet Strand at Portmarnock, recalling the pioneer aviators who took off from here.

Useful web addresses

THE CASINO AT MARINO	www.heritageireland.ie/en/dublin/casinomarino
PICASSO RESTAURANT, HOWTH	Tel: 01853 1120 www.picassorestaurant.ie
CLONTARF CASTLE HOTEL	Tel: 01 833 2321 www.clontarfcastle.ie
ST. ANNE'S, RAHENY	www.clontarf.ie
AQUA RESTAURANT, HOWTH	Tel: 01 832 0690 www.aqua.ie
HOWTH CASTLE	www.howthcastle.com/visiting
THE IRISH TRANSPORT MUSEUM, HOWTH	www.nationaltransportmuseum.org
KING SITRIC RESTAURANT, HOWTH	Tel: 01-832 5236 www.kingsitric.ie
MALAHIDE CASTLE AND GARDENS	www.malahidecastleandgardens.ie
SIAM THAI RESTAURANT, MALAHIDE	Tel: 1 845 4698 www.siamthai.ie/restaurant/malahide
THE GARDEN HOUSE CAFE, MALAHIDE	www.thegardenhouse.ie
NEWBRIDGE HOUSE, DONABATE	www.newbridgehouseandfarm.com
ARDGILLAN CASTLE, BALBRIGGAN	www.ardgillancastle.ie
BLUE BAR RESTAURANT, SKERRIES	Tel: 01 849 0900 www.bluebar.ie

Howth harbour is a busy fishing and pleasure port and a favourite place of Dubliners.

The High Cross at Monasterboice is regarded as one of the best surviving examples

A cannon looks out over the town of Drogheda from the top of Millmount Tower.

BOYNE VALLEY DRIVE -
A DRIVE THROUGH 6,000 YEARS OF HISTORY

The Boyne Valley could probably be best described as Ireland's 'Valley of the Kings'. Included on the Greek geographer, Ptolemy's, map of Ireland in the 2nd century which included the River Boyne, the history of the area around the river goes back a lot further than that. As far back as 4,000 BC in fact – that's 6,000 years ago making some of the sites that you can visit today older than the Pyramids of Gisa. But don't think the Boyne Valley drive is just a collection of tumbling ruins, it's not, and here you will find activities to seduce the most varied of tastes and interests.

DROGHEDA
Drogheda, whose name comes from the Irish, *Droichead Átha,* meaning 'bridge of the ford', is one of Ireland's oldest towns. It is located in County Louth on the east coast, some 56 km (35 miies) north of Dublin. It is the last bridging point on the River Boyne before it enters the Irish Sea, and the UNESCO World

Heritage Site of Newgrange is located 8 km to thewest of the town.

The River Boyne divides the dioceses of Armagh and Meath, and as a result Drogheda was founded as two separate towns, Drogheda-in-Meath (for which a charter was granted in 1194) and Drogheda-in-Oriel (or 'Uriel') as County Louth was then known. In 1412 these two historic towns were united into one fortified town. Today Drogheda is a busy town and there are several places of interest well worth visiting.

Millmount Museum and Tower overlooks Drogheda and is an artificial hill that may once have been a prehistoric burial ground. The Normans built a motte-and-bailey fort here and this was later replaced by a castle and in 1808 by the present round tower. Parts of what were once the army barracks on the site now house the Millmount Museum that among much else, tells the story of the brutal siege of Drogheda by Cromwell and also of the nearby Battle of the Boyne. A visit is highly recommended. St.Peter's Church of Ireland on William Street, also bears witness to the brutality of the Cromwellian forces as its spire was burned by Cromwell's men, an action that resulted in

The cross, known as Muiredach's High Cross, is 5.5 metres high, and is generally acknowledged to be the finest surviving High Cross in the whole of Ireland. The panels on the cross feature biblical carvings from the Old and New Testaments of the Bible.

Millmount Tower and Museum are built on an artificial hill that once may have been a prehistoric burial ground.

the death of over one hundred people who had sought sanctuary inside.

At the eastern end of the town's main street is the 13th Century St. Laurences's Gate, the best surviving portion of the walls that once extended for 3 km around the city.

MONASTERBOICE

Monasterboice contains the ruins of an early Christian settlement, founded in the late 5th century by Saint Buithe. It was an important center of learning and religion until it was eclipsed by nearby Mellifont Abbey founded in 1142 AD. The site contains the ruins of two churches built in the 14th century and an earlier round tower, and a 10th century High Cross for which it is best known.

MELLIFONT ABBEY

Mellifont Abbey was the first Cistercian Abbey to be built in Ireland. It was founded in 1142 AD and sits on the banks of the River Mallock about 10 km north-east of Drogheda. The Abbey soon grew in importance and by 1170 AD there were 100 monks and over 300 lay brothers living there. Other Cistercian Abbeys built in Ireland were modeled on it and it remained the main abbey in Ireland until it was closed in 1539, when it was turned into a fortified house.

William of Orange, who fought the Battle of the Boyne nearby, used Mellifont as his headquarters during the battle in 1690. Today the site of the abbey is a ruin. Interestingly, New Mellifont Abbey, located in the nearby village of Collon, is today home to the Cistercian Order in County Louth.

Where else can you come face-to-face with the soldiers who fought in the Battle of the Boyne except at the impressive Battle of the Boyne Visitor Centre near Drogheda.

THE BATTLE OF THE BOYNE VISITOR CENTRE

Opened in May 2008 by the then Taoiseach, Mr. Bertie Ahern and the then First Minister of Northern Ireland, Dr. Ian Paisley, the Battle of the Boyne Visitor Centre, is located near Drogheda on the banks of the River Boyne at Oldbridge and is open all year round for visitors.

The battle was fought on 1st July (old calendar) 1690 and was the largest attended battle in the history of Ireland with around 60,000 European troops on the field. On the Jacobite side were about 24,000 soldiers from Ireland, England and France and facing them on the Williamite side were 36,000 men from Ireland, England, France and other European countries that were part of a 'grand alliance' against Louis XIV of France. Two kings met in person at the Boyne, King James II and his son-in-law King William III. At stake was power in Ireland, the crown of England and French dominance of Europe.

Today, the battle site is managed by the Office of Public Works and features a visitor centre located in the 18th century Oldbridge House, with original and replica weaponry of the period, a very impressive laser model of the battle site and a 15 minute film in multiple languages. There are also walks through the battle site over several hundred acres, a recently restored Victorian Walled Garden and a shop and Tea Room serving light fare and refreshments. Highly recommended. And don't miss the superb laser model of the battle site.

NEWGRANGE - *BRÚ NA BOINNE*

Newgrange is a UNESCO World Heritage Site and part of a complex of monuments built along a bend of the River Boyne known collectively as *Brú na Bóinne.* The other two principal monuments in the complex are Knowth (the largest) and Dowth, but throughout the area there are as many as 35 smaller mounds.

Newgrange is a Neolithic (Stone Age) monument and was constructed about 5,200 years ago (3,200 BC) and thus is older than Stonehenge and the Great Pyramids of Giza. Newgrange consists of a large circular mound 85 meters (93 yards) in diameter and 13.5 meters (15 yards) high with a 19 meter (21 yard) stone passageway and chambers inside. The mound is circled by 97 large kerbstones, some of which are engraved with megalithic art symbols. A passage measuring 19 meters (21 yards) leads into a chamber and has three alcoves. Famously the passage and chamber are aligned with the rising sun on the occasion of the Winter Solstice.

Access to the Newgrange monument is via the *Brú na Bóinne* Visitors Centre where there are also displays explaining the complex, as well as an excellent café. A visit to Newgrange is an essential component of any visit to Ireland. Allow plenty of time for your visit and take the tour that also includes the Knowth complex. Highly recommended.

SLANE/HILL OF SLANE/SLANE CASTLE

Slane village is situated on a steep hillside on the northern bank of the River Boyne. The surrounding area contains many historic sites dating back over 5,000 years. The village centre owes its distinctive layout to the Conyngham family and is an excellent example of town planning in the 18th century. Its most distinctive features are the four identical houses that stand at the intersection of the two main streets of the village.

North of the village is the Hill of Slane some 518 metres high and there are a number of historic ruins on its summit. Legend has it that St. Patrick lit a Paschal fire on the hill top in defiance of the High King Laoire who had forbidden any fires other than his pagan festival fire on the Hill of Tara. So impressed by Patrick's devotion was Laoire when he investigated that he allowed Patrick to continue his missionary work in Ireland. The hill became a centre of religion after St. Patrick and the ruins of a friary and chuch can be seen there today. On the western slopes of the hill can also be seen the ruins of a 12th century Norman motte and bailey, built by the Flemings, at that time Barons of Slane.

The Flemings were replaced by the Conyngham family during the Williamite confiscations, and it was they who built Slane Castle on the River Boyne, most notable in recent years as the site of many large rock concerts.

NAVAN

The county town of Meath, Navan on the River Boyne is the fifth largest town in Ireland. Interesting to note that Navan is one of the few towns to have a palindromic name. The name is thought to have derived from the Irish *An Uamhain,* meaning 'the cave'.

Europe's largest lead and zinc mine is located literally in Navan, extending deep under the town and it's outskirts. The town is a busy centre for shopping and has a large commuter population travelling daily to Dublin.

KELLS

Kells – or *Ceannanas Mór* meaning 'Head Fort' – was the site of a monastery founded around 800 AD by monks from St. Columkille's monastery on the Scottish island of Iona fleeing the attacks of Viking raiders. There are many sites associated

The UNESCO World Heritage site of Newgrange was built before the pyramids, some 5,200 years ago.

Slane Castle on the River Boyne at the attractive village of Slane has been the site of several major Rock concerts down the years.

with the monastic settlement. Perhaps the most imposing are the Round Tower and the town's five High Crosses, four of which are located with the Round Tower in the churchyard of St. Columba's Church. Nearby is the small oratory with a stone roof known as St. Columncille's House and built sometime in the 11th century.

North of Kells on the Oldcastle Road is the 'People's Park' with the strange Tower of Lloyd that dominates the hilltop on which it is situated. This 18th century folly in the form of a Doric column with a glazed lantern at its top – an inland lighthouse – was erected in memory of Thomas Taylor, the 1st Earl of Bective.

LOUGCREW CAIRNS

The Loughcrew Cairns form the largest complex of passage graves in Ireland, megalithic burial chambers built around 4,000 BC, making them older than the well-known Newgrange site. The cairns are in two locations: Carnbane West

The Hill of Slane has a number of important ruins on its summit.

where there are about fifteen cairns including Cairn L which is roofed and where there are impressive and well-preserved carvings. From the car park the Carnbane West Cairns are a 2 km walk on gently sloping ground. Carnbane East contains another roofed cairn, Cairn T that also has some excellent carving. The walk to this group of cairns is shorter but much steeper. If you have the good fortune to visit Loughcrew on a good summer day the views are magnificent. And after your walk there is an excellent café as you descend from the car park. Recommended.

HILL OF TARA

The Hill of Tara is an archaeological complex that runs between Navan and Dunshaughlin and contains a number of ancient monuments and, according to tradition, was the seat of the High King of Ireland.

At the summit of the hill, to the north of the ridge, is an oval Iron Age hilltop enclosure, known as *Ráith na Ríogh* (the Fort of the Kings), In the middle of the *Forradh* is a standing stone, which is believed to be the *Lia Fáil* (Stone of Destiny) at which the High Kings of Ireland were crowned. According to legend, the stone would scream if a series of challenges were successfully met by the would-be king. At his touch the stone would let out a screech that could be heard all over Ireland. To the north of the ring-forts is a small Neolithic passage tomb known as *Dumha na nGiall* (the Mound of the Hostages), which hs been dated to around 3,400 BC.

A traditional shopfront in Kells.

The Tower of Lloyd just outside the historic town of Kells is an 18th century folly.

To the north, just outside the bounds of the *Ráith na Rí*. excavations there have discovered Roman artefacts dating from the 1st–3rd centuries, while farther north is a long, narrow rectangular feature known as the Banqueting Hall (Teach Miodhchuarta).

To the south of the Royal Enclosure lies a ring-fort known as *Ráith Laoghaire* (Laoghaire's Fort), where the legendary king is said to have been buried in an upright position. Half a mile south of the Hill of Tara is another hill fort known as *Rath Maeve*, the fort of either the legendary Queen Medb, who is more usually associated with Connacht, or the less well-known legendary figure of *Medb Lethderg*, who is associated with Tara.

A church, called Saint Patrick's, is on the eastern side of the hilltop. This modern church was built in 1822–23 on the site of an earlier one. The earliest evidence of a church at Tara is a charter dating from the 1190s. In 1212, this church was 'among the possessions confirmed to the Knights Hospitallers of Saint John of Kilmainham by Pope Innocent III'. The building is now used as a visitor centre. During the rebellion of 1798, United Irishmen formed a camp on the hill but were attacked and defeated by British troops. Some 400 rebels died on the hill on that day.

In 1843, the Irish Member of Parliament

The majestic Trim Castle is, to my mind, the most impressive Norman fortress, to tour. A visit is highly recommended.

Daniel O'Connell hosted a peaceful political demonstration on Hill of Tara in favour of repeal of the Act of Union that drew over 750,000 people.

TRIM CASTLE

Trim Castle is the largest Anglo-Norman castle in Ireland, and was constructed over a thirty-year period by Hugh de Lacy and his son Walter. Hugh de Lacy was granted the Liberty of Meath by King Henry II in 1172 in an attempt to curb the ambitions of Richard de Clare, the Norman warrior known as Strongbow. Just four years later construction of the massive three storied Keep, the central stronghold of the castle, was begun on the site of an earlier wooden fortress. This massive twenty-sided tower, which is cruciform in shape, was protected by a ditch, curtain wall and moat. During the late Middle Ages, Trim Castle marked the outer northern boundary of The Pale – the area around Dublin controlled by the English. By the 16th and 17th centuries it had declined in importance and was allowed to deteriorate. During the 15th century the Irish Parliament met in Trim Castle seven times and a mint operated in the castle.

The Castle was refortified during the Irish Confederate Wars in the 1640s. In 1649 after the sacking of Drogheda, the garrison of Trim fled to join other Irish forces and Trim Castle was occupied by the army of Oliver Cromwell.

Expert guided tours of the keep are available and are highly recommended. The guides are exceptionally good at imparting the history of the fortress and the views from the rooftop are splendid.

FOURKNOCKS

Fourknocks is a Passage Chamber Tomb built about 5000 years ago. It is located 10 miles southeast of Newgrange between Ardcath in County Meath and The Naul in County Dublin. Fourknocks has a short passage leading into a wide circular-shaped chamber with three smaller side chambers. Originally the roof was probably a wooden structure supported by a central pole. The current concrete roof was constructed in 1952 at the end of a 2-year excavation. Fragments of 65 burials were found in the tomb, both cremated and un-burnt remains of adults and children. Decorated pottery and vessels and personal ornaments including pendants and beads were also found. All of the items found are in the National Museum of Ireland.

Just inside the main chamber to the left of the entrance is one of the few representations of a human face from the Neolithic Period in Ireland. The face is about 3 feet high. Highly recommended.

An aerial view of the Tara complex set in the rich, rolling countryside of County Meath.

The Loughcrew Cairns near Oldcastle form the largest complex of passage graves in Ireland and were constructed around 4,000 BC.

Useful web addresses

DROGHEDA	www.drogheda.ie
NEWGRANGE	www.newgrange.com
MONASTERBOICE	www.discoverireland.ie/arts-culture-heritage/monasterboice-high-cross-and-round-tower/52774
MELLIFONT ABBEY	www.boynevalleytours.com/mellifont-abbey.htm
SLANE	www.visitslane.ie
THE HILL OF SLANE	www.visitslane.ie/the-hill-of-slane/
SLANE CASTLE	www.slanecastle.ie
KELLS	www.heritage towns.com/kells.shtml
LOUGHCREW CAIRNS	www.loughcrew.com/cairns/
HILL OF TARA	www.hilloftara.org
TRIM CASTLE	www.mythicalireland.com/ancientsites/tara/ www.heritageireland.ie/en/midlands-eastcoast/trimcastle/
FOURKNOCKS	www.knowth.com/fourknocks.htm

Ancient carved symbols on an entrance stone at Newgrange.

Historic Carlingford enjoys an idyllic location on the Cooley Peninsula.

THE COOLEY PENINSULA - ALONG LEGENDARY PATHS

For so many like myself who regularly travel the Dublin to Belfast road the Cooley Peninsula is easily overlooked. And that is a missed opportunity for it has secrets aplenty. This is a particularly historic landscape that played a central role in the story of The Brown Bull, The *Táin Bó Cuailinge* legend from early Irish literature, as well being associated with Finn MacCool. Numerous raths as well as much evidence of the Norman presence in this area are to be seen throughout the varied landscape.

Having turned off the main Dublin to Newry road as it enters Newry at Drumalane onto the B79 and following the signs for Omeath and Carlingford, the road runs beside the old Newry Canal that once brought ships into Newry itself. Victoria Lock, now an amenity area with picnic tables and car parking, at the head of the Newry Canal is a good place to start your journey. The Newry Canal was the first summit level canal built in Britain or Ireland (1742) and facilitated the passage of goods from Carlingford Lough to Lough Neagh. Heading towards Omeath

the B79 becomes the R173 as we cross the border. The dark bulk of Slieve Foye (579m), the highest mountain in the Carlingford range, now rises ahead of us with its smaller companion, The Eagles Rock (528 m), closer to us. Across Carlingford Lough can be seen Warrenpoint as our view of the lough opens out for the first time revealing the Mournes in all their glory on the opposite shore.

Carlingford, with it's pubs and restaurants, is an ideal base for exploring the Cooley Peninsula.

Tranquil scene near Carlingford.

CARLINGFORD

This is a very attractive road now hugging the coastline as it leads us to historic Carlingford. Few Irish towns have so much history woven into their structure as Carlingford with its Norman fortress of King John's Castle, medieval Tholsel and 15th and 16th century townhouses, as well as portions of its medieval wall. As a centre for walking, sailing and other outdoor pursuits, modern Carlingford is an ideal base for anyone who wishes to explore the Cooley Peninsula.

After Carlingford, continue along the R173 turning inland towards the road junction at The Bush, or alternatively one can continue alongside the coast for another few kilometers by taking the R176 towards Greenore. This road ends in a junction with the R175, which taken in a south-west direction will lead us to the same junction at The Bush. At this junction of five roads take the road for The Windy Gap to begin the most spectacular part of your journey through this varied landscape. As with so much of this peninsula, The Windy Gap is associated with Connacht's legendary Queen Medb and her fabled raid into Cooley in search of the Brown Bull. Her route took her through the Cooley Mountains and she is credited with having gouged out The Windy Gap or *Bearnas Bó Cuailinge* as a form of insult to the warriors of Ulster.

The impressive ruins of the Norman fortress of King John's Castle above Carlingford.

Sailing is popular all the way around the coast of the Cooley Peninsula.

THE WINDY GAP

The road from The Bush to The Windy Gap is mostly straight climbing the heather-coloured slopes gently until it reaches the narrow Gap itself. The road now begins a descent towards the town of Omeath providing spectacular views across the lough and back towards the Cooley Mountains. However, about 2 1/2 kms from The Windy Gap watch for a narrow road branching left. This road, while its first 2 kms are not the greatest surface (but certainly traversable without difficulty or damage), leads up towards the 508 m Black Mountain. The road soon improves and along the way are several parking places with spectacular views across Carlingford Lough, and, once the highest point of the road is passed, west towards Slieve Gullion described elsewhere in this guide.

The wooded slopes on the western side lead down to the end of our journey at Carrickcarnan on the main Dundalk to Newry road close to where the old customs posts were once located. Arrival back on the busy main road yet again brings home to one that it is still possible in Ireland to be in a wilderness location yet only minutes from busy areas of human activity.

The Windy Gap is associated with Queen Medb and her fabled raid in search of the Brown Bull.

PROLEEK DOLMEN

Before leaving the Cooley Peninsula, take the opportunity to visit the Proleek Dolmen, one of the finest examples of a Portal Tomb anywhere in Ireland. The dolmen is located in the grounds of the golf course attached to the Ballymascanlon Hotel, itself signposted from the nearby M1 motorway. Park in the hotel's car-park and follow the signs from the car park to the dolmen. Don't forget to throw a stone up onto the capstone of the dolmen for tradition says that 'if the stone stays there, you'll be married within a year.'

The Cooley Peninsula is an exploration worth making and will reward anyone who forsakes the main road for Medb's ancient and unexpected landscape. Recommended as a day trip.

The Proleek Dolmen at Ballymascanlon is one of the finest examples of a Portal Tomb anywhere in Ireland.

Useful web addresses

THE COOLEY PENINSULA
www.irelandseden.ie/explor-eden/carlingford-the-cooley-peninsula/

CARLINGFORD   www.carlingford.ie

KING JOHN'S CASTLE, CARLINGFORD
www.curiousireland.ie/king-johns-castle-carlingford/

THE CATTLE RAID OF COOLEY
www.tinmarch.net/index.php/en/tain-bo-cuailgne.html

PROLEEK DOLMEN   www. Curiousireland.ie/proleek-dolmen/

Useful maps: Ordnance Survey Discovery Series – Sheets 29 and 36

Wicklow abounds in great places to walk - here seen above Glendalough's Upper Lake.

The statue of Pegasus in the ornate Powerscourt Gardens.

WICKLOW - QUITE SIMPLY, THE GARDEN OF IRELAND

One of the features of the Irish landscape is how quickly it changes from one type to another. Sometimes the landscape is similar to, say, western Scotland but the distance one travels before there is a marked change in landscape is far shorter than in Scotland. Nowhere in Ireland is this more readily demonstrated than in Wicklow, long called the Garden of Ireland. Its an apt title for within Wicklow – and the county stretches from the southern suburbs of Dublin to the edge of northern Wexford, there is a variety that is unparalleled anywhere else on this island. Wild mountains, deep lakes and woodland, mix harmoniously with towns and villages of character and history. Ah yes, history, for everywhere in Wicklow are the reminders of the failed rebellion of 1798 that was fought in every corner of the county and also in Wicklow Gaol where life ended for many of the insurgents. By contrast to the mountainous interior of Wicklow are the towns that straddle it's coast for this county also has a maritime tradition kept alive today. So, allow plenty of time to explore Wicklow, explore not just the famous sites such as Glendalough but also the brown signs that point to other lesser-known attractions that, I guarantee, will surprise and delight.

BRAY

Appropriatly known as the 'Gateway to Wicklow', Bray is Ireland's oldest seaside town. Indeed, in the mid-19th century, because of its rapid tourist development, Bray was known as the 'Brighton of Ireland'.

Modern Bray has many attractions including a mile long promenade built in 1859 as well as some very fine Georgian style terraces. There is a Martello Tower built when Britain was at war with France during the reign of Napoleon and the young James Joyce lived at No 1 Martello Terrace between 1887 and 1891.

During the summer, Bray is a busy seaside town with all the attractions that go

Bray beach is a popular destination for Dubliners throughout the Summer.

There is a free Air Spectacular each year held along Bray's seafront.

with that. To the south of the town is Bray Head. It's a twenty minute climb from the car park to the top but well worth the effort as the views, particularly towards Greystones are stunning.

KILRUDDERY HOUSE
Kilruddery House is a large Elizabethan style country house on the southern outskirts of Bray about 20 km south of Dublin. The present building is a south facing multi-bay mansion, originally dating from the 17th century, but remodelled and extended in 1820 in the Elizabethan style. To the north an office wing incorporates the 17th-century building and to the south and west is a large domed conservatory.

Kilruddery House and it's grounds close to Bray are a very popular destination.

The house sits within a large landscaped demesne that features a pair of long parallel canals in front of the house.

The House and it's grounds are a very popular attraction with a wide range of activities taking place there throughout the year. There is a farm market every Saturday. As one of the few remaining 17th century gardens in Ireland or Britain, the gardens of Kilruddery House are of significant importance.

Sailing is polular along the coast of Wicklow and is well served by the counties harbours.

GREYSTONES
Greystones is a coastal town about 8 km south of Bray. The town is bordered by the Irish Sea to the east, Bray Head to the north and the Wicklow Mountains to the west.

The town was named after the one-kilometre stretch of grey stones between two beaches on the sea front. The harbour area and the Greystones railway station are at the northern and southern ends respectively. The North Beach, which begins at the harbour, is a stony beach, and some of its length is overlooked by the southern cliffs of Bray Head. The South Beach is a broad sandy beach about one kilometre long. It is a Blue Flag beach and receives many visitors and tourists, mainly in summertime. In 2008, Greystones was named as the world's 'most liveable community' at the LivCom Awards in China.

Powerscourt Waterfall should be on every visitor's list of places to see. The Waterfall has featured in several episodes of the popular TV series 'The Vikings'.

POWERSCOURT HOUSE AND GARDENS, WATERFALL, ENNISKERRY

Powerscourt Gardens, just outside the attractive village of Enniskerry, is one of the most beautiful gardens in Ireland, a fact recognized when they were voted No.3 in the World's Top Ten Gardens by National Geographic. The Gardens stretch over 47 acres and offer visitors a blend of formal gardens, sweeping terraces, statues and ornamental lakes, secret hollows and rambling walks. The Gardens were designed from 1731 onwards, with the intention of creating a garden which formed part of the wider surrounding landscape. Today, the Powerscourt Gardens include The Walled Gardens, The Italian Garden, The Dolphin Pond, The Japanese Gardens, Pets Cemetery and Pepperpot Tower, among other features and attractions which include the excellent Avoca Handweavers shop. The Gardens are open all-year round with the exception of December 25th and 26th. Recommended.

Also within the grounds of the estate is Powerscourt Waterfall - Ireland's highest at 121 m (398 ft.) and it is situated 6 km

Powerscourt House is one of the jewels of County Wicklow and a visit is highly recommended.

from the Main Estate. Driving from the gate-lodge towards the Waterfall you travel by beech, oak, larch and pine trees, some of which were planted over 200 years ago. Look out for the giant redwoods, which are native to Northern California where they may grow up to 80 m high and live for 4,000 years.

The Waterfall is an ideal location for summer picnics and barbecues. The whole area surrounding the waterfall is a haven for wildlife – Chaffinch, Cuckoo, Raven and the Willow Warbler. Other inhabitants include the Sika Deer which were introduced to Ireland in 1858 and you may even be lucky enough to see a red squirrel or two.

Take time to explore the pathways that meander through the flora and fauna, walk along the woodland pathways and listen to the birdsong.

MOUNT USHER GARDENS
Mount Usher Gardens, with its Avoca Garden Café and Courtyard Shops is situated in the village of Ashford, just 35 minutes south of Dublin city, and close to the seaside towns of Bray, Wicklow and Arklow. The popularity of the gardens, café and shops during the summer season is such that the car park can become very full but additional parking is available in Ashford village a short walking distance away.

Mount Usher is one of the finest examples of an authentic 'Robinsonian' style garden combining a fine collection of trees and shrubs with informal floral planting schemes in a sheltered valley setting. A detailed Tree Trail Guide is provided to visitors to help locate the many superb examples in the Gardens. Recommended as is the excellent Avoca Garden Café.

Mount Usher Gardens on the outskirts of Ashford are an excellent example of a 'Robinsonian' Garden.

Time to check the map in the attractive village of Enniskerry.

WICKLOW TOWN AND GAOL

Wicklow Town is the ccounty town of County Wicklow. The town owes its origins to the Vikings who began plundering the east coast of Ireland around 795 AD and in the mid-9th century they established a settlement here taking advantage of the natural harbour at Wicklow. The Black Castle ruins that overlook the harbour are a reminder of the Norman invasion. Wicklow was granted to Maurice FitzGerald who built the Black Castle that played a significant role in the town's history.

The harbour and its surrounds play an integral part in the life of the town, both commercially and from a tourist point of view. Enjoy a stroll out either of the piers or further along The Murrough, a coastal

Wicklow Gaol has a dark past and was the final destination of many Irish insurgents.

wetland, very popular with walkers and nature lovers where you can enjoy views of the town and coastline. Wicklow is a pleasant town and in recent years has developed it's historic Gaol as a tourist attraction.

A visit to Wicklow's Gaol is to experience prison life as it was endured by its 18th

River as it makes its way from the Vartry Reservoir to nearby Ashford village. The site hosts a mixture of broad leaf and conifer forest with fine stands of beech, Spanish chestnut and ash. The steep rock face of the gorge has been colonised by various species of plant life: lichens, mosses and the polypody fern and the area is home to Sika deer, fox, otter,

The 'Military Road' runs through the heart of Wicklow and via the 'Sally Gap'.

century inmates. Using experienced actor guides, the story told in this interactive tour is of the harshness of prison life in the 18th century and of the cruelty of the transportation ships that took prisioners to a new life in Australia. Very though-provoking and recommended.

ASHFORD/DEVILS'S GLEN
Ashford is an attractive village on the outskirts of which are two notable attractions – the Mount Usher Gardens (mentioned already elsewhere) and The Devil's Glen.

The Devil's Glen boasts a dramatic landscape that was fashioned at the end of the Ice Age when the melt waters of the ice sheet created the valley. The resultant gorge affords a swift decent for the Vartry

badger and squirrel. The site was once part of the Glanmore estate, former ancestral home of John Millington Synge. There are walks through the Devil's Glen accessed by two car parks, one at the start of the Seamus Heaney Way and the other at the start of the Waterfall Walk. Recommended but don't lose your way!

THE MILITARY ROAD
The Military Road runs north-south across the heart of the Wicklow Mountains. It was constructed over nine years between 1800 and 1809, following the 1798 rebellion, with the purpose of opening up the Wicklow Mountains to the British Army to assist them in putting down insurgents who were hiding there. The road runs from Glencree through Sally Gap to Glenmalure and on to

Aughavanagh where it ends. It was one of the first purpose-built roads in Ireland and four barracks were built along the way at Glencree, Laragh, Glenmalure, and Aghavannagh. The engineer in charge of its construction was Alexander Taylor (b. 1746), who was also responsible for many other roads in the country, including some early toll roads.

Throughout Wicklow are many poignant memorials remembering those who fell in successive rebellions agains English rule, in particular the failed 1798 Rising.

SALLY GAP

Sally Gap is a cross-roads on the Military Road that leads you North to Dublin, West to Blessington, South to Glendalough or East to Roundwood. From the road there are spectacular views of the surrounding blanket bog and the Wicklow Mountains. It is one of two east-to-west passes across the Wicklow Mountains.

Close by are the Glencree valley, the dark waters of Lough Tay, Kippure Mountain and Glenmacnass Waterfall.

LUGGALA

Luggala, also called Fancy Mountain, is a 595 metres (1,952 ft) mountain east of Sally Gap. Its cliffs are situated above a spectacular lake, Lough Tay, and are a popular location for rock climbing. The mountain is part of the Luggala Estate (also known as the Guinness Estate), which is owned by wealthy arts patron Garech Browne, a member of the Guinness family. The buildings on the estate, including the luxurious Luggala Lodge are rented commercially all year-round.The estate has been used as the location of some major films, including Zardoz, Braveheart and Excalibur, as well as the historical drama television series Vikings.

LARAGH

Laragh is a small, pictureesque village at the junction of three roads through the Wicklow Mountains and close to Glendalough. There are several good places to eat but it is most notable for it's proximity to the ancient monastic settlement of Glendalough, one of Ireland's most popular tourist attractions.

Luggala and Lough Tay are an area of great natural beauty and tranquility.

An unusual view of the Valley of Glendalough and the two lakes after which it is named.

GLENDALOUGH

Glendalough is a glacial valley in the heart of the Wicklow Mountains and is renowned for it's early medieval monastic settlement founded in the 6th century by St Kevin. Some time in the sixth century, St. Kevin crossed the mountains from Hollywood to Glendalough. And over a period of one hundred years the area developed into one of the most important monastic sites in Ireland. The monastery continued to flourish after St. Kevin's death in 617 AD and by the end of the eighth century, the monastery employed up to 1000 laypeople to help grow crops and tend livestock. Monasteries were wealthy. In addition to stores of treasure, most monasteries maintained substantial stocks of food and were able to survive periodic famines. Such rich sites were often plundered and Glendalough's remote location made it an easy target, and between 775 and 1095 AD it was plundered many times by both local tribes and Viking invaders. Usually the churches and houses were burned, but each time the monastery was rebuilt, only declining after it was annexed to the diocese of Dublin in 1152 AD.

Today the ruins of the ancient monastic site are scattered throughout the valley, and many are around 1000 years old. The main sites are located in the area known as the Monastic City, beside the OPW Visitor Centre, where Guided tours are available. Further afield are the ruins of other churches, extending from St. Saviour's Church in the far east of the valley, to *Temple na Skellig* beside the Upper Lake.

The Monastic City is the name given to the main monastic site at the eastern end of the valley, close to the OPW Visitor Centre and the Glendalough Hotel. The following monuments can be seen in the Monastic City. The Gateway stands at the entrance to the Monastic City, and is perhaps one of the most important monuments as it is now unique in Ireland. The building was originally two-storied, probably with a timber roof. Inside on the west wall, is a cross-inscribed stone. Visitors entering the Monastic City from the road still pass through this ancient entrance,

The Round Tower at Glendalough in the Monastic City.

walking on some of the original stone paving.

Perhaps the most noticeable monument, is the Round Tower which is about 30 metres high. The entrance is about 3.5 metres from the base. Originally there were six wooden floors with ladders. The roof had fallen in many years ago, but was rebuilt in 1876 using the original stone. Round towers were multi-functional. They served as landmarks for visitors, bell-towers, store-houses, and as places of refuge in times of attack.

The Cathedral is the largest of the churches, and was constructed in several phases. Of note, are an aumbry or wall cupboard under the southern window, and a piscina - a basin used for washing sacred vessels. Outside the Cathedral is St. Kevin's Cross - a large early granite cross with an unpierced ring. The Priest's House is a small Romanesque building which was almost totally reconstructed using the original stones in 1779. The east end has a decorative arch. The original purpose of the building is unknown, but it may have been used to house the relics of St. Kevin. In the 18th and 19th centuries, it was used as a place to inter priests.

St. Kevin's Kitchen is a church most notable for its steep roof formed of overlapping stone, supported internally by a semi-circular vault. The belfry has a stone cap and four windows facing north, south, east and west, and is reminiscent of a round tower. Only the low walls of St. Kevin's Church remain. It was uncovered in 1875, and probably commemorates the founder of Clonmacnoise, the monastic settlement on the banks of the River Shannon, that had associations with Glendalough during the 10th century.

Quite apart from it's historic value, Glendalough and it's surroundings are areas of great natural beauty and there are many walks to be discovered in the surrounding landscape. A visit here is a must. Highly recommended.

BLESSINGTON

In 1667, Michael Boyle (the younger), Archbishop of Dublin and Lord Chancellor of Ireland, received a Royal Charter to establish the town of Blessington. Construction of Blessington House began in

Lake. The reservoir was created when the waterfall at Poulaphouca on the River Liffey (which flows from the Wicklow Mountains to Dublin) was dammed to create a hydro-electric plant that is still in use today. The valley was flooded and the resulting lakes extend over approximately 5,000 acres . In doing so a small village was submerged by the damming of the waterfall, and the remains of roads can still be seen leading down into the lake.

In addition to electricity, the lakes also provide water for the locality and the Dublin region as well as providing a leisure resource. The lake is also extensively used by boatmen and fishermen, and is a training location for the Irish Air Corps HQ divisions from Baldonnel, 15 km north of Blessington, and also Local Civil Defence Water rescue teams.

RUSSBOROUGH HOUSE

Russborough House is situated 5 km south of Blessington, on the road from Blessington to Ballymore Eustace. Built by the Leeson family, Earls of Milltown, it became the home of philanthropist Sir Alfred Beit,

Russborough House, situated 5 km south of Blessington, houses an important art collection.

1673 and shortly afterwards St. Mary's Church in Blessington, which was completed in 1683.

The town is situated beside Poulaphouca Reservoir, also known as the Blessington

Russborough is a treasure trove for any lover of art, culture and social history.

The house has survived two forced occupations (in 1798 and in 1922), two fires (in 1964 and in 2010) no less than four art rob-

Interior of Russborough House.

beries (in 1976 by the IRA and in 1986 by Martain Cahill ('The General') and also in 2001 and in 2002. It's a stunning place to visit and there are a range of activities and tours to make your visit memorable.

AVONDALE

Avondale House, close to Rathdrum, was the birthplace of Charles Stewart Parnell, one of the foremost politicians in Irish history. Avondale House and Forest Park includes the Charles Stewart Parnell Museum. There are over 500 acres of mature woodland with tree's from all over the world including the tallest collection of trees in Ireland. There are walking trails from an easy 1 hour walk to a tough 5 hour trek. Avondale House was designed by James Wyatt and was built between 1777 and 1779. In 1846 Charles Stewart Parnell, one of Irelands greatest political leaders in modern Irish history, was born in the house. There is an American Room dedicated to Admiral Charles Stewart – Parnell's American grandfather who manned the USS Constitution during the 1812 war. There is also a licensed cafe, book shop, picnic areas, children's play area, three orienteering courses and numerous walking trails. In 1904 the state purchased the Avondale Estate to develop modern day forestry in Ireland, and today it is regarded as the historic home of Irish Forestry. The walking trails are particularly recommended.

Avondale House, near Rathdrum, was the birthplace of Charles Stewart Parnell, one of the greatest of Irish politicians.

The Meeting of the Waters, immortalised in song by Thomas Moore.

THE MEETING OF THE WATERS

The Meeting of the Waters, is where the Avonmore and Avonbeg rivers come together to form the Avoca River. Inspired by the beauty of the place, it was here that Thomas Moore penned the famous Irish melody, 'The Meeting of the Waters.

"There is not in this wide world a valley so sweet

As that vale in whose bosom the bright waters meet!

Oh the last rays of feeling and life must depart

Ere the bloom of that valley shall fade from my heart"

The remains of Black Castle overlooks Wicklow Harbour.

Useful web addresses

BRAY	www.bray.ie
KILRUDDERY HOUSE	www.kilruddery.com
GREYSTONES	www.greystonesguide.ie
POWERSCOURT	www.powerscourt.com
MOUNT USHER GARDENS	www.mountushergardens.ie
AVOCA GARDEN CAFÉ	www.mountushergardens.ie/gardencafe/
WICKLOW GAOL	www.wicklowshistoricgaol.com
WICKLOW TOWN	www.visitwicklow.ie/item/wicklow-town/
THE DEVIL'S GLEN, ASHFORD	www.coillteoutdoors.ie
THE MILITARY ROAD	www.visitwicklow.ie/item/old-military-road/
LUGGALA	www.luggala.com
GLENDALOUGH	www.glendalough.ie

WICKLOW MOUNTAINS NATIONAL PARK
www.wicklowmountainsnational park.ie

BLESSINGTON	www.visitwicklow.ie/item/blessington
RUSSBOROUGH HOUSE	www.russborough.ie

AVONDALE HOUSE
www.visitwicklow.ie/attractions/avondale-house-forest-park/

The Meeting of the Waters   www.visitwicklow.ie/item/meeting-of-the-waters/

**Useful maps: Ordnance Survey Discovery Series - Sheets 56, 62 and 69
Fir Tree Aerial Maps - Wicklow**

Wicklow roads are relatively traffic-free and afford visitors a view over a constantly changing landscape.

Experience Kilkenny the Pembroke way

In the heart of the city centre, just minutes' walk from Kilkenny's most famous landmarks including Kilkenny Castle, St Canice's Cathedral & Ireland's Medieval Mile, Pembroke Kilkenny is the perfect base to enjoy the sights and sounds of Kilkenny. Explore the thriving arts culture and rich medieval heritage of Ireland's Ancient East on a variety of driving routes.

The hotel stands on the site of the well-known Statham's Garage and the 1930's Statham's Ford Special race car is on display. Visit our website to see footage of the car racing in the 1935 Limerick Grand Prix.

PEMBROKE
Kilkenny

Tel: 00353 56 77 83500
www.pembrokekilkenny.com

The site of Kilkenny Castle has been fortified since Strongbow, the legendary Norman warrior, built a fort here in the 12th century.

IN AND AROUND KILKENNY - IRELAND'S FRIENDLY MEDIEVAL CITY

If there is one city in Ireland that I delight in returning to again and again, it is the city of Kilkenny. Abounding in history, Kilkenny is neither too big or too small – in other words it retains a human dimension and can easily and comfortably be explored on foot. I love its narrow streets filled with restaurants and coffee shops, the mystery of places like Kytler's Inn with its links with medieval witchcraft and the modern Kilkenny, as evidenced by the Kilkenny Design Workshops, a leader in modern silver design.

But most of all it's a place to walk, either through it's streets or along the banks of the River Nore by the side of the impressive Kilkenny Castle. Do blend the old with the new when you visit Kilkenny – climb the Round Tower beside St Canice's Cathedral and take the Smithwick's Experience in the famous local brewery. Perhaps, like me, you'll fall under the spell of the place and want to return again and again. I hope so.

THE MEDIEVAL MILE
Once the medieval capital of Ireland, Kilkenny's origins predate existing medieval landmarks. St Canice founded a monastic settlement here in the 6th century. The 9th century round tower beside

the cathedral of St Canice's, is a remaining monastic landmark from this settlement. Built in the 13th century and a showcase for ornate stonemasonry skills, St Canice's is the second longest Cathedral in Ireland.

Strongbow, the legendary Norman invader, built a fort here in the 12th century

Kilkenny's Medieval streets are a joy to explore.

Kilkenny is a compact city, making its exploration easy and enjoyable.

on the site where Kilkenny Castle stands today. William Marshall (Strongbow's son-in-law, the 4th Earl of Pembroke) fortified the city walls, built a stone castle on the site and consolidated the Norman's position of power in the city.

Ireland's only witch trials took place in Kilkenny in 1324 and are believed to be Europe's first witchcraft trials. Dame Alice Kyteler (an innkeeper and moneylender) was accused of using poison and sorcery against her four husbands, having in the process amassed a fortune from them. Before she could be tried, Alice fled to England, but her maid was flogged and burned at the stake, which hardly seems to have been justice!

The city prides itself on its lively culture and entertainment scene with a range of live music and theatre events available throughout the city's pubs and music venues. There's a range of festivals held annually, including the renowned Kilkenny Arts Festival (August) which features a variety of classical music events, art exhibitions, literary readings, workshops, jazz and folk sessions. Other festivals include Smithwick's Kilkenny Roots Festival - Music Festival (May); the renowned

Kilkenny Cat Laughs - a Comedy Festival (June); the International Gospel Choir Festival (August/September); Greystock Festival - (September) and the famous Savour Food Festival (October).

Kilkenny is also renowned as a world class craft centre, having its origins in the Design workshops of the late 1960s, the story of which can be explored in the Castle Yard site.

One of the best and unique features of Kilkenny is its compactness allowing you explore everything it has to offer on foot, just be sure to allow yourself enough time to experience it all.

KILKENNY CASTLE

Kilkenny Castle stands dramatically on a site that commands a crossing on the River Nore and dominates the 'High Town' of Kilkenny City. Over the eight centuries of its existence, many additions and alterations have been made to the fabric of the building, making Kilkenny Castle today a complex structure of various architectural styles.

The original Anglo-Norman stone castle was built for William Marshal, 4th Earl of Pembroke (c.1146-1219) during the first

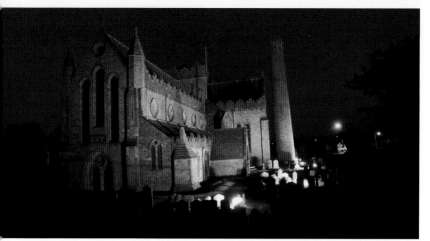

The Cathedral of St. Canice's is the second longest in Ireland and was built in the 13th century.

decade of the 13th century. Kilkenny Castle later became the principal Irish residence of the powerful Butler family for almost 600 years. The Butler ownership began when James, the 3rd Earl of Ormond, purchased the castle in 1391, and lasted until 1967 when Arthur, 6th Marquess of Ormonde, presented it to the people of Kilkenny in return for a token payment of £50. The buildings have been in the care of the Office of Public Works since 1969, and much important archaeological excavation,

Rothe House is a unique Tudor merchant's townhouse built between 1594 and 1610. Full of surprises, a visit is highly recommended.

conservation, and restoration have been carried out there. Guided tours of the castle are available and are highly recommended.

ROTHE HOUSE

Rothe House is one of the surprises of Kilkenny! It's a unique Tudor merchant's townhouse, built between 1594 and 1610, and actually comprises three houses, three enclosed courtyards and a large garden to the rear. The property is a lot bigger than it looks from the street. To accommodate his growing family, on this long, narrow plot, John Rothe Fitzpiers built three houses, one behind the other, with cobbled courtyards in-between. To the rear is a half-acre garden that runs all the way back to the old City Wall.

The property is now owned by Kilkenny Archaeological Society and is home to their large collection of artefacts relating to Kilkenny city and county. The garden has been painstakingly reconstructed to reflect the Rothe Family garden and is planted with heritage varieties of vegetables, herbs, flowers and fruit. A visit is highly recommended. Self-guided tours are the norm but guided tours are available for larger groups.

Outdoor dining in Kilkenny.

SMITHWICKS

The Smithwick's Experience was named as 'one of the Top 25 Hot New Attractions in the World to Visit in 2015' by *The Lonely Planet*. There are brewery tours and there are brewery tours and this one is definetly recommended. Follow the story of Smithwicks from the first batch of malt to the final tasting of a delicious pint on a guided tour. Not to be missed.

DUNMORE CAVE

I first visited Dunmore Cave many years ago long before it was ever developed as a visitor attraction. It was an unforgettable experience made even more memorable by the knowledge that the cave had been the site of a Viking massacre in ancient times.

Today access is much easier and there is an interesting exhibition centre telling the history of the cave and it's geology. The cave consists of a series of chambers formed over millions of years, containing some of the finest calcite formations found in any Irish cave. The cave has been known to man for many centuries and is first mentioned in the 9th century Irish Triads. The most interesting reference however, comes from the Annals and tells of a Viking massacre at the cave in the year 928 AD. Archaeological finds within the cave confirm Viking activity. Guided tours are available and are recommended for a unique experience.

A guided tour of the Smithwick's Brewery is not to be missed.

The Statham-Ford Special in action in the Leinster Trophy Race at the Skerries road circuit in 1934 driven by MJ Hynes.

STATHAM-FORD SPECIAL

The 1930s were a very special era in Irish Motor racing. The three successful Irish International Grand Prix held in Dublin's Phoenix Park between 1929 and 1931 encouraged many enthusiasts to become involved and led to races being held on street and road circuits throughout Ireland.

For those that could not afford a purpose-built racing car, there was an alternative – designing and building your own 'Special'. This was a very popular route into motor racing for Irish enthusiasts and these 'Specials' were often of a very high standard and very competitive.

One of the most famous 'Special's was the Statham-Ford Special built in the garage of the same name on which the Pembroke Hotel on Patrick Street now stands. Designed and built by George Statham, the car was taken to several notable successes by MJ Hynes, who drove it throughout its career.

Powered by a Ford V-8 engine it had a notable success at the 1934 Phoenix Park Senior Race that it won outright in a new record time. But it's greatest success came in the 1935 Limerick Grand Prix, a street race that attracted the cream of international drivers and their cars to this island. There it placed 7th overall against some of the finest purpose-built racing cars of the day built by such legendary names as ERA, MG and Bugatti.

Today, this historic racing car, the Statham-Ford Special, can be seen at classic car events in the area and is recalled at the Pembroke Hotel.

The plaque on the exterior of the Pembroke Hotel marking the birthplace of the Statham-Ford Special.

GRAIGUENAMANAGH

Graiguenamanagh is a gorgeous village on the banks of the River Barrow and at the foot of Brandon Hill. There's kayaking on the river, good places to eat and once a year the 'Town of Books' Festival takes place here. What's not to love?

Visit the Cistercian Duiske Abbey and the nearby village of St. Mullins, an oasis of calm and a sense of timelessness or enjoy coffee and dessert at the famed Mulican Café. Spending a few hours lingering in Graiguenamanagh is strongly recommended

Night life at the Left Bank pub, Kilkenny.

The lovely village of Graignamanagh nestles on the River Barrow at the foot of Brandon Hill.

Kayaking on the River Barrow at Graignamanagh.

JERPOINT ABBEY
Jerpoint Abbey, on the road south from Thomastown, is a very impressive religious ruin. There is a visitors centre explaining the long history of the site. Its probable that the present Cistercian building dating from between 1180 and 1200 AD was erected on the site of an earlier Benedictine abbey sometime around 1158 AD by Donal MacGilla Patrick, King of Ossory. The oldest part of the surviving structure is the Irish-Romanesque transepts and chancel where Bishop O'Dulany who died in 1202 AD lies. The abbey was dissolved in 1540 and its 1880 acres were given to the Earls of Ormonde. Recommended.

Enjoy a coffee and dessert at the famed Mulican Cafe.

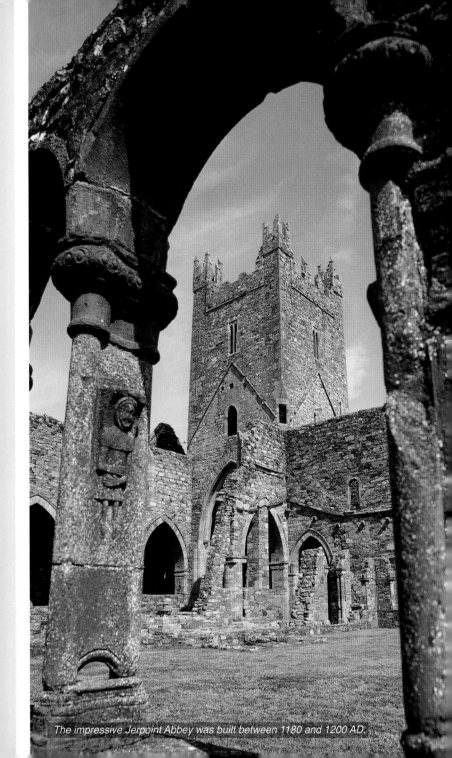

The impressive Jerpoint Abbey was built between 1180 and 1200 AD.

The extensive ruins of Kells Priory are somewhat undiscovered by visitors. Take the time to explore this remarkable complex.

KELLS PRIORY

Kells Priory is an Augustinian Priory founded in 1193. It is situated alongside King's River beside the village of Kells, about 15 km south of the medieval city of Kilkenny. Perhaps its most striking feature is the collection of medieval tower houses spaced at intervals along and within walls which enclose a site of just over 3 acres. These give the priory the appearance more of a fortress than of a place of worship and from them comes its local name of 'Seven Castles'.

There is also a Celtic cross dating from the 9th century that stands over the burial site of *Niall Caille*, High King of Ireland. Kells Priory is a very impressive site that is only at the early stage of being developed to make it more accessible to visitors. At the moment it's still a well-kept secret' and I would strongly recommend seeking it out.

Useful web addresses

KILKENNY	www.visitkilkenny.ie
KILKENNY CASTLE	www.kilkennycastle.ie/visitorinformation/
ROTHE HOUSE	www.rothehouse.com
PEMBROKE HOTEL, KILKENNY	www.pembrokekilkenny.com
JERPOINT ABBEY	www.visitkilkenny.ie/jerpoint_abbey
GRAIGENAMANAGH	www.visitkilkenny.ie/graigenamanagh
KELLS PRIORY	www.visitkilkenny.ie/kells_priory
DUNMORE CAVE	www.visitkilkenny.ie/dunmore_caves

Wexford at dusk, viewed across the River Slaney.

WEXFORD, WATERFORD AND THE COPPER COAST - WHERE VIKING AND NORMAN LEFT THEIR MARK

Ireland's sunny south-east, as it is called with good reason is one of my favourite regions of Ireland. Look solely at the map and you might feel that there are few reasons to attract the visitor when compared to the wild beauty of the west of Ireland, but you would be wrong for there is here a wealth of experiences to delight and to bring you back again and again. There's history galore but there are also wonderful beaches, fishing villages and great places to eat as well as surprises like coming face-to-face with a Mercury Space Capsule at the JFK Memorial Centre, or experiencing the Dunbrody Famine Ship at New Ross. The best way to enjoy Ireland is to set out with a loosely defined plan to go to a particular place but to then let yourself be persuaded to follow all the signs that you come across to interesting places you've yet to discover. Wexford and Waterford abound in such opportunities so allow yourself plenty of time and take all the oppoprtunities that will present themselves.

WEXFORD
Wexford is the county town of County Wexford and is on the south side of the estuary of the Slaney River. Founded around 800 AD, Wexford is yet another Irish town that owes its origins to the Vikings. For the next three hundred years Wexford was a Viking town, however in 1169 AD it was besieged by Dermot MacMurrough, the King of Leinster and his Norman ally Robert Fitz-Stephen. The Vikings put up a fierce resistence but eventually were persuaded to accept a settlement.

Through the Middle Ages Wexford was a English town and following the Crusades, the Knights Templar had a presence in Wexford. Today, their presence is perpetuated in the old Knights' Templar chapel yard of St. John's Cemetary, on Wexford's Upper St. John's Street. Wexford was one of the key centres of the 1798 rebellion when the town was held by rebels throughout the conflict.

Today Wexford is a bustling town with a stong interest in the arts. The annual Wexford Opera Festival every October is recognised internationally and there are many theatre groups active in the town. Wexford is an excellent shopping centre and its cuisine is distinct from the rest of Ireland, in particular its seafood with smoked cod, mussels and rissoles being favourite dishes.

Johnstown Castle contains a fascinating museum telling the history of agriculture from the 18th century onwards.

Wexford has several interesting attractions. The Wexford Wildfowl Reserve is just outside the town on the eastern side of the River Slaney. From early October to the middle of April, the north and south slobs and the harbour are home to thousands of ducks, geese, swans and waders making this a site of major international importance for wildfowl and waders. It's a wonderful place for a walk and there is an observation tower from which to view the birds without disturbing them. Situated three miles from Wexford town on the Rosslare Road is the Irish National Heritage Park depicting man's settlement in Ireland from around 7,000 BC up to the arrival of the Normans. There is an excellent audio-visual telling the story and many reconstructions of the dwellings of the time and other objects. Like a visit to the Wexford Wildfowl Reserve, a visit to the Irish National Heritage Park is highly recommended.

Johnstown Castle was built by the Esmonde family who came to Wexford in 1169 AD. The walled gardens were first laid out between 1844 and 1851 and

Vinegar Hill, just outside Enniscorthy, was the site of the rebels last stand during the Rebellion of 1798.

pathways throughout the grounds of the castle meander through a woodland garden and around the lakes. In addition there is a Museum displaying the history of Irish Agricultural life from the start of the 18th century onwards. This is a fascinating museum and a visit, combined with a visit to the gardens is recommended.

The attractive town of Enniscorthy is one of the longest continuously occupied sites in Ireland.

ENNISCORTHY

Enniscorthy is the second largest town in County Wexford and is one of the longest continuously-occupied sites in Ireland with a history going back as far as 465 AD.

Situated on the River Slaney, Enniscorthy is an attractive place to visit with much to interest the visitor. Wexford and in particular Enniscorthy played a key role in the failed rebellion of 1798 and the story of the Wexford rebels is dramatically told in the National 1798 Rebellion Centre. The rebels final stand at nearby Vinegar Hill is told in a 4D Experience and the whole history of the rebellion comes to life in dramatic detail. Not to be missed – the 1798 Rebellion was a seminal event in Irish history – and highly recommended. (Note: the Centre is closed during the winter months).

At Enniscorthy Castle there are exhibitions exploring the development of the Castle and town from its earliest Anglo-Norman origins up until its use as a family home in the early 20th century. Unique displays include areas dedicated to the 1916 Rising in Enniscorthy, (the only town to rise outside of Dublin), as well as the work of the renowned Irish furniture designer and architect, Eileen Gray.

Enniscorthy Castle is one of the few Irish Castles to offer access to its roof where a spectacular view of the surrounding countryside awaits. Or you can descend to the deeps of its dungeon and view the wall art depicting a medieval soldier who was imprisoned in the dungeons over 400 years ago. Recommended.

Wells House is a Victorian House and Gardens situated between Gorey and Wexford.

Winterval in Waterford.

WELLS HOUSE AND GARDENS

Wells House and Gardens, is a Victorian House and Gardens situated on the R741 about 18 km from Gorey on the Gorey to Wexford road.

Built in the late 1600s, this Daniel Robertson designed house was remodeled in the 1830s. Wells House and Gardens has much to enjoy with two woodland walks, a living house tour, daily garden tours, a craft courtyard, terrace gardens, archery, clay pigeon shooting, falconry, an adventure playground and an animal farm with falconry centre. The house and gardens are open all year round.

NEW ROSS

No visit to the town of New Ross on the River Barrow would be complete without experiencing the Dunbrody Famine Ship. Situated on the New Ross quayside, the award winning Dunbrody Famine Ship Experience is unique, transporting you back to the journey of Irish emigrants fleeing the diastrous Irish Famine that began in the mid-1840s. As well as the ship's tour, the Dunbrody Visitor Centre houses an excellent river-view restaurant and the Irish America Hall of Fame. The Hall of Fame commemorates the critical contribution made by Irish men and women to US history, as well as acknowledging the continuing contribution of contemporary Irish Americans. The guided tour of the ship features costumed performers and themed exhibitions providing a unique insight into the bravery and fortitude with which Irish people faced up to a desperate situation. Stroll along the newly developed quayside featuring public art and sculptures, and incorporating The John F. Kennedy Memorial Wall and statue and the spectacular Emigrant Flame, which was lit from the American President's grave at Arlington National Cemetery.

JFK MEMORIAL PARK AND ARBORETUM

THE John F. Kennedy Park and Arboretum is dedicated to the memory of John Fitzgerald Kennedy, the 35th president of the United States of America until his assassination on 22nd November 1963. It is located a short distance south of New Ross and consists of 622 acres including 4,500 types of trees and shrubs, 200 forest plots, rhododendrons and dwarf conifers. Special features include an Ericaceous Garden, (with 500 different rhododendrons, and many varieties of azaleas and heathers), dwarf conifers, hedges, ground covers and climbing plants. The lake is the most popular part of the Arboretum, and is a haven for waterfowl.

A road provides access to the 271m summit of Slieve Coillte from which there are panoramic views. A Visitor Centre houses exhibitions and an audio visual show. Recommended.

The award winning Dunbrody Famine Ship is an essential stop on any visit to New Ross.

KILMORE QUAY

Kilmore Quay is a fishing village near Duncormick. Its leisure facilities such as sailing, and sea angling charters are significant and the village holds a seafood festival during the summer with seafood served everyday, live music in the local pubs, and activities such as raft races, and family fun days.

The Saltee Islands lie off the coast near Kilmore Quay, and boat trips to these islands are available from the village. The two islands, Great Saltee and Little Saltee, are mainly known for being Ireland's largest bird sanctuary with gannets, gulls, puffins, cormorants, razorbills, and guillemots living on the islands.

HOOK HEAD

The lighthouse on Hook Head is an almost unique example of a near-intact Medieval lighthouse, dating from early in the 13th century. Purpose-built as a lighthouse it has served mariners and shipping for 800 years and is thought to be one of the oldest operational lighthouses in the world. When the light was automated in 1996 it was decided to open the facility to the public.

Hook Head also offers superb opportunities for whale watching. The Irish Whale and Dolphin Group run a sighting scheme and you should consult their website for further information. The most commonly observed cetacean species observed from Hook Head are small Harbour porpoise while Common and Bottlenose dolphins are sometimes observed. During the winter months of November to February Humpback and Fin Whales – some of the largest animals on our planet, can also be seen. To improve your chances of seeing these creatures be sure to have a pair of binoculars available.

Kilmore Quay is a busy fishing village notable for its summer seafood festival.

A visit to the Visitor Centre at the JFK Memorial Park and Arboretum will surprise and delight.

The lighthouse at Hook Head is a near-intact Medieval lighthouse, dating from early in the 13th century.

WATERFORD

Waterford is Ireland's oldest city, having been founded by the Vikings in the 9th century. It has survived seiges, invasions, famine and economic highs and lows. Today its rich history is celebrated in the area known as the Viking Triangle. It is so called because of the 1000-year-old Viking walls which once surrounded it. Perhaps the most famous building in the triangle is Reginald's Tower (which contains the Viking Museum) but the triangle is also the site of the Medieval Museum and the Bishop's Palace Museum, collectively known as Waterford Museum of Treasures. Reginald's Tower is situated on the quay-

side and contains an exhibition of stunning Viking treasure. It is named after the Viking who founded Waterford in 914 AD. Any visit to Waterford should incude an exploration of the iconic Reginald's Tower. Very highly recommended.

Also within the Viking Triangle is the Medieval Museum where you can see the medieval Cloth-of-Gold Vestments as well as the 1373 AD Great Charter Roll of Waterford that was viewed by Quees Elizabeth II during her visit to ireland in 2011. Again, highly recommended.

The other must-see location in the Viking

Reginald's Tower, on the Waterford Quayside, dates back to the Viking foundation of the city, Ireland's oldest.

Triangle is the Bishop's Palace, an authentic 18th century Georgian grand residence built in 1743. While there be sure to see the only surviving gold mourning cross commissioned by Napoleon's mother on the Emperor's death in 1821 and also the oldest surviving piece of Waterford Crystal (1789) in the world. Other places within the Viking Triangle worth visiting are the 13th century Franciscian Friary, Greyfriar's Church and the Greyfriar's Gallery – Waterford's Municiple Art Gallery.

On The Mall, adjacent to the Viking Triangle is a modern attraction that brings visitors from all over the world, the House of Waterford Crystal. Two hundred years of

The plaque in Catherine Street that marks the side of WF Peare's Garage, Ireland's first purpose-built garage, where there is still a garage today.

crystal making is celebrated there and a guided factory tour is available where you can experience the intricate manufacturing processes that go into the making of this world famous product. There is also an opulant retail store with the world's largest collection of Waterford Crystal.

Two other attractions I must mention are firstly Mount Congreve, one of the great gardens of the world. Mount Congreve House was designed by local architect John Roberts, and is an 18th century Georgian mansion. Curraghmore House, near Portlaw, is around 30 minutes from Waterford City and is the historic home of the Marquis of Waterford. It was the last of four castles built in Ireland by the Le Peor family after their arrival in Ireland in 1167 AD. With over 2,500 acres of formal gardens, woodland and grazing lands it is the largest private demesne in Ireland. A sitka spruce planted on the estate in the 1830s is among the tallest trees in Ireland and stands guard over King John's Bridge. Built in 1205 this stone-arched structure, spanning the Clodagh River, is the oldest bridge in Ireland. Twelve miles of famine relief boundary walls and four sturdy wrought iron gates surround the estate. Gnarled pink chestnut trees line the approach to the big house and original castle tower. Group tours of the main reception rooms of Curraghmore House can be arranged by prior appointment. This tour takes in some of the finest neo-classical rooms in Ireland which feature the magnificent plaster work of James Wyatt and grisaille panels by Peter de Gree. Recommended.

Finally, before we travel on from Waterford City, I'd like to mention the Waterford and

Waterford's Medieval Museum is a treasure house of the cities past and a visit is highly recommended.

The opulent retail store at the House of Waterford Crystal in Waterford city.

Suir Valley Railway, a narrow gauge heritage railway that follows 8.5 km of the old Waterford to Dungarvan route. The railway runs from Kilmeaden Station to Gracedieu Junction providing an elegant way to see some of the best scenery along the River Suir. Recommended.

TRAMORE

Tramore (from the Irish, *Trá Mhór,* meaning 'big strand') is a seaside town that has continually expanded since the arrival of the railway in 1843. Initially the town flourished as a tourist destination but in more recent years it has developed as a seaside satellite town of Waterford City, which is 13 km to the north. Waterford Airport is located about 6 km northeast. The town is situated on the north-western corner of Tramore Bay on a hill that slopes down to the strand that divides the bay. Behind the spit lies the tidal lagoon known as the Back Strand. Tramore has an imposing Gothic Revival Catholic Church, dominated by an asymmetrical tower and spire, on a monumental site overlooking the town. The area within a 16 km (10 mi) radius of Tramore is an area rich in megalithic structures including Ballindud Cromlech; Ballynageeragh Cromlech; Knockeen Dolmen and Gaulstown Dolmen, all indications of the settlement of the area long before Christianity.

DUNGARVAN

Dungarvan is a market town arranged around its own bay in the west of County Waterford. Dungarvan has an excellent reputation for food and good restaurants and there is choice aplenty to suit all tastes overlooking the Quays and in the town Square. Dungarvan Museum explains the history of the whole area and the Old Market Art Centre holds art exhibitions throughout the year. King John's Castle opens its gates and exhibition to the public during the summer months and you can see traditional crystal crafting and glass cutting at Comeragh Crystal. But above all else, do be sure to sample

Dungarvan is noted for its many fine seafood restaurants.

One of the many activities on Tramore's fine beach,

the local sesfood when you are in this pleasant seaside town.

ARDMORE

Ardmore is a seaside resort and fishing village along the coast of County Waterford not far from the town of Youghal in County Cork. It is believed to be the oldest Christian settlement in Ireland. St Declan lived in the area at some time between 350 and 450 AD and brought the Christian message before the coming of St. Patrick. There is a fine 30 m high 12th century Round Tower and the ruins of a 12th century cathedral on a hill above the village. On the outer walls of the cathedral are images saved from an earlier 9th century building.

Also nearby is the superb Cliff House Hotel, a small boutique style hotel and restaurant.

LISMORE

Lismore is located in the west of County Waterford on the River Blackwater at the foot of the Knockmealdown Mountains, the mountain range that divide Waterford and Tipperary. The town traces its origins to the arrival of St Carthage in the area in 636 AD. The town developed and was at one time a celebrated university city attended by scolars from all over Europe. But the town attracted the attentions of the Vikings who sacked it, plundering its riches and burning it to the ground. With the arrival of the Normans to Ireland, Prince John, the son of King Henry II, built Lismore Castle in 1185 AD. For four centuries the castle was an Episcopal residence, until in 1589 it was leased with its lands to Sir Walter Raleigh. Richard Boyle, later the great Earl of Cork, purchased Sir Walter Raleigh's estates in 1602. His famous son Robert Boyle, the father of modern chemistry, was born in Lismore Castle in 1626. In 1748, the castle and its lands passed to the 4th Duke of Devonshire through the marriage of Lady Charlotte Boyle. The battlements and turrets of the present day castle date from a mid-nineteen century refurbishment. The present owner of Lismore Castle is the 12th Duke of Devonshire. Whilst the Gardens and Gallery are open to the public, the Castle itself remains a private family home.

St Carthage's Cathedral lies beyond tall gothic gates and has been a place of worship since 636. Gravestone slabs from monastic times may be found inside the Cathedral. The first stone Church on this site was build about 1207 but the present church dates from 1630. The Earl of Cork had the building restored at the time but naturally the structure has been altered and extended since. A superb tower and ribbed spire were added by the Pain Brothers in 1827. The remarkable table-tomb of the McGraths dating from 1486 is worth viewing and in the graveyard around the Cathedral many old and interesting gravestones may be found.

The beautiful setting of Lismore Castle on the banks of the River Blackwater.

The 'Hindu-Gothic' Dromana Gate, near Villerstown, is a curious mixture of styles, designed by a local architect Martin Day and built in 1849.

Trawnamoe Cove, on the Copper Coast, is one of many beautiful inlets waiting to be discovered.

The Waterfall in the Comeragh Mountains, an area of outstanding beauty just inland from the Copper Coast.

THE COPPER COAST

The Copper Coast takes its name from the 19th century copper mines that lie at its heart. In 2001 the area wa awarded European Geopark Status in recognition of its outstanding volcanic geology and in 2004 this was followed by UNESCO Global Geopark status.

To follow the Copper Coast take the R675 coastal drive to Tramore. The Cooper Coast extends from Fenor (just outside Tramore) to Stradbally (just before Dungarvan), It's a beguiling place that rewards taking the time to explore its many coves, caves and harbours. There are a string of interesting villages along the Copper Coast including Stradbally, Bunmahon, Boatstrand with its charming harbour, Annestown, Fenor and Dunhill. From several of these villages guided walks are available along parts of the Copper Coast and joining one of these is recommended so as to gain the most from your visit to the area.

COMERAGH MOUNTAINS

From the end of the Copper Coast at Dungarvan, the R672 heads inland around the Monavullagh and the Comeragh Mountains. Both provide ideal walking territory and be sure not to miss seeing the Mahon Falls in the Comeragh Mountains and Ormonde Castle if you venture on to the town of Carrick-on-Suir.

Useful web addresses

WEXFORD VISITOR GUIDE
www.visitwexford.ie/sites/default/files/content/VisitWexford-Wexford-Visitor-Guide-2016.pdf

ENNISCORTHY	www.enniscorthytourism.com
WELLS HOUSE AND GARDENS	www.wellshouse.ie
JOHNSTOWN CASTLE	www.wexfordweb.com/johnstown/
IRISH AGRICULTURAL MUSEUM	www.irishagrimuseum.ie
KILMORE QUAY	www.visitkilmorequay.com
WATERFORD	www.southeastireland.com/pwaterford-ireland.html
REGINALD'S TOWER	
MEDIEVAL MUSEUM	
BISHOP'S PALACE MUSEUM	www.waterfordtreasures.com
WATERFORD CRYSTAL	www.waterfordvisitorcentre.com
CURRAGHMORE HOUSE	www.curraghmorehouse.ie
MOUNT CONGREVE	www.mountcongreve.com
WATERFORD & SUIR VALLEY RAILWAY	www.wsvrailway.ie
FITZWILTON HOTEL, WATERFORD	www.fitzwiltonhotel.ie
ARDMORE	www.ardmorewaterford.com
CLIFF HOUSE HOTEL	www.cliffhousehotel.com
LISMORE HERITAGE CENTRE	www.discoverlismore.com
LISMORE TOWN	www.lismoreheritagetown.ie
TRAMORE	www.southeasternireland.com/ptramore.html
DUNGARVAN	www.dungarvantourism.com/welcome/web
THE COPPER COAST	www.coppercoastgeopark.com
	www.copper-coast.com

ORMONDE CASTLE
www.discoverireland.ie/arts-culture-heritage/ormonde-castle/8443

Useful maps: Ordnance Survey Discovery Series – Sheets 76 and 77

The Copper Coast.

A view of Carlow Town, situated on the confluence of the Rivers Barrow and Burrin.

THE GORDON BENNETT TRAIL - MIDLAND SURPRISES

This route takes you along the figure eight course that was used for the Gordon Bennett Race of 1903, and in doing so takes you on a journey through the counties of Laois, Kildare and Carlow. Along the way you'll learn the history of this important motor race as well as travelling through spectacular Irish countryside and into the picturesque towns and villages of these midland counties. You'll find the entire route very well signposted with signs bearing the 'Gordon Bennett Route' logo and along the way you'll find activities to interest everybody. So let's get started.

A number of years ago I wrote what I hope will prove to be the definitive history of this important motor race (The 1903 Irish Gordon Bennett – *The race that saved Motor Sport*, published by Bookmarque). As a result I was asked to provide text for a guide to the race route when the official Gordon Bennett Route was being established by the tourism bodies in Counties Laois, Kildare and Carlow. I was very happy to do so, not simply because the race was very important in the history of international motor

sport as well as Irish motoring, but also because following the route the racers took seems to me to be an ideal way to see three of the most beautiful midland counties in Ireland.

There's a great deal to see and do along this route and much of it will surprise you, so take your time, explore everything that takes your fancy and enjoy the variety of the Irish Midlands.

The Gordon Bennett Trail is marked by easy to follow signs.

Ernest Shackelton, the great leader and explorer of the Antarctic, was born in Kilkee, close to Athy and his achievements are remembered at the Athy Heritage Centre.

OLD KILCULLEN VILLAGE

This spectacular ecclesiastical site is located on the top of a small hill. Tradition links it with St. Patrick and although this is uncertain, it is known that the settlement established there was raided by Vikings in both 936 and 944 AD. According to the Annals of the Four Masters, the 936 AD raid saw 1,000 prisoners being taken. Despite this the town grew in size into a walled town during the time of the Normans. During the 1798 rebellion the site saw the Battle of Kilcullen, initially a success for the rebels but which, within hours became a costly slaughter by government troops.

The building of a bridge over the River Liffey at another site nearby brought about the decline of Old Kilcullen and the rise of the modern town of Kilcullen.

Today there is a Round Tower, High Cross and the remains of a church to be seen on the site.

A model of Shackelton's ship Endurance in the Athy Heritage Centre.

THE STORY OF THE 1903 RACE..

The great Breton driver, Fernand Gabriel, at speed during the race in his French Mors racing car.

In 1903 an event took place in Ireland that was to set the pattern that led to international motor racing and the Grand Prix series that we know today. That event was the fourth Gordon Bennett race.

The history of this remarkable race began in 1899 with the presentation by James Gordon Bennett, millionaire owner of the *New York Herald,* of a silver trophy to the Automobile Club de France to be awarded for an international motor race, the first such race in the history of motorsport. The first Gordon Bennett race took place in 1900 and for several years the races remained insignificant. What saved the event from oblivion was the totally unexpected victory in 1902 of Selwyn Francis Edge driving a British Napier.

Under the rules of the contest the winning country had to host the following years race, and that provided the British club with a dilemma. In Britain there was a strong anti-motoring lobby and a blanket speed limit of 20kph (12mph). Clearly the race could not happen in Britain. Irish enthusiasts proposed that the race should be held in Ireland as it would bring visitors to the island, thus helping the depressed economy.

A figure eight course was eventually decided upon centered on Athy, and legislation was passed in Parliament repealing the speed limit for the day of the race – 2nd July 1903. The course was unusually to be held on a closed circuit over a total distance of 545.8 kms (327.5 miles) to be traversed three times with an extra circuit of the western loop.

Entries were received from the USA, Germany, France and England and for the first time cars were to be painted in national colours. America choose red, Germany white and France blue while the English team choose emerald green in honour of the host country. The track was prepared and arrangements were made for the circuit to be marshaled by members of the Royal Irish Constabulary.

At 7 am on race day Edge led the field of twelve cars away from the start at Ballyshannon Crossroads. By the second lap the great Belgian driver, Camille Jenatzy, driving a Mercedes for Germany had moved into a lead he was never to lose. Disaster befell Charles Jarrott when the steering of his Napier broke on a fast downhill section and the car overturned trapping his *mécanicien*, Bianchi, underneath. Happily, he was soon freed and suffered non-life treatening injuries.

The official programme of Automobile Fortnight in Ireland - the two weeks of events whose highlight was the Gordon Bennett race.

Camille Jenatzy, the Belgian driver, who won the Irish race driving a Mercedes.

By the end of a long days racing, Jenatzy brought his Mercedes home first, followed by De Knyff, followed in turn by Henry Farman, both driving French Panhards.

The race and its organisation demonstrated how a major race could be run safely and efficiently and set the pattern for the races that were to follow, until 1906 when the Autoimobile Club de France introduced a revised format, to be known as the Grand Prix.

143

Carlow Courthouse, designed by William Vitruvius Morrison, is said to be modelled on the Temple of Llissus in Athens.

A visit to the Athy Heritage Centre, located in the 18th century Market House in the Centre of the town is highly recommended.

KILGOWAN LONGSTONE

Kilgowan Longstone is a standing stone situated on a small hill just off the N9 near Kilcullen. It is 2.5 metres high and is unusual in having a small cross cut into its granite. The site has never been properly excavated but it is believed that there were Iron Age and later, Christian burials at the site.

BALLITOR QUAKER MUSEUM

The charming village of Ballitore developed in the 17th century as a Quaker settlement when two Quakers, John Bancroft and Abel Strettel established farms in the area. Originating from Yorkshire, the Quakers who settled there developed the town as the only planned and permanent Quaker settlement in Ireland.

In 1975 the Meeting House of the Society of Friends was restored by Kildare County Council and today houses a library and museum. The museum contains many items of Quaker interest and a visit is highly recommended.

MOONE HIGH CROSS

At Moone there is evidence of settlement going back at least 6,000 years, making it one of the oldest inhabited places in Irland. In the sixth century, St. Colmcille founded a monastry there.

The Moone Cross is one of the finest High Crosses surviving and dates back to the 8th century and stands within the ruins of the Medieval church. It was discovered buried in the Moone Abbey churchyard in 1835 and measures 17 and a half feet from its platform to its summit.

CARLOW TOWN

Situated on the confluence of the Rivers Barrow and Burrin, Carlow is a busy market town. Its courthouse is a particularly fine building, having been designed by William Vitruvius Morrison in 1839, and is said to be modeled on the Temple of Llissus in Athens. By contrast, its basement is s maze of cells and dungeons. There is a cannon captured during the Crimean War on its steps outside.

Carlow Castle is thought to have been built by William de Marshal, Lord of Leinster, between 1207 and 1213. Today it is a ruin owing to the efforts of a local physician who in 1814 tried to remodel it as an asylum. Attempting to demolish the interior he used explosives that destroyed all but the west wall and towers. Located on the Athy Road just outside Carlow is the Carlow Military Museum, well worth a visit, but check the opening hours first.

The Barrow Walk – a beautiful riverside trail – can be joined at Carlow and offers much of architectural interest to the visitor as well as a varied flora and fauna. The full Barrow Walk stretches from Lowtown to St. Mullins and is 113 kms in length.

ARDSCULL MOTTE

About 5 kms from Athy on the road to Kilcullen is the great earthworks that mark the location of an Anglo-Norman Motte and Bailey timber castle. The castle was probably built towards the end of the twelfth century by William Marshall, Earl of Leinster. It may surprise visitors to learn that one of the battles of the Scottish War of Independence was fought in the vicinity of Ardscull. A Scottish army, led by Edward Bruce, brother of Robert Bruce, King of Scotland, was moving towards Castledermot when it encountered an English army. Despite a significant advantage in numbers the English were defeated and as a result, Edward Bruce was crowned King of Ireland soon afterwards on the Hill of Faughart in County Louth.

During the Gordon Bennett race the site was a favourite viewing place for many spectators and there is a memorial to the race beside the picnic area at the foot of the Motte.

ATHY

Athy takes its name from *Ae*, the son of *Deargabhail,* who was slain in a second century battle at a ford on the River Barrow. Thereafter, the ford was called *Ath-Ae*, which was later anglicised into Athy.

White's Castle was built in 1417 AD by Sir John Talbot, Viceroy of Ireland, to protect the bridge over the River Barrow and was

White's Castle in Athy was built to protect the important bridge over the River Barrow in 1417 AD.

one of the outposts guarding the Pale, the area of Ireland centered on Dublin controlled by the English.

Located in the former 18th century Market House, Athy Heritage Centre has a number of dispays telling the story of Athy, some of it's famous sons and the events that took place there. There is material on the Gordon Bennett race as well as artifacts relating to Sir Ernest Shackelton and his Antartic expeditions including

an original sledge and harness together with a 15 ft model of his ship Endurance.

A visit to the Heritage centre is something that should not be missed.

KILCULLEN

The town of Kilcullen came into being around the new bridge built over the River Liffey in 1319 AD. As Kilcullen prospered, Old Kilcullen declined. Ireland's first toll road, opened in 1729, ran to the 'bridge at

Veteran cars in a rally in County Kildare.

Kilcullen' – its maintenance and administration were at times questionable and caused amending legislation to be enacted several times in its history.

THE CURRAGH

The Curragh of Kildare is a flat, open plain of common land some 5,000 acres in size between the towns of Newbridge and Kildare. It is well-known for horse breeding and training and the Curragh Racecourse located there is Ireland's premier Flat racecourse, hosting all five of the classic races in the Irish calender.

The Curragh was a regular site for the mustering of the armies of the English forces of the Pale. During the 1798 rebellion there was a massacre at the place known as Gibbet Rath, while in the natural bowl-shaped amphitheatre known as Donnolly's Hollow the Irish champion boxer Dan Donnelly, defeated the English champion George Cooper in 1815.

Today the Curragh Camp, the main trainging camp of the Irish Defense Forces is located on the southern edge of the Curragh.

KILDARE

Kildare town has much to offer the visitor.

An excellent Heritage Centre is located in the towns 18th century Market House, while the Irish National Stud and the world famous Japanese Gardens are located on the edge of the town. Also close by is Kildate Village, an excellent collection of mainly outlet boutiques and restaurants located in a very attractive setting.

IRISH NATIONAL STUD AND JAPANESE GARDENS

The Irish National Stud and Japanese Gardens are on the outskirts of Kildare town. The National Stud provides an opportunity to see some of the world-class thoroughbreds, mares and foals for which County Kildare is world famous. There is also a small but interesting horse museum teling the story of some of the most famous horses produced there.

At the same venue is the internationally famous Japanese Gardens, widely regarded as the finest such gardens in Europe, and created between 1906 and 1910 by the Japanese gardener Tassa Eida and his son. The gardens are a must-see but beware the sometimes torturous paths they follow at times. There is also an Irish water and rock garden with a monastic cell as its centrepiece dedicated

Horses racing at the Curragh, Ireland's premier Flat Racing racecourse.

Atop the Rock of Dunamaise are the ruins of a castle. Its a romantic site of mystery and much beauty.

to the patron saint of Irish gardeners, St. Fiachra.

KILDARE VILLAGE

Kildare Village is a designer outlet mall on the edge of Kildare town. Its presented in an authentic village setting and is home to 80 fashion and lifestyle boutiques and a number of restaurants.

MOORE ABBEY WOOD

Moore Abbey Wood is a wooded area of around 250 acres of conifer and broadleaf trees at Monastrevin. There are many well laid-out pathways and the woods are notable for their fabulous display of Bluebells in early summer. There are a number of self-guided trails laid out through the woods.

DUNAMAISE

The Rock of Dunamaise is a rocky outcrop in County Laois with the ruins of a castle on it commanding a fine view over the surrounding countryside. The earliest authenticated reference to the castle is in the Annals of the Four Masters who state that *Dun Mase* was attacked and plundered by the Vikings in 843 AD. Recognising the strategic importance of the site, the Normans enlarged its fortifications, before it began a slow decline, finally becoming a stronghold of the Cromwellian forces in Ireland. Now in ruins, it is an fascinating site and a visit is recommended.

STRADBALLY

The largely 18th century town of Strad-

bally was developed by the Cosby family. Today this pretty Laois village is best known for the Electric Picnic festival held there each year and for the Narrow Gauge Railway opearated at Stradbally Hall. There is also St. Colmans monastry which is thought to be the place where the Book of Leinster, now preserved in Trinity College, was made. The nearby Windy Gap offers great views of the surrounding countryside.

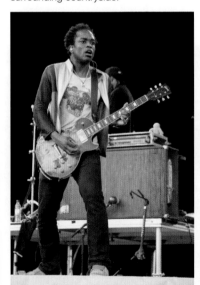

The annual Electric Picnic Festival at Stradbally is one of Ireland's most popular music festivals.

Traditional Irish shop front near the Athy Heritage Centre.

Useful web addresses

THE QUAKER MUSEUM, BALLITORE
www.discoverireland.ie/Arts-Culture-Heritage/ballitore-library-quaker-museum/13670

THE MOONE HIGH CROSS www.kildare.ie/southkildareheritagetrail/moone.htm

GORDON BENNETT TRAIL BROCHURE
www.gordonbennettroute.com/brochure.pdf

ATHY HERITAGE CENTRE www.athyheritagecentre-museum.ie

MOTTE OF ARDCSULL www.kildare.ie/southkildareheritagetrail/ardscull.htm

KILDARE HERITAGE CENTRE www.kildare.ie/kildareheritage/

THE IRISH NATIONAL STUD AND JAPANESE GARDENS
www.irishnationalstud.ie

THE JAPANESE GARDENS www.japanesegardens@eircom.net

MOORE ABBEY WOODS
www.discoverireland.ie/arts-culture-heritage/moore-abbey-wood/44732

THE ROCK OF DUNAMAISE www.megalithicireland.com/dunamaise.html

STRADBALLY www.stradbally.com

Useful maps: Ordnance Survey Discovery Series – Sheets 55 and 61

Ulster

Rathlin Island

The castle at Narrow Waters was an English stronghold built in 1560.

THE MOURNE COASTAL DRIVE - FOREST PARKS AND THE MOURNES

Great efforts have justifibly been made in recent times to attract visitors to the Causeway Coast of Northern Ireland but as a result the Mourne Coastal Drive perhaps tends to be somewhat over-looked. This is a great pity for it combines some very interesting places with several areas of great natural beauty. The Mournes were immortalised by Percy French when he wrote of the place *'Where the Mountains of Mourne sweep down to the sea"*. And the Mournes do sweep down to the sea, most particularly at the bustling town of Newcastle which nestles at the foot of the highest of the Mournes, Slieve Donard. But between the town of Newry and the village of Strang-ford on the southern shore of the lough of the same name, there is a world of inter-esting places waiting to be discovered on this quiet coastal road.

NEWRY

Newry occupies the gap between Slieve Gullion and the Carlingford Mountains and it may surprise visitors to learn that it owes its origins to a group of Cistercian monks who were its founders in 1144 AD.

But it was as a garrison town guarding the narrow Northern Gap on the southern borders of the province of Ulster that Newry prospered. The town sits on the River Clanrye and a canal to Lough Neagh was completed in 1741 to allow

Murlough Beach, near Newcastle is actually an ancient sand dune system some 6 kms. in length.

In Tullymore Forest, County Down, in the Mourne Mountains.

The town of Warrenpoint is situated at the mouth of Carlingford Lough, viewed here from the Cooley Peninsula.

the produce of the inland towns to be brought to market here. Incidentallly, that canal was the first in the British Isles, being completed some 20 years before the Bridgewater Canal became the first to be built in England.

WARRENPOINT

Taking the coast road out of Newry quickly brings you to the town of Warren-point, a traditional seaside resort with a beach and a marina from where there are boat trips to Omeath. Carlingford Lough, on which Warrenpoint is situated, marks the border between Northern Ireland and the Republic, and has the appearance of a narrow fiord. The town was named by the Vikings who probably felt at home in its fiord-like waters and they were recorded here as early as 841 AD, using the waters as a base for raiding nearby Armagh. In 1560 an English garrison was established when they built a stronghold at Narrow Waters.

ROSTREVOR

The pictureesque town of Rostrevor lays claim to being the 'most sheltered place' in Northern Ireland, nestling as it does between the mild waters of Carlingford Lough and Slieve Martin. This is an area of forest pines and also a native oak woodland and its well-worth making the short diversion to Rostrevor Forest Park and Kilbroney Park, both of which have fine forest drives.

In Kilbroney churchyard, there's a granite obelisk commemorating Major General Robert Ross who in 1814 captured Washington DC. It is said that he ate the dinner prepared for President Madison who had hastily departed!

THE SILENT VALLEY

From Rostrevor the coastal road travels through Greencastle to Killkeel, from where one should follow the signs heading inland to The Silent Valley. Here are the two reservoirs and dams that provide water to the Greater Belfast area. There's a fascinating visitors centre that tells the story of the construction of this massive

project in the early years of the last century. Although you cannot take your car up to the reservoirs the area has been landscaped and is a pleasing walk among the surrounding mountains. Here also is the start and finish of the Mourne Wall – a 22 mile structure that crosses the summits of some 15 mountains and encloses the entire Mourne water catchment area having been built between 1904 and 1922. A visit to The Silent Valley is highly recommended.

SPELGA DAM

If you feel like continuing your inland detour a little further to the west, then head for Spelga Dam, just above which is the highest road in Northern Ireland. It's a good place to access the so-called 'inner Mournes', the circle of mountains around the beautiful Lough Shannagh.

ANNALONG

Annalong's tiny harbour is protected by two rocky clefts in the coastline and is a

The beautiful surroundings of the Silent Valley reservoir

Annalong's tiny harbour nestles between two rocky clefts.

Newcastle's Festival of Flight thrills holiday crowds every August.

pleasant place to explore or to simply take a break, watching the world go gently by.

NEWCASTLE

Between Annalong and Newcastle the road rises as it travels along the coast and is where the Mourne Mountains truly *'sweep down to the sea'*. Slieve Donard – the highest of the Mourne Mountains – dominates but this prettily situated seaside resort bustles with activity. There's a fine beach that stretches from Dundrum Bay to Newcastle's harbour and borders Royal County Down, the championship golf course. The sea-side of the town is dominated by the massive Victorian Slieve Donard Hotel, a monument to the

importance of Newcastle as a holiday resort in times past. The Mourne Heritage Trust is situated in the town and provides information about all aspects of the Mournes and the many activities available there.

Every year in early August there is a superb Air Display here when the aircraft perform parallel to the natural amphitheatre of the bay. I recommend a visit to it highly. The sight of the now-grounded Avro Vulcan approaching at low level between the Mourne peaks during a recent display is just one memory that will remain with me forever!

Before leaving Newcastle can I recom-

The Victorian Slieve Donard hotel is one of Newcastle's great landmarks - here photographed during the August air display.

155

Kilclief Castle was built for the Bishop of Down, John Sely, in 1413.

mend travelling the two miles west to Tollymore on the slopes of Slieve na Brock and Luke's Mountain. This very attractive Forest Park in the Valley of the Shimna River has attractive walks and numerous follies.

DUNDRUM

Leaving Newcastle we soon come to the interesting village of Dundrum, where John De Courcy built a castle in the 13th century on a rocky site – the Fort of the Ridge' - that commands superb views over the surrounding countryside and the coast.

The nearby sand dunes at Murlough have produced abundant evidence of Stone-age and Bronze-age settlements, while just south of Dundrum village is the 4,000 year old Sliddery Dolmen or portal tomb.

STRANGFORD

The drive from Dundrum to Strangford along the coast and through Ardglass provides excellent scenary and passes the well-preserved Kilclief Castle, built in 1413 by John Sely, Bishop of Down. He lived there until 1443 when he was sacked for an adulterous liasion.

The pretty village of Strangford is situated at the narrowest part of the entrance to Strangford Lough and is where the ferry departs for nearby Portaferry on the northern shore of the lough. During the Anglo-Norman occupation the site was considered of supreme importance and no less than four castles commanded this stretch of coastline. In recent times the production of the successful *Game of Thrones* television series has been based around the village. Highly recommended as an eating place in Strangford village is *The Cuan,* where one might rub shoulders with members of the cast of *Game of Thrones* who regularly eat here during filming.

The regular ferry service between Strangford and Portaferry.

Useful web addresses

THE CUAN GUEST INN	Tel: 028 4488 1222 www.thecuan.com

DUNDRUM CASTLE   www.discovernorthernireland.com/dundrum-castle-dundrum-newcastle-p2866

MORELOUGH NATIONAL NATURE RESERVE
www.nationaltrust.org.uk/morlough-national-nature-reserve

NEWRY   www.carlingfordandmourne.com/newry

NEWCASTLE   www.carlingfordandmourne.com/newcastle

TOLLYMORE NATIONAL OUTDOOR CENTRE   www.tollymore.com

TOLLYMORE FOREST PARK   www.discovernorthernireland.com/tollymore-forest-park-castlewellan-p2888

THE SILENT VALLEY   www.silentvalley.gov.in/silenthome/php

SLIEVE DONARD HOTEL
www.hastingshotels.com/officialsite/slieve-donard-resort-and-spa/

WARRENPOINT   www.carlingfordandmourne.com/warrenpoint

NEWCASTLE FESTIVAL OF FLIGHT   www.newcastleairshow.wordpress.com
www.niaviation.co.uk

Useful maps: Ordnance Survey Discovery Series – Sheets 21 and 29

Portaferry, on the northern shore of Strangford Lough.

The Ring of Gullion is an example of a Ring Dyke produced when the active volcano's caldera underwent collapse. Slieve Gullion is a part of the Ring of Gullion.

SLIEVE GULLION - THE GIANT'S LAIR

The 'Troubles' were not kind to South Armagh, but the years since the Good Friday Agreement have worked wonders for this neglected area where there is much for the motorist to discover. Perhaps the most dramatic and scenic part of South Armagh is the area around Slieve Gullion (Holly Mountain) just a few short kilometers south-west of Newry. Surprisingly few people are familiar with this ancient mountain that is mentioned in the epic *The Cattle Raid of Cooley.* At its 576 m summit – the highest in Armagh - is a 5,000 year-old passage grave and nearby is the small *Calliagh Bernas* Lough – The Witch's Lake – which is associated with the enchantment of Finn McCool by a witch.

Approaching from Dublin along the M1 continue to the slip road for Newry. Turning to the east will bring you into the town of Newry but turning to the west will take you along the B113 through the village of Meigh and shortly afterwards to the modest entrance to Slieve Gullion Forest Park. A short drive takes you to the Courtyard Buildings that were originally built by the Chambre family in 1820 and are now managed by The Slieve Gullion Courtyard Development Group, who provide environmental education and tourist facilities. For younger visitors there is the opportunity to play in the Adventure Playpark; explore the Giant's Lair in the wonderful Hawthorn Hill Forest Nature Reserve and woodland trails. There are also the ornamental walled garden, where you will find picnic benches, an outdoor performance stage, an *al fresco* coffee bar (open in the summer) and a wildlife pond with covered seating areas.

I should explain the Giant's Lair. It's simply the most ambitious children's arts project ever commissioned in Northern Ireland,

and is open to boys, girls, elves and fairies alike. The Giant's Lair Story Trail takes young visitors on an unforgettable journey of intertwined fairy house and arts features creating a childhood land of mystery, dragons, giants, witches and fairies. The art in the Giant's Lair is all in-spired by the rich tapestry of local legend and mythical folklore and is spread over a mile of woodlands in the Forest Park.

Children can follow in the footsteps of Flynn the mischievous fairy, who has one important job – not to allow anyone to wake Slieve Gullion; It might look like a mountain but it's really a sleeping giant! Drop in for a cup of dandelion tea, grab a seat at the Giant's Table, stroll along to the Ladybird House and sneak a peek at local witchy trickster, The *Cailleach Beara*. The Giant's Lair without a doubt, captures a genuine sense of enchant-ment and mystery in the beautiful setting of Slieve Gullion Forest Park.

For the entire family, signposted from the Courtyard car park is the 13 k Slieve Gullion Drive which is one-way throughout its length. For the first kilo-meter or two the road takes you through a heavily wooded area before breaking out into open moorland which turns an amazing purple in Summer and reveals the most spectacular views as the road rapidly ascends. The mountains of the Cooley Peninsula and the Mournes rise up in the distance to provide a spectacular backdrop to the rolling countryside of south Armagh.

As the road swings first north-west and then due north it reveals more spectacular views towards the rugged nearby hills of Slievenabolea, Carricka-stickan and Croslieve – all reflecting, like Slieve Gullion itself, their origins in volcanic activity many millennia ago. While looking towards these spectacu-lar hills a brief glimpse is caught of a

As the road climbs to its highest point, Slieve Gullion's unusual surrounding landscape is revealed.

Peregrine Falcon – the perfect addition to a magnificent landscape.

The Slieve Gullion Drive continues to its most northerly and highest point from where one can continue on foot to the passage grave on its summit. The road now doubles back on itself while descending all the while providing new and equally spectacular views and confirming the realization that this is a very beautiful part of Ireland.

Having reached its most southerly point the drive now swings back towards the northeast returning to the point where we began close to the Courtyard. All in all a memorable drive of discovery and somewhere that will live long in the memory.

Useful web addresses

RING OF GULLION www.ringofgullion.org
www.ringofgullion.org/living-history/
www.wikipedia.org/wiki/Slieve_Gullion
www.voicesfromthedawn.com/slieve-gullion/
www.carlingfordandcooleypeninsula.ie/index.php/attractions-carlingford-cooley-peninsula/ring-of-gullion-aonb

Useful Maps: Ordnance Survey of Northern Ireland Discoverer Series Sheet 29

The Giant's Lair takes young visitors on an unforgettable journey through a land of mystery.

The view over Belfast from Cave Hill.

IN AND AROUND BELFAST -
A LOT MORE THAN TITANIC

Visiting Belfast, as befits it's industrial and engineering past, is a different experience to other cities on the island of Ireland. It's not a very big city and was deeply scarred by the 'Troubles'. However, in recent times since the signing of the historic Peace Agreement, the city has rediscovered its gaiety and it is now a vibrant and intersting city to visit.

There is much of interest to see and explore here, most particularly of course, the Titanic Experience which draws visitors from all over the world and was recently named as Europe's top visitor attraction. But there are many other places to see and when you add to that good shopping, excellent restaurants and a vibrant night life, its easy to see why Belfast has become such a popular destination in recent times.

THE TITANIC EXPERIENCE
Costing a whopping £77 m to create, the Titanic Experience is Northern Ireland's largest visitor attraction, and tells the story of the creation of the White Star Lines' SS Titanic, the hopes it carried and it's tragic fate. Housed in an extraordinarily dramatic aluminum-clad building, the Titanic Experience is rightly at the top of 'must-see' places for visitors to Belfast.

How it is done is really quite remarkable across nine galleries spread over three floors. Beginning with the shipyard and 'booming Belfast' of 1910. The building of the Titanic is brought imaginatively to life and the highlight of this part of the story – and perhaps of the entire exhibition – is the six minutes Shipyard Ride exploring the life of the ordinary men who built the ship, often in very difficult and dangerous conditions.

Replica cabins explore the class differences of the time and the finished ship is explored before attention turns to its fated voyage and sinking. The sinking in particular is brought vividly to life by a series of imaginative exhibits, as is the inquiry held afterwards. Finally, the discovery of the wreck of the Titanic is told in the Ocean Exploration centre where additionally marine biologists explain life under the sea around our coastline. If you've the time there is also a one hour walking tour that includes the original slipways and the Drawing Offices.

All in all, an amazing experience and highly recommended.

BELFAST CITY HALL

The centerpiece of Belfast is undoubtedly the massive Portland stone City Hall located in Donegall Square. It's an imposing building and is the civic building of Belfast City Council, having been completed in 1906, at a time when Belfast was booming and flexing its new-found industrial wealth. Today it is regarded as one of the finest and most important examples of Classical Renaissance style anywhere in the United Kingdom.

Do check out the many statues in it's grounds and the Titanic Memorial Garden. Free public tours are available with an experiences and knowledgeable guide exploring the history and key features of the building.

BELFAST CATHEDRAL

The Cathedral Church of St. Anne, as well as being a place of worship, is a

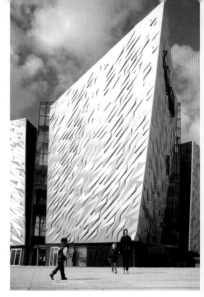

The dramatic Titanic Experience building houses Ulster's biggest visitor attraction.

treasure throve of art, culture and music. The Cathedral was consecrated in 1904 and has been expanded down the years, the most recent addition being the Spire of Hope added in 2006. In it's interior are

The heart of Belfast - City Hall in Donegall Square.

mosaics by Sir Charles Nicholson and sculptures by Rosamund Praegar and Maurice Harding. The mosaic over the font is said to contain ,more than 150,000 pieces. In addition there is a labyrinth, some spectacular stained glass windows and fine needlework including the poignant Titanic Pall.

ST. GEORGE'S MARKET
St. George's Market is claimed to be one of the best markets in the UK or Ireland and is also one of Belfast's oldest attractions. Indeed, the Friday Variety Market, that was held on this site, dates back to 1604. On Saturdays the market has speciality foods from around the world as well as handmade crafts, flowers, plants and local artwork, while on Sunday there is an emphasis on local arts and crafts giving local craftspeople the opportunity to

Belfast Cathedral, the Church of St. Anne, was consecrated in 1904.

display their talents.

All of this activity takes place against weekend backdrop of local bands and solo musicians. Well worth a visit.

BLACK TAXI TOURS

And now for something totally different! All through the 'Troubles' Belfast's taxi drivers plied their trade in their London-style black taxies. Today, some of these same drivers offer tours of some of the landmarks of those dark times. The tours include all areas of Belfast and you can learn about the conflict from the point-of-view of the Republicans, the Loyalists, the British and 'the truth'! Includes many of the most famous murals that dot the Loyalist and Republican areas of the city and provides a free hotel pick-up service. Good value and recommended.

BELFAST CASTLE

To the west of Belfast rises Cave Hill and it is here that the Victorian Belfast Castle is located on the lower slopes. From the castle there are stunning views over the city and this fact has made it a popular venue for weddings. You can also visit the Cave Hill Visitor Centre and, if you're feeling sufficiently energetic, climb Cave Hill itself.

ULSTER FOLK AND TRANSPORT MUSEUM

I have to make a confession regarding the Ulster Folk and Transport Museum. Although I have been many times to the Transport Museum I have never visited the Folk Museum. I'm sure I'm the poorer for not having visited the outdoor collection of lovingly re-created and restored 18th century buildings representative of life in Ireland at that time. Costumed guides are on hand to bring the whole experience to life and a visit there is an omission I hope to put right in the near future.

The Transport Museum, on the other side of the Belfast to Bangor Road at Cultra, is somewhere with which I am very familiar. With an idyllic hillside setting, entry to the museum starts in the Railway pavilion. In many ways this is the most impressive part of the Museum and it is built around a turntable that enables the exhibits to move outside to join the track close to nearby Cultra Station. The highlight here is without a doubt the mighty Maedb, built at the CIE Inchicore works. A personal highlight for me is the excellent example of one of the beloved Hill of Howth trams of which I have fond memories. The Train section is followed by a road

St. George's Market is one of Belfast's oldest attractions.

Belfast Castle, is situated high on the slopes to the west of Belfast.

The Train Collection at the Ulster Folk and Transport Museum is outstanding.

transport section and then a motoring section. For me the motoring section has never lived up to its potential given Northern Ireland's key role in the development of motoring in Ireland. But to some extend, that is nit-picking, for there is much of great interest to see here.

Finally, at the bottom of the hill, a short walk from the other pavilions, is the aviation section, where again, given Ulster's preeminence in the development of flying in Ireland, there is much to see. Curi-

ously, there are a number of motoring exhibits here as well including a small display on RJ Mecredy, the Dublin pioneer of motoring, who is regarded as the Father of Motoring in Ireland.

Finally, if you take in the Folk Museum as well as the Transport Museum, you should allow for a very enjoyable day's outing. Recommended.

ULSTER MUSEUM

Located in the Botanic Gardens off the Stranmillis Road, the eye-catching Ulster

In addition to the Train Collection, the Museum displays motoring and aviation material.

Museum building houses a varied and highly interesting display of artifacts ranging from an Egyptian mummy, Spanish Armada gold and even a six meter long Edmontosaurus dinosaur skeleton. Many of the exhibits are designed to educate and are interactive so this is a great place for inquisitive children to go. Recommended.

THE DISCOVERY CENTRE

The Discovery Centre is a science and discovery collection with over 250 interactive exhibits spread across its four levels and located in the Odyssey Complex. The various sections are called DISCOVERY, SEE and DO, which tells you something about their content. Especially

THE SOMME MUSEUM

The Somme Museum opened in 1994 and tells of Ireland's role in the Great War and in particular in the three volunteer Divisions raised in Ireland – the 10th and 16th (Irish) Divisions and the 36th (Ulster) Division. The 10th (Irish) Division saw action in Suvla Bay in the Gallipoli campaign of 1915 and later in the Middle East. The 16th (Irish) Division drew many recruits from the ranks of the Irish Volunteers, an organisation that had been formed to fight for Irish self-government. The Volunteers were mainly Roman Catholic and came from all over Ireland. The Division distinguished itself in the Battle of the Somme and suffered some 4,000 casualties. The 36th (Ulster) Division was formed

The impressive Stormont building was opened in 1932 and is home to the Northern Ireland Assembly.

noteworthy is Climbit, described as a cross between a maze and a jungle gym, and claimed to be the first structure of its kind in the UK and Ireland.

This really is a great place for kids where they can learn in the best possible way – by seeing and doing. Highly recommended.

largely from the Protestant Ulster Volunteer Force raised to fight the imposition of Home Rule in Ireland. During the Battle of the Somme, the Division lost 5,500 men in the first two days of July 1916, in capturing the supposedly impregnable Schwaban Redoubt at Thiepval.

The Somme Museum is a timely reminder

of the futility of war and the part played by ordinary Irishmen of all persuasions who made the ultimate sacrifice in the Great War. Highly recommended.

STORMONT

Yet another imposing building of Portland stone is the Stormont Parliament Building set in the 164 acre public park that is Stormont Estate. The building was opened by Edward, Prince of Wales in 1932 and is home to the Northern Ireland Assembly.

The building stands at the top of a mile long Prince of Wales Avenue behind a statue of Lord Edward Carson, the Unionist MP regarded as the founding father of the Northern Ireland state. Also in the grounds, reflecting perhaps, more recent times is a water sculpture of a couple embracing across a divide.

There are free guided tours on Monday to Friday and it is also possible to watch proceedings in the Assembly Chamber from the public gallery.

Useful web addresses

TITANIC	www.titanicbelfast.com
TITANIC BOAT TOURS	www.laganboatcompany.com
BELFAST CITY HALL	www.belfastcity.gov.uk/cityhall/tours.asp
CITY CENTRE WALKING TOURS	www.Belfasthiddentours.com
BELFAST CATHEDRAL	www.belfastcathedral.org
ST. GEORGE'S MARKET	www.belfastcoty.gov.uk/stgeorgesmarket/
BLACK TAXI TOURS	www.blacktaxitours.com
BELFAST CASTLE	
www.discovernorthernireland.com/belfast-castle-estate-belfast-P3028	
ULSTER FOLK & TRANSPORT MUSEUM	www.nmni.comuftm
ULSTER MUSEUM	www.nmni.com/um
THE DISCOVERY CENTRE	www.w5online.co.uk
THE SOMME MUSEUM	
www.discovernorthernireland.com/somme-heritage-centre-newtownards-p2864	
STORMONT	www.assembly.gov.uk/visit-and-learning/visiting /tours

'Winterfell' is located on the edge of Strangford Lough.

GAME OF THRONES TOUR -
A JOURNEY THROUGH TIME AND WESTEROS

George R.R. Martin's extraordinarily successful book series *'A Song of Ice and Fire'* has brought a whole new dimension to tourism in Ulster. This medieval fantasy epic – a depiction of two powerful families, both playing a deadly game for control of the Seven Kingdoms of Westeros, where the victor will sit atop the Iron Throne. The bulk of the locations for this mega-budget TV series are in Northern Ireland and it is also filmed in Malta, Morocco, Iceland and Croatia.

Such is the interest by fans of the TV series, that there are now several commercial operators offering 'Game of Thrones Tours' on some of which you'll even dress in the garb of Westerros to get you into a medieval mood. (We've included links to their web-sites at the end of this section). But of course you may wish to drive

around the various locations so here is the information you need. If you're not a fan of *Game of Thrones,* move on quickly to the next route, because what follows will mean very little to you...

The best place to start your tour is at Tollymore Forest Park, the 'Haunted Forest' of the TV programme. It's a mesmerising place, with caves, follies, grottos and forest all set on the foothills of the Mourne Mountains. In the story this is where the White Walkers begin their journey into the realms of men, so its an appropriate place to start.

Inch Abbey, to the northeast of Tollymore is our next destination, the setting for where the Starks came to negotiate with the Freys at The Twins. Do walk along the River Quoile here – it's the location of the

George RR Martin's epic story has been brought to life in the Ulster landscape.

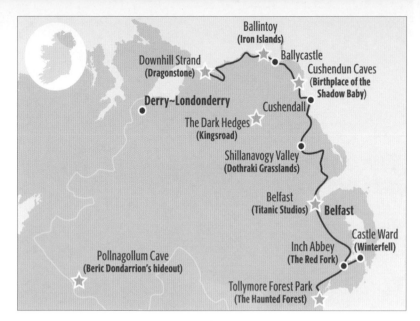

Riverlands and also the Red Fork. Our next stop is Winterfell, or Castle Ward to give it it's real title. Here on the edge of Strangford Lough the tale of Game of Thrones began. Castle Ward's historic farmyard is the location of Winterfell, the backdrop for the series and much of the first season. Here you will find the Whispering Wood and key scenes were shot here including Robb Stark's Camp, the Baelor battle and when Brienne confronts the Stark men. Eight weeks were spent at Castle Ward building the elaborate set of Winterfell ahead of the pilot episode and hundreds of actors and crew have worked on the filming here. Nearby Audley's Castle was also used as a backdrop to Robb's camp.

The iconic 'Dark Hedges' provide one of the most memorable backdrops to the story.

Castle Wards historic farmyard is the setting for 'Winterfell', where much of the first season was shot.

A certain amount of shooting is also done in the Titanic Studios at Belfast but we continue our tour at the Shillanovogy Valley which serves as the Dothraki Grasslands. A detour from here to the northwest will take you to the iconic Dark Hedges, 'Kingsroad' with it's extraodinary avenue of Beech trees, the vision of which, I promise, will haunt you for a long time after your visit.

After the Dark Hedges its back to the coast and the caves at Cushendall, where Melisandre birthed the Shadow Assassin. Continuing along the coast we reach Ballintoy, close to the Giant's Causeway, and it's little harbour from where you can see Pyke, one of the Iron Islands. The white cliffs lead from here to the eastern part of Larrybane Bay – the 'Stormlands' – before we finish our tour at Downhill Beach, the 11 km (6.8 mile) stretch of sand that serves as the epic 'Dragonstone', a fitting place for our journey through time to end.

Useful web addresses

GAME OF THRONES TOURS	www.gameofthronestours.com
	www.stonesandthrones.com
	www.seniccartours.com
	www.gameofthronestoursireland.com
	www.stonesandthrones.com
THE CAUN, STRANGFORD	www.thecuan.com
(Where the cast sometimes eat during filming)	
CASTLE WARD	www.nationaltrust.org/castle-ward
	www.seniccartours.com

The impressive Carrickergus Castle is the oldest and best preserved Norman citadel in Ireland.

THE CAUSEWAY COAST -
A SPECTACULAR COASTAL DRIVE

Coastal roads have provided some of the world's great driving roads and one thinks immediately of the legendary 'Big Sur', Highway 1 from Leggett, California to Los Angeles, or The Corniche along France's Mediterranean coast. Coastal roads, it seems, have an additional indefinable 'something' not apparent on inland roads. Perhaps it's the combination of man's age-old fascination with the sea together with the freedom of the road which combines to give them a special attraction: whatever it may be, every country with a coastline seems to have a special coastal road. In Ireland, there are several candidates and for me the Causeway Coast Route from Carrickfergus to Portrush provides a near-perfect coastal drive.

CARRICKFERGUS
Situated on the shores of Belfast Lough, between the ports of Larne and Belfast, Carrickfergus is the gateway to the Causeway Coast and Antrim Glens. Carrickfergus is an excellent starting point for any visitor planning to drive along the Causeway Coast.

The town itself is dominated by the famous Carrickfergus Castle, built in the 12th Century, and the oldest and best-preserved Norman citadel in Ireland. Also worth seeking out are the historic town walls, built by Chichester in the 1600's, that demonstrate the quality and consistency of the Jacobean builders and are worth a visit in their own right. Another place to visit is the Andrew Jackson Cottage and also the US Rangers Centre located at Boneybefore, and the 800-year old St. Nicholas Church with its famous stained glass windows.

WHITEHEAD
This pretty seaside town roughly half way between Carrickfergus and Larne is known as the 'town with no streets' as all

roads have been named without using the word 'street'. The town is a Victorian railway village and today is home to steam trains and the County Antrim Yacht Club.

THE GOBBINS

The Gobbins is something unusual – a mile long coastal walk first created in 1902 by Berkeley Deane Wise, Chief Engineer of the Belfast and Northern Counties Railway Company, in a successful attempt to use the recently expanded railway line to attract visitors to this spectacular piece of coastline.

The original path fell into disuse when insufficient funds were available to maintain it, a continuous requirement owing to its expoure to the harsh elements of the exposed cliffs of this part of the coast. However, in 2011 Larne Borough Council made funds available for its renewal and the reimagined path was created in 2014 and opened to the public once again, offering unique and spectacular views along its route. A visit is highly recommended. If you're tempted be sure to read the information on the website for this attraction as it's a strenuous walk not suitable for everyone and suitable clothing is essential.

LARNE

Larne is a deepwater port from which ferry services leave for Troon and Cairnryan in Scotland, the latter being just 34 miles distant. That short distance probably accounted for Larne and the surrounding district being one of the first places in Ireland to be inhabited. Flintwork and other artefacts found in the area have been dated to the Mesolithic era of about 6,000 BC

BALLYGALLY

A couple of miles along the coast from Larne is the village of Ballygally located on the headland of the same name. Ballygally beach is a popular destination for locals and tourists alike especially during the summer months, and Ballygally Castle, situated in the middle of the village at the junction with the road to Cairncastle is reputed to be the oldest occupied building in Ireland. In addition it has a reputation for being haunted and despite this, today contains a 4-star hotel. The castle was built around 1625 for James Shaw of Greenock and is regarded as one of Ireland's best-preserved Scottish baronial style plantation houses.

The Gobbins is a mile long spectacular costal walk that clings to the cliffs.

Some of the magnificent scenery along the Causeway Coast.

GLENARM

Glenarm is one of those places where there is much to see including Glenarm Castle and its Barbican, Walled Garden, the Glenarm Forest and Sculpture Trail and, of course, the village itself with its immaculately preserved Georgian streets and sandy beach from which on a clear day can be seen the coast of Scotland. The village lies at the foot of Glenarm Glen, the first of the nine Glens of Antrim and which we explore in detail in a later section.

It's also an ancient place and is recorded in history from the 5th centuryAD. There is a tradition that sometime around 1200 AD, King John of England granted to Glenarm a 'municipal charter'. If true, this would make Glenarm one of the oldest towns in Ireland.

Glenarm Castle is the ancestral home of the McDonnels, Earls of Antrim, who have been in Glenarm for some 600 years. The castle, which is a private residence, is open for occasional guided tours and the castle website should be consultated to check availability. The Castles Barbican, built at the later date of

The Causeway coast provides mile after mile of winding coastal roads with often spectacular views.

1825, is complete with porcullis, gothic windows and stone turret staircase and is marketed as holiday accomodation. The Castle's Walled Garden was created in the 18th century and is highly recommended for a visit.

CUSHENDALL

Cushendall village is the place where three of the nine Glens of Antrim meet: Glenann, Glenballylemon and Glencorp. This location makes it an ideal place from which to explore the Glens and it deserves its title of the Capital of the Glens. Its a picturesque village, where preserved Georgian houses line the four streets, and the Curfew Tower is still a centrepiece. It's a perfect place to walk along the beach, ramble around the glens, sit by the river or explore both stone-aged monuments and its more recent historical, sword-producing, past. In the past Cushendall looked towards Scotland – the Mull of Kintyre is only 14 miles away – as it was easier to cross the sea than the surrounding mountains.

CUSHENDUN

Cushendun, at the mouth of the River Dun, stands on an elevated beach at the outflow of the Glendun and Glencorp valleys.

Its yet another pretty village and was designed by Clough William Ellis in 1912 at the request of Ronald John McNeill, Baron Cushendun. Its picturesque Cornish appearance was deliberate, and was intended to please the Baron's Penzance-born wife, Maud. Ellis designed a village square with seven houses that are today run as craft shops and tea rooms. When Maud died in 1925, Ellis designed a row of whitewashed cottages in her memory. Baron Cushendun also commissioned the neo-Georgian Glenmona .

In ancient times Cushendun was a safe landing place and harbour for the frequent travellers between Ireland and Scotland who landed on the beach near Carra Castle. Built in the fourteenth century over a Mesolithic flint site, the ruins of the castle remain today. Close to the ruins, lie several Bronze Age standing stones. The poets Moira O'Neill and John Masefield lived in Cushendun and found the landscapes and settings inspirational.

The village of Cushendun is one of several pretty hamlets along the Causeway Coast.

The Carrick-a-rede rope bridge was originally used by fishermen to check their salmon nets.

TORR HEAD

From Cushendun, it's possible to take the road directly to Ballyvoy near Ballycastle but the more interesting road is that which follows the coastal route along Torr Head before swinging westwards to Ballyvoy.

The road is narrow and climbs and dips around Carnanmore (379 m). However you'll be rewarded by some magnificent views all the way to the Mull of Kintyre. Recommended.

BALLYCASTLE

Ballycastle is situated on the most north-easterly tip of County Antrim, and enjoys popularity amongst holiday maker. The town lies in the district of Moyle and has

views of the surrounding mountain ranges, forest parks, glens, lakes and coastline. There is a real choice of activities to pursue and places to explore in and around Ballycastle.

This is an area of outstanding natural beauty, and, of course, is another excellent base to explore the famous Nine Glens of Antrim. If you decide to use Ballycastle as a base, there are many exciting sights in the locality to experience. The famous Giant's Causeway , Bushmills Distillery and the Carrick-a-Rede rope bridge are all less than 10 miles from Ballycastle, while towering above the town itself, is Knocklayde Mountain (514 m) which can be seen for miles around. On the side of this mountain you will find Ballycastle Forest which has two entrances and whose peace can be enjoyed while enjoying a picnic or a walk. Fifteen miles across the Irish Sea, you may well be able to see the Mull of Kintyre, the fifteen-mile long peninsula at the narrowest stretch of water between Scotland and Ireland.

RATHLIN ISLAND

Raithlin Island is only seven miles off the coast from Ballycastle, and its possible to take a short ferry trip to this, the only inhabited island off the north coast of Ireland. An unusually shaped isle - eight miles long and less than a mile wide - it has a history that is full with legend. Legend tells that it owes its existence to the mother of the giant Fionn MacCool. Fionn drained Ireland of its whisky and so his mother travelled to Scotland to find some. Taking a mountain with her to use as a stepping stone, she tripped and fell, dropping this mountain into the sea and so it became the island we see today. There are daily ferries to the island and as a result the island has become popular with visitors and also with divers as there are over forty shipwrecks lying in the waters surrounding it. It's also popular with

popular visitor attractions in Northern Ireland. If like me, you don't have a head for these sorts of heights, you may fail to see the attraction! However, on the way, there are some wonderful vantage points to stop and take in the natural beauty of the place, and it's worth noting that the geology, flora and fauna have won Carrick-a-Rede recognition as an area of special scientific interest. Vast colonies of fulmars, kittywakes, guillemots and razorbills breed on the islands close to the rope bridge. It was fishermen who erected the bridge to Carrick-a-Rede island over a 23m-deep and 20m-wide chasm to check their salmon nets.

The rope bridge originally consisted of a single rope hand-rail that has been replaced by a two-hand railed bridge by the National Trust. Once you reach Carrick Island, there is only one way off the island - back across the swaying bridge! You have been warned!

THE GIANTS CAUSEWAY

The world-famous Giant's Causeway is an area of about 40,000 interlocking basalt columns, and is located about three miles (4.8 km) northeast of the town of Bush-

Seals basking in the sunshine on Rathlin Island.

ornithologists also visit the island from all over the world to study the impressive selection of puffins, guillemots, kittiwakes and razorbills on shores. Recommended.

CARRICK-A-REDE ROPE BRIDGE

A short coastal footpath leads to Carrick-a-Rede Rope Bridge, one of the most

mills, and was declared a World Heritage Site by UNESCO in 1986, and a National Nature Reserve in 1987. The tops of the columns form stepping stones that lead from the foot of the cliff and disappear under the sea. Most of the columns are hexagonal, although there are also some with four, five, seven or eight sides. The

The world famous Giant's Causeway is a UNESCO World Heritage site.

The Bushmills Railway provides a link between the town of Bushmills and the famous Giant's Causeway site. It was built to the Irish narrow gauge of 3 feet (0.91 m) and runs for two miles along the track of the former Giant's Causeway tram.

tallest are about 12 metres (39 ft) high, and the solidified lava in the cliffs is 28 metres (92 ft) thick in places.

In 1986 the Giants Causeway Visitors centre opened, coinciding with the World Heritage Conventions addition of the Causeway to its coveted list of sites, which are of exceptional interest and universal value.

The facilities at the Causeway Centre now include Tourist Information offices, Bureau De Change, Accommodation Booking Service, an Interpretive Audio-Visual Presentation and a Souvenir Shop, and the Causeway Coaster bus service from the centre to the Causeway operates in conjunction with the opening hours of the centre. Highly recommended.

BUSHMILLS

South of the Giant's Causeway is the little village of Bushmills, site of Irland's oldest working distillery. Individual and group tours are available with the exception of January and February when the distillery is closed to visitors. The tour is very popular with visitors and is well worth taking.

PORTRUSH

With it's spectacular location, situated on a mile long peninsula extending into the Atlantic Ocean, Portrush is a very popular holiday destination. Its location affords

panoramic views over the Causeway Coast towards Scotland and the Donegal hills.

As befits a family holiday destination there are restaurants, night clubs, quality hotels and family entertainment venues aplenty in Portrush. The spectacular Airwaves Airshow takes place every September when up to 200,000 spectators gather along the sea shore to watch the action and is highly recommended. Also based around a road circuit that runs from Portrush to Portstewart and down to Coleraine is the North West 200 Motor Cycle Races held in May each year. This annual motorcycle extravaganza is Ireland's largest outdoor event and draws followers from all over the island and abroad and is highly spectacular. Recommended.

PORTSTEWART

Portstewart, which marks the end of our trip along the Causeway Coast, is most notable for the nearby Portstewart Strand and Barmouth Wildlife Reserve:

Between Portstewart and the mouth of the River Bann lie the golden sands and sand dunes of Portstewart Strand. This area of natural beauty and of scientific interest is owned and managed by the National Trust. A year round destination for holiday makers, Portstewart Strand holds the prestigious Blue Flag award for the management, cleanliness and quality of water and it is also one of the few remaining beaches in Ireland where cars still have access and permission to drive onto the beach, ideal for families who wish to picnic on the golden shores.

The dramitacilly situated ruin of Dunluce Castle, a part of which fell into the sea during a storm in 1639.

The North West 200 is Ireland's largest outdoor event attracting up to 200,000 spectators every May.

Useful web addresses

CARRICKFERGUS
www.discovernorthernireland.com/Carrickfergus-Carrickfergus-P7124

WHITEHEAD   www.whiteheadnorthernireland.com

THE GOBBINS   www.thegobbinscliffpath.com

GLENARM CASTLE   www.glenarmcastle.com

GLENARM
www.discovernorthernireland.com/downloads/GlenarmVisitorGuideAndMap.pdf

CUSHENDALL
www.discovernorthernireland.com/Cushendall-Cushendall-P12588

TORR HEAD   www.causewaycoastalroute.com/torr-road.html

BALLYCASTLE   www.discoveringireland.com/ballycastle-town/

RATHLIN ISLAND   www.rathlinballycastleferry.com
http://www.discovernorthernireland.com/Rathlin-Island-Ballycastle-P8209

CARRICK-A-REDE   https://www.nationaltrust.org.uk/carrick-a-rede

THE GIANTS CAUSEWAY   http://www.giantscausewayofficialguide.com

BUSHMILLS   www.bushmills.com

DUNLUCE CASTLE   http://www.discovernorthernireland.com/Dunluce-
Castle-Medieval-Irish-Castle-on-the-Antrim-Coast-Bushmills-P2819

PORTRUSH   www.portrush.org.uk

AIRWAVES AIRSHOW   www.airwavesportrush.co.uk

NORTHWEST 200   hwest200.org/about-the-nw200/

PORTSTEWART   http://www.discovernorthernireland.com/Portstewart-
Strand-and-Barmouth-Portstewart-P2921

Useful Maps: Ordnance Survey of Northern Ireland Discoverer Series
Sheets 4, 5, 9 and 15.

The nine gentle Glens of Antrim are a walkers paradise and deserve to be explored at a leisurely pace.

THE ANTRIM GLENS - THE GENTLE GLENS

There are nine Glens of Antrim. They are in order with their translated names, as follows:

Glenarm   *The Glen of the army*

Glencloy   *The Glen of the hedges*

Glenariff   *The arable Glen*

Glenballyeamon   *Edward's town Glen*

Glenann   *The Glen of the colt's foot*

Glencorp   *The Glen of the slaughtered*

Glendun   *The Glen of the brown river*

Glenshesk   *The Glen of the reeds or sedges*

Glentaisie *The Glen of the Princess Taisie of the bright sides*

GLENARM AND GLENCLOY

Travelling from the sea along the B97 into Glenarm, the land is at first marshy before opening out to a landscape of small farms and stone-walled fields. This, in turn gives way to open moorland and to the south-west can be seen the slopes of Slemish Mountain, where, in the 5th century, a young man was brought tto work tending pigs. The young man was to become Ireland's venerated patron saint, St. Patrick.

From the slopes of Slemish head back along the northern Glencloy along the A42. Along the northern edge of this rtoad rises Garron Plateau, the nearest thing to wilderness that still exists in Northern Ireland. The A42 rejoins the coast road at Carnlough. This attractive village is home to the Londonderry Arms Hotel that was built in 1850 and is notable for having once been owned by Sir Winston Churchill, when he was Secretary of State of War, having been left to him as an inheritance from his grandmother, the Marchioness of Londonderry.

GLENARIFF AND GLENBALLYMEAMON

Glenariff, which runs inland from just past the village of Waterfoot on the coast road has bestowed on it the additional title 'Queen of the Glens'. Described by the Writer William Thackeray as 'Switzerland in miniature', Glenariff is a spectacular glen, a classic U-shaped valley created by a glacier and with many tumbling waterfalls dropping down to feed the river of the same name that flows along its valley bottom.

The glen shows its most attractive face at its southern end and a short excursion can be made to Glenariff Forest park from where some of the best views of the area can be seen, before returning via Glenballymeamon to Cushendall and the coast.

GLENANN, GLENCORP AND GLENDUN

In the main street of the village of Cushendall follow the A2 as it continues inland through Glencorp – the Glen of the Slaughtered, so named as far as I have been able to discover for the slaughter of the McQuillan clan, in the peat bogs of

Dramatic seascape at Ballintroy.

Each year in June the Glens Walking Festival draws walkers from all over Ireland and further afield to the Nine Glens.

The beautiful Glenariff Waterfall is one of the 'must-see' places in the Glens.

Orra Beg. There the McQuillans were lured into concealed pits dug in the marshy ground, slaughtering them as they floundered in the marshy pools. At Glendun Viaduct turn left to follow the road southwest along Glendun before turning back along Glenann to travel back to rejoin the A2. The viaduct by which the road crosses the Dun river is known locally simply as 'The Big Bridge'. Designed by Charles Lanyon, the architect of Queen's University, the bridge was built between 1834 and 1839 with all the stone for its construction being drawn from the Layde quarry near Cushendaun by horse and cart. It really is a most impressive structure and a short diversion will take one to its base from where it can be better appreciated. We ended this part of our journey at the waters edge in Cushendun beside an unusual and poignant memorial, a sculpture of the goat 'Johann', commemorating the last animal to be culled in the Foot and Mouth outbreak of Spring 2001.

GLENSHESK AND GLENTAISIE

Glenshesk is a well-wooded glen and lies along the B15 road out of Ballycastle. About five miles along the road there is a small car park. The signs here point to Breen Wood, meaning the 'place of the fairies'. A walk of about 2 km will take you to an enchanting place, an ancient oak wood that is a rare survivor of 2,000 year old woodland of the type that once covered all of Ireland.

Finally, travel back to Ballycastle along the road from Amoy traveling part of the way through Glentaisie.

The Glens of Antrim, are superb motoring roads well worth exploring and discovering for oneself. Journey over them and you will not be disappointed.

Useful web addresses

Useful maps: Ordnance Survey of Northern Ireland Discoverer Series Sheets 4, 5, 8 and 9.

On Glenariff has deservedly been bestowed the title of 'Queen of the Glens'.

The view from the coastal road over Knockglass and Soldier's Hill is among the best to be found anywhere in Ireland.

MALIN HEAD - BREATHTAKING VIEWS AT IRELAND'S MOST NORTHERLY POINT

The Inisowen Pensiula is a large stretch of land bordered to the west by Lough Swilly and to the east by Lough Foyle while it's northern tip – Ireland's northernmost point - reaches out into the Atlantic. There are many beautiful stretches of road along the peninsula but in this route we're going to explore the area from the town of Malin to the very tip of Malin Head, a route of extraodinary wild beauty.

We'll start our drive from the pretty 17th century plantation town of Malin, situated on an inlet of Trawbreaga Bay. Leaving the town by way of the R242 and heading northwest and following the signposts for Lag and Malin Head, the road follows the sea-shore for several kilometres before turning inland, a change of direction that also signals a change of terrain.

To the east of the road is Cranny Hill while a short road to the left passes Lag Church with its unusual location amongst the sand dunes.

LAG CHURCH

Built in 1784, Lag (sometimes spelt 'Lagg') is one of the oldest Catholic churches still in use today, and also the second most northerly church in Ireland. Just outside the church is an ancient baptismal font that is believed to date from the sixth century and was taken from the old monastery at St. Mura's, Fahan.

The road past the church continues to Five-fingers Beach, to my mind one of the most beautiful beaches on this island.

Malin Head, the very northern tip of the island of Ireland, is a rugged place jutting out into the Atlantic.

St. Mary's church at Lag, one of the oldest Catholic churches in Ireland, nestles among the sand dunes.

FIVE FINGERS STRAND

Five Fingers Strand - its name comes from five finger-like rock pinnacles jutting out into the sea - is quite simply breathtaking! Its sand dunes are amongst the highest in Europe and to walk along its unpoilt shore is a joy. Well worth visiting and lingering over!

Spectacular Aurora Borealis over Linsfort Church at Desertegney, County Donegal. The Aurora can be see from many places in Donegal.'

KNOCKAMANY BENDS

Back on the R242, one soon comes to a road marked with a brown 'Inisowen 100' sign that leads sharply up Knockglass Hill, Soldiers Hill and on around a narrow but perfectly adequate coastal drive. The views along this road are quite simply magnificent, amongst the best to be found anywhere along Ireland's coastline, and look out across the entrance to Trawbreaga Bay to Doagh Island (not actually an island at all) where there is a very large concentration of Megalithic remains located on its eastern side. All too soon the road drops down again to sea level and rejoins the R242 just before another turn close to the Coastal Radio Station with its high radio mast providing a landmark.

MALIN HEAD

This road leads onto Malin Head itself where there is a small car park at the most westerly point. Once again the views to the west are impressive. Continue on to the most northerly point of the road, marked by a short stretch of road down to a car park beside a military watchtower built here in 1805 during the Napoleonic War. In 1902 a signal tower was built and the remains of both these buildings are still standing. The most northerly point of the island of Ireland is the headland named Banba's Crown located at 55.38°N. (Further north are the islands of Inishtrahull and Tor Beg rock). The word 'EIRE' was spelt out in stones nearby as a sign to airmen that they were approaching the coastline of neutral Ireland, a relic of 'The Emergency' when the battle for the North Atlantic was fought from the northern side of Lough Foyle.

Rejoining the road, we return after a short distance to the R242 at the tiny village of Bulbinbeg and now point our car towards the town of Malin once more. Before coming to the point where we diverted along the coast road just past the church at Lag, the road once again passes through a surprisingly wide variation of landscape – something one encounters again and again in Ireland. After Lag, the road once more travels along the sea shore, offering new aspects of Trawbreaga Bay to be enjoyed, before finishing our exploration in the town of Malin.

This is not a particularly long drive; rather it is one to be enjoyed at a leisurely pace with many stops to enjoy the beauty of the many magnificent views you will encounter along its route.

The glorious Five Fingers Strand - its sand dunes are amongst the highest in Europe.

The author enjoying the views, and the sunshine, at Soldier's Hill in his Daimler SP250.

Useful web addresses

LAG CHURCH
www.welovedonegal.com/ch-stmarys-lagg-malin-head-inishowen.html

FIVE FINGERS STRAND   www.visitinisowen.com/five=fingers-strand/

MALIN HEAD   www.ireland.com/en-gb/articles/waw-malin-head/

INISHOWEN PENINSULA   www.visitinishowen.com

MALIN TOWN   www.welovedonegal.com/malin-town.html

Useful maps: Ordnance Survey Discovery Series – Sheet 3

The Guildhall has been at the heart of Derry city life since 1890.

DERRY CITY AND ITS SURROUNDINGS - THE WALLED CITY

Derry and Londonderry are one and the same place, something that you may find confusing, so let me straight away attempt to explain this anomaly that you will no doubt encounter should you visit this fascinating city. Like so much in Ireland, it's about history. Derry, whose official title is Londonderry, is the second-largest city in Northern Ireland and the fourth-largest city in Ireland. In 1613, the city was granted a Royal Charter by King James I and gained the 'London' prefix to reflect the funding of its construction by the London guilds. While the city is more usually known colloquially as Derry, Londonderry is also commonly used and remains the legal name.

The old walled city lies on the west bank of the River Foyle, which is crossed by two road bridges and one footbridge. The city has grown and now covers both banks (Cityside on the west and Waterside on the east). The city is close to the border with County Donegal, with which it has had close links for many centuries. Derry is the only surviving completely intact walled city in Ireland and one of the finest examples of a walled city in Europe. Its interesting to note that the walls constitute the largest monument in State care in Northern Ireland and, as the last walled city to be built in Europe, they stand as the most complete and spectacular.

THE CITY WALLS

The Walls were built between 1613 and 1619 by The Honourable The Irish Society as defences for early 17th century settlers who came mainly from England and Scotland. The Walls, which are approximately 1.6 km in circumference and vary in height and width between 3.7 and 10.7 metres, are completely intact and form an interesting walkway around the inner city. They provide a unique promenade to view the layout of the original city that still preserves its renaissance style street plan. The four original gates to the Walled City

Derry retains many narrow streets, particularly within the city walls.

within the walls include the 1633 Gothic cathedral of St Columb, the Apprentice Boys Memorial Hall and the Courthouse.

Derry is one of the few cities in Europe that never saw its fortifications breached, withstanding several sieges including the most famous in 1689 which lasted 105 days, and gave rise to the city's nickname, The Maiden City.

Now that we have that bit of history out of the way, let me say that Derry (as I shall call it) is a vibrant city, full, as you might imagine, of history. It's a great place to visit and has really blossomed as a result of The Peace Process in the last twenty years.

THE GUILDHALL
The Guildhall describes itself as 'the heart of the city', and in many ways it is having been at the heart of city life since 1890. One of the cities most recognisable landmarks, it is home to the Council's Chamber and the Mayor's Parlour. In recent times it has been restored and refurbished winning architectural awards in the process. It contains stunning stained glass windows, an exhibition exploring the history of the Plantation of Ulster and a noteworthy Main Hall and an organ,

are Bishop's Gate, Ferryquay Gate, Butcher Gate and Shipquay Gate. Three further gates were added later, Magazine Gate, Castle Gate and New Gate, making seven gates in total. Historic buildings

A stroll along the intact city walls is a fascinating experience.

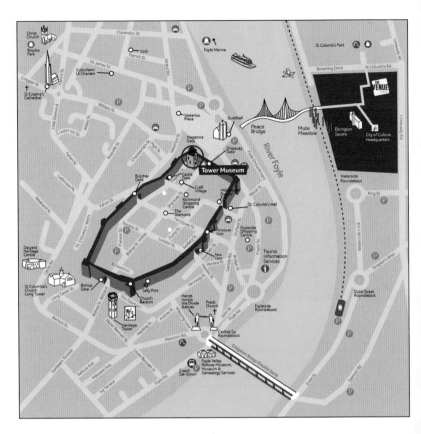

built in 1891 and one of the largest in Ireland.

I must also mention the Guildhall Clock that was designed as a replica of London's 'Big Ben' and is the largest of its kind in Ireland. Recommended.

TOWER MUSEUM
The Tower Museum tells two very disparite stories – the story of Derry and also the story of a Spanish Armada shipwreck – *La Trinidaf Velencera*. The museum is located within the historic city walls and also has a unique open air viewing facility that provides stunning views of the city and the River Foyle.

The Story of Derry exhibition tells the story from the earliest settlement on the site through to the Plantation of Londonderry and its growth as a city during the

18th and 19th centuries. The history of the city in the 20th century is also explored including the development of the Civil Rights Movement and the impact of The Troubles on the city and its people.

By contrast, the story of the *La Trinidad Valencera* is the story of the shipwreck in 1588 of one of the largest ships in the Spanish Armada. The *La Trinidad Valencera* sank in Kinnegoe Bay in County Donegal and its final resting place was discovered some 400 years later by divers from the City of Derry Sub Aqua Club. Highly recommended.

MUSEUM OF FREE DERRY
The Museum of Free Derry exists to remember and understand the local history of the city and its contribution to the ground breaking civil rights struggle

The 'Hand's across the Divide' statue symbolises the cities hope for the future.

that erupted in Derry in the mid-1960s and culminated in the events of Bloody Sunday.

It puts the Free Derry period into a wider Irish and international context so that visitors can see the events depicted not just in relation to the communal conflict in the North or the conflict between Britain and Ireland. They are invited to make comparisons with the civil rights movement in the USA as well as other massacres such as Wounded Knee, Sharpeville and Fallujah. Thought provoking and recommended.

APPRENTICE BOYS MEMORIAL HALL AND SEIGE MUSEUM

The Siege of Londonderry in 1689 was an important event in Irish history.

For 105 days up to 30,000 Protestants held the walled city of Londonderry in the face of the Catholic King James II, until the relief fleet broke the boom across the River Foyle on July 28 and the Jacobite forces commenced their retreat on August 1, 1689. The new Siege Museum tells the story of this heroic defence of the city and also of the Associated Clubs of the Apprentice Boys of Derry.

The first Apprentice Boys Club was formed on 1st August 1714 by Colonel John Mitchelburne, Governor of the City, towards the end of the Siege. Although this club ceased to exist after his death, the memory of the Siege was always celebrated each year in some form right through the 18th Century. In 1814, Benjamin J Darcus formed the Apprentice Boys of Derry Club, and over the next 40 years other clubs were founded to commemorate the Siege. The Museum is open Monday to Saturday between 10.00 am and 5.00 pm and is a particularly interesting place to visit.

The Halloween Banks of the Foyle Festival, colourful and entertaining.

The large wall murals that are such a feature of Derry are to be found in several parts of the city.

THE MURALS

Throughtout the city of Derry you will find many murals relating to the city's history and life during 'The Troubles'. Three local artists –Tom Kelly, Kevin Hasson and William Kelly - have created The People's Gallery in the Bogside area. It is a series of large-scale murals depicting the key events in Northern Ireland since 'The Troubles' and the paintings present a window into the politics, people and history of Northern Ireland. The majority of the murals in the Bogside reflect events that occurred in the past and one mural – The Peace Mural – looks to the future with hope.

In the Fountain Estate close to the city walls is one of the oldest 'King Billy' murals together with many others linked to the famous siege of Derry in 1689. There are also an extensive range of wall murals in the Bond Street area. Well worth a look.

Left: The 'Peace Bridge' spans the River Foyle and is popular with visitors to the city.

The Tower Museum includes a fine display telling the story of one of the largest ships of the Spanish Armada - La Trinidead Valencera - that sank in Kinnegoe Bya in nearby County Donegal.

Ferguson flying over the broad sands of Magilligan during the summer of 1911. (Painting by aviation artist Vincent Killowrey).

Harry Ferguson - First to Fly in Ireland

The distinction of being the first to fly in Ireland belongs to Harry Ferguson, a remarkable young man from Dromara in County Down. He grew up hating the hard work of farm life and joined his brother, Joe, in setting up an engineering business in 1901. By 1908, Harry, like many of his generation was excited by the developments taking place in Europe and America in the field of aviation. Harry travelled to several aviation meetings in Europe and on his return, decided to design and build his own aeroplane. His first design had a wingspan of 26 ft. and was powered by an 8-cylinder JAP engine producing 35 hp. Harry successfully flew a short distance on the last day of 1909 at Lord Downshire's Old Park at Hillsborough, becoming the first to fly in Ireland and the first British subject to fly in a machine of his own design and construction. The following April, May and June of 1911 he made several flights over the wide-open spaces of Magilligan Strand. However, in October 1911 he abandoned his flying experiments due to strained relations with his brother, who felt their business was being neglected as a result, and turned his attention to motoring.

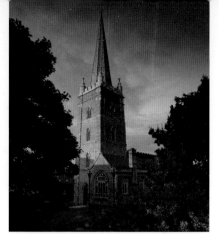

St. Columb's Cathedral pictured at dusk.

ST. COLUMB'S CATHEDRAL

St. Columb's Cathedral is noteworthy as the first cathedral to be built in the British Isles after the Reformation and it is regarded as the city's oldest and most historic building. The Cathedral Chapter House contains displays of artefacts from the Siege of Derry and also of the famous composer of hymns, Cecil Francis Alexander.

MAGILLIGAN

Magilligan is an area of both historic and conservation significance. The Martello Tower at Magilligan Point built in 1812 during the Napoleonic wars is an example of the small defensive forts which were built as a defence against a possible attack by the forces of Napoleon during the 19th

Century. It is one of about fifty such towers built around the Irish coast to deter an attack.

Magilligan Beach is a much studied coastal landform, and is an area of both historic and conservational significance. Harry Ferguson, the first man to fly in Ireland, carried out many of his flying experiments from the beach. Fittingly, today the Ulster Gliding Club is based at Bellarena Airfield in the same area.

FORT DUNREE

Fort Dunree is located about 10 km north of Buncrana on the Inisowen Peninsula along the shore of Lough Swilly over which it commands a majestic view of the Lough and it's shorelines. The Fort houses a military museum, an exhibition centre and a wildlife discovery room as well as scenic walks with breathtaking views. Highly recommended.

INISHOWEN MARITIME MUSEUM AND PLANETARIUM, GREENCASTLE

The Inishowen Maritime Museum and Planetarium is located at the Old Coast Guard station over looking Greencastle Harbour on the banks of Lough Foyle. A new Planetarium system has recently been added and together with the many and fascinating maritime displays and and items to be found in the Museum makes this an essential stop. Very highly recommended.

The impressive City Walls - the last to be built in Europe - dominate the city.

199

SEAMUS HEANEY HOMEPLACE

In the village of Bellaghy mid-way between Derry and Belfast is the newly opened Seamus Heaney HomePlace, where the life and literature of the poet and Nobel Laureate are celebrated.

Seamus Heaney was born in 1939 near the village of Bellaghy, and published his first collection of poems, *Death of a Naturalist*, in 1966, the same year he was appointed to the faculty of Queens University Belfast, as lecturer in English. Subsequently, he was also a professor at Harvard University and Oxford University. Throughout his life he published poetry, plays, essays and translations and in 1995 was awarded the Nobel Prize in Literature, sealing his reputation as one of Ireland's literary and cultural giants. He died in 2013 and is buried at Bellaghy. At the HomePlace there are exhibitions on his life and works and a visit is very highly recommended.

The Seamus Heaney HomePLace is to be found in the village of Bellaghy.

Inside the Seamus Heaney HomePlace are exhibitions about the poet's life and the plays, poetry, essays and translations he published during his lifetime.

Amelia Earhart with the Lockeed Vega in which she became the first woman to fly solo across the Atlantic. She landed in a pasture near the the village of Culmore, close to Derry.

'Lady Lindy'

Aviator Amelia Earhart was born on July 24, 1897 in Atchison, Kansas. In 1923, Earhart, fondly known as 'Lady Lindy,' became the 16th woman to be issued a pilot's license. She made several notable flights, becoming the first woman to fly across the Atlantic Ocean in June 1928 as passenger on the Fokker aircraft named *Friendship*. Earhart later confided that she felt she *'was just baggage, like a sack of potatoes.'* Then she added,

'*... maybe someday I'll try it alone.*' Early in 1932 she announced that on the fifth anniversary of Charles Lindbergh's flight across the Atlantic, she would attempt the same crossing. Thus on the morning of May 20, 1932, she took off from Harbour Grace, Newfoundland, with that day's copy of the local newspaper to confirm the date of the flight.

Almost immediately, the flight ran into diffi-culty as she encountered thick clouds and ice on the wings. After about 12 hours the conditions became worse, and the plane began to experience mechanical difficulties. She knew she wasn't going to make it to Paris as Lindbergh had, so she started look-ing for a new place to land. She found a pas-ture just outside the small village of Culmore, in Londonderry, Northern Ireland, and successfully landed there. Amelia went on to become the first person to fly over both the Atlantic and Pacific. In 1937, she mysteriously disappeared while trying to circumnavigate the globe from the equator. Since then, several theories have formed re-garding Earhart's last days, many of which have been connected to various artefacts that have been found on Pacific islands - howwever the mystery of her disappearance remains unsolved.

Useful web addresses

THE GUILDHALL
www.derrystrabane.com/Subsites/Museums-and-Heritage/Guildhall

THE TOWER MUSEUM   www.derrystrabane.com/towermuseum

MUSEUM OF FREE DERRY   www.bloodysundaytrust.org/

THE SEIGE MUSEUM   www.thesiegemuseum.org
www.discovernorthernireland.com/Siege-Museum-Londonderry-Derry-P3324

MUSEUM OF FREE DERRY   www.bloodysundaytrust.org/content/museum

GASYARD HERITAGE CENTRE   www.gasyardheritagecentre.com

ST. AUGUSTINE'S CHURCH
www.discovernorthernireland.com/Saint-Augustines-Church-Londonderry-Derry-P3323

AMELIA EARHART   www.ameliaearhartlegacyassociation.co.uk

ST. COLUMB'S CATHEDRAL   www.stcolumbscathedral.org

LIMAVADY
www.discovernorthernireland.com/Limavady-Visitor-Information-Centre-Limavady-P6900

INISHOWEN MARITIME MUSEUM & PLANETARIUM
http://inishowenmaritime.com

FORT DUNREE   www.dunree.pro.ie

ULSTER GLIDING CLUB   www.ulsterglidingclub.org/

SEAMUS HEANEY HOMEPLACE
www.seamusheaneyhome.com/home-place/

Useful maps: Ordnance Survey Discovery Series: Sheet 3
Fir Tree Series of Aerial Maps: County Donegal and North West Ireland

Ballynastocker Beach on the lovely Fanad Head Peninsula.

DONEGAL -
THE MOST BEGUILING OF COUNTIES

Donegal is vast by Irish standards and made to seem even larger by it's geography and the abundance of mountains within its borders. A part of the ancient provience of Ulster, Donegal, to my mind, stands apart from other parts of Ireland and has a unique charm that takes time and patience to explore and understand. A holiday spend in Donegal should not be rushed for there is so much to see and do, and if you can only spend time in one location in Ireland, well, Donegal would be a good choice. Its people are friendly, its roads are good and the scenery is spectacular but as always in Ireland, for me its attraction lies in the unexpected discoveries you make along the way. Its difficult to know where to base yourself to best facilitate your explorations: Buncrana for the Inishowen Peninsula; Milford for the Fanad, Rosguill and Horn Head Peninsulas; Dunglow for the Rosses and Gweedore; letterkenny for Glenveagh National Park and Killybegs or

Donegal town for Glenties, Glencolumncille and soaring Slieve League. Perhaps now you'll have some idea of the vastness of Donegal. But don't be put off by the sheer size of Donegal – head up there, find a base that suits what you want to see and discover your own piece of this most beguiling of counties.

CARNDONAGH

We've aleady devoted one of our routes to a small part of the Inishowen Peninsula – Malin Head – but there is much more than Malin Head to the Inishowen Peninsula. Inishowen is the largest of the Donegal peninsulas and its position close to the city of Derry has a major impact on life there. There are excellent drives along the coast along Lough Foyle through Moville and on to Dunagree Point on the eastern side of the peninsula and on the western side from Burnfoot through Fahan and the delightful town of Buncrana and on up to Carndonagh and to Malin itself.

If you've an interest in history there is an intrigueing High Cross in Carndonagh that seems to mark the tranistion around the 7th century from crosses carved on stone slabs to crosses on stone slabs first carved into the shape of a cross. A look is recommended.

BUNCRANA

Buncrana is located on the eastern shore of Inishowen on the River Crana and on the shores of Lough Swilly. Buncrana enjoys a delightful situation and is the second largest town in County Donegal. During the 1798 Rebellion, the patriot Wolfe Tone was captured after a British and French sea battle off the coast of Donegal and was held in Buncrana before been taken to Derry.

Another interesting historical connection with Buncrana is that of John Newton and his shipmates on *The Greyhound* who found a safe haven in Lough Swilly in 1748 during a devastating Atlantic storm. Newton saw his survival as divine intervention, the answer to prayer and the refuge of the Swilly and Buncrana area laid a spiritual foundation for a reformed later life. In 1764 Newton became a Church of England clergyman and subsequently, as curate at Olney in Buckinghamshire, he became an anti-slavery activist and renowned hymnist who is today remembered for writing *'Amazing Grace'*.

GRIANAN OF AILEACH

While on the Inishowen Peninsula, be sure not to miss the stone fort called

Fanad Head Lighthouse.

Grianan of Aileach. It's sited on a hilltop 250 m above sea level, and the stone fort was probably first built on an earthen rath. The view from *Aileach* is simply breathtaking. The blue waters of Lough Foyle and Lough Swilly can be clearly seen, as can the outline of the entire peninsula.

The origins of the *Grianán of Aileach* fort date back to 1700 BC. It is linked to the *Tuatha de Danann* who invaded Ireland before the Celts and built stone forts on top of strategic hills. They worshipped *Dagda* (the Good God) and he too is associated with the origins of *Aileach*. Legend says it was he who ordered the building of a stone fort to act as a burial monument to his dead son. Very highly recommended.

'Murder Hole' on Rosguill Peninsula.

Spectacular view at the Mamore Gap.

LETTERKENNY

Letterkenny is the location of Donegal's only Catholic Cathedral and is nicknamed 'the Cathedral Town'. It is the largest and most populous town in County Donegal, and lies on the River Swilly. Along with the nearby city of Derry, Letterkenny forms the major economic core of the north-west of Ireland. It's a lively town with good restaurants and nightlife and a good centre from which to tour.

it's Irish name being *Baile na nGallóglach* meaning 'town of the *gallóglach*. The *gallóglaigh* (the angilicised name being gallowglass) were an elite class of mercenary warrior who descended from the Gaelic-Norse clans in Scotland between the mid-13th century and the end oif the 16th century. As a result of a battle between the Irish – helped by the *gallóglaigh* - and the English on a hill where the town is now, gave rise to the town's modern name.

MILFORD

Milford is a tranquil small town located at the head of Mulroy Bay and Broadwater. The origins of its name are interesting,

FANAD HEAD

The Fanad Peninsula contains some of the most spectacular scenery and

coastal roads in the northwest and should not be missed. Milford is the natural centre for touring the peninsula and the road around Knockalla is especially spectacular. In addition there are many fine beaches around the peninsula.

Highlights of the Fanad Peninsula include the plantation villages of Ramelton and Rathmullan, where 'Red Hugh' O'Donnell, Earl of Tyrconnell, was lured on to an English merchant ship for a drink, only to be seized and taken to Dublin as a prisoner.

Horse riding on Dunfanaghy Strand.

ROSGUILL PENINSULA

The smallest of the north Donegal peninsulas, Rosguill, features an 11 km circular spectacular route called the Atlantic Drive that is signed and passes dunes and good beaches.

DUNFANAGHY

Dunfanaghy is a seaside village near an excellent sandy beach offering windsurfing and canoeing, and a blowhole called Mc-Swyne's Gun that 'explodes' periodically in rough weather. Not far from Dunfanaghy be sure to visit Doe Castle; a 15th-century fortress rebuilt in Victorian times. Views from the battlements overlook Sheephaven Bay. Lackagh Bridge provides another vantage point.

HORN HEAD PENINSULA

The sheer, quartzite cliffs of Horn Head provide terrific views and a windy home for many thousands of seabirds. Sheep Haven is particularly attractive, and Marble Hill Strand has a fine beach.

GLENVEAGH NATIONAL PARK

No visit to Donegal would be complete without a visit to the Glenveagh National Park, some 16,540 hectares (40,873 acres) of mountains, lakes, glens. woods, and the home of a herd of red deer. The Scottish style castle (built between 1870 and 1873) is surrounded by one of the finest gardens in Ireland, which contrast with the rugged mountain surroundings. It is built around a four storey rectangular keep. Access to the interior is by tour only. There is a fine Visitor Centre with exhibitions and an audio-visual show. Recommended.

FALCARRAGH

The area surrounding Falcarragh is one of great natural beauty, with the Derryveagh mountains to one side and the beautiful unspoilt beaches of Drumnatinney, Ballyness Bay and Magheroarty on the other. The islands of Tory and Innisboffin are just off the coast.

An Grianan of Aileach Burt from where there are spectacular views in all directions.

Magnificent Mount Errigal, Donegal's highest mountain.

BUNBEG

Bunbeg is a small village situated between Derrybeg and Dore and is the location of the ferry service to the nearby Tory Island.

GWEEDORE

Gweedore is densely populated, with new bungalows springing up along the coast. The most scenic part of the coastline is Bloody Foreland, a mass of red granite that glows a brilliant red colour at sunset.

BURTONPORT

Burtonport is a small fishing village on the western coast of Donegal. From here a ferry operates to the nearby island of Arranmore with sailings daily. The name, like so many places in Donegal derives from that of a landowner in earlier times. Burton Conyngham was responsible for building houses on nearby Rutland Island and crossed to the island from a small pier he had built for his use and which became referred to as 'Burton's port'.

DUNGLOE

Dungloe developed as a town in the middle of the 18th Century, and now serves as the administrative and retail centre for the west of Donegal, and in particular the Rosses, and have the only mainland secondary school for the area.

The town attracts many tourists every July and August when the 'Mary From Dungloe International Festival' takes place.

The picturesque Dungloe Bay and surrounding hills are very popular with visitors and have enabled Dungloe to develop a healthy tourism industry. In addition to the 'Mary from Dungloe' international festival there is another festival dedicated to the

The unspoilt horseshoe shaped beach at Malin Beg.

socialist writer Peadar O'Donnell held each autumn. A little to the north of the town is the site of the ancient church of Templecrone.

KILLYBEGS
Killybegs is the largest fishing port on the island of Ireland and is located on the south coast of the county, north of Donegal Bay and near Donegal Town. The town is situated at the head of a scenic harbour and at the base of a vast mountainous tract extending northward and westwards to Slieve League. Each summer, there is a street festival celebrating the fish catches and incorporating the traditional 'Blessing of the Boats'.

SLIEVE LEAGUE
For me, Slieve League is one of the most spectacular places to visit in Ireland. The sea cliffs here rise to 609 m above the Atlantic, making them twice the height of the cliffs of Moher and one of the highest sea cliffs in Europe. The views in every direction are spectacular and this really is one of the wildest and most remote places in Ireland.

Before you come to the cliffs themselves, you'll come across the Slieve League Cliffs Centre. Inside this family-run centre there is information about local history and culture, and, in summertime, you can even catch a traditional Irish music session. Very highly recommended.

MALIN BEG
Malin Beg, on what is very nearly the

Killybegs is Ireland's busiest fishing port.

most westerly point of Donegal (nearby Rossen Point is the most westerly) is the location of a beautiful horse-shoe shaped beach anmed The Silver Strand not far from Glencolumbcille. It's a wonderful unspoilt beach in one of the remotest places in Ireland. Highly recommended.

DONEGAL TOWN
A busy shopping and tourist town, Donegal is situated where the River Eske flows into Donegal Bay. It will surprise many to know that it was invaded by the Vikings in the 8th century and that they established a port there. This invasion is where the town got its Gaelic name, *Dun na nGall,* which means 'Fort of the Foreigners'. The Vikings established an important garrison at the

A broad view of the magnificent Glenveagh National Park.

The sea cliffs at Slieve League in western Donegal are amongst Europe's highest.

site, thought to have been where O'Donnells Castle now stands. Human remains have been found in the grounds of the Castle and these are thought to be Viking.

The centre of the town is called 'The Diamond' and markets were held here until 1967. In the Diamond stands an obelisk in memory of 'The Four Masters', four monks who compiled and wrote the *Annals of the Four Masters* between 1632 and 1636 AD. The *Annals of the Four Masters* covers the history of Ireland from 2242 BC to 1616 AD and remains one of the most important historical writings in Ireland. The chief author was Micheal O'Cleirigh, who was assisted by Peregrine O'Clery, Fergus O'Mulconry

and Peregrine O'Duignan, and their names appear on the lower part of the Obelisk. Micheal O'Cleirigh would travel around Ireland during the summer months gathering information both historical and mythological, and return to the Friary in Donegal Town at the end of summer where the winter months would be spent correlating and writing up the annals.

BALLYSHANNON

Ballyshannon takes its name from 'The Mouth of Seannach's Ford' after a 5th century warrior, *Seannach,* who was slain there, and is situated at the mouth of the River Erne. To the west of the town, the River Erne widens into a long sandy estu-

Master of all he surveys, seen at Dunlewey.

Surfing at Pollan Beach.

ary, whose northern bank of the river rises steeply away from the riverbank, while the southern bank is flat with a small cliff that runs parallel to the river. From its pretty setting, Ballyshannon looks out over the estuary and has fine panoramic views of mountains, lakes and forests.

Perhaps the most famous son of Ballyshannon was guitarist and singer Rory Gallagher. The town centre contains a statue erected in his memory that, on occasion, has been known to be dressed in a Donegal jersey.

Coast road on the oddly named Bloody Foreland.

Useful web addresses

CARNDONAGH HIGH CROSS
www.megalithicireland.com/High%20Cross%20Carndonagh.html

LETTERKENNY   www.letterkennyguide.com

FANAD HEAD LIGHTHOUSE
www.greatlighthouses.com/lighthouses/fanad-head/

ATLANTIC DRIVE
www.irelandnorthwest.ie/pThe-Donegal-Atlantic-Drive.html

GRIANán OF AILEACH
www.discoverireland.ie/Arts-Culture-Heritage/grianan-of-aileach/73795

GLENVEAGH NATIONAL PARK
www.heritageireland.ie/en/north-west/glenveaghnationalpark/

FALCARRAGH   www.falcarraghvisitorcentre.com

BURTONPORT   www.welovedonegal.com/burtonport.html

KILLYBEGS   wwwkillybegs.ie

SLIEVE LEAGUE   www.slieveleaguecliffs.ie

BALLYSHANNON   www.welovedonegal.com/ballyshannon.html

DONEGAL TOWN   www.welovedonegal.com/donegal-town.html

Useful Maps: Ordnance Survey Discovery Series Sheets 1,2, 3, 6,10, 11 and 16.
Fir Tree Aerial map of County Donegal and North West Ireland

Glencolumbcille Folk village, situated in one of the remotest parts of Donegal.

Connacht

Elly Beach on the Mullet Peninsula.

The beautiful Glencar waterfall.

The poetry of WB Yeats is recalled in a sculpture at Drumcliffe Churchyard.

IN AND AROUND SLIGO -
IN THE SHADOW OF THE POET

It is hard to think of another locality in Ireland that bears the imprint of one of it's sons as Sligo and it's surroundings does. Sligo and it's environs were central to the life and work of Ireland's national poet, William Butler Yeats, and it's associations with him make it a unique place to visit. Here, one can see and experience the places that influenced his life and that of his artist brother, Jack Yeats. Not surprisingly, the Yeats influence is everywhere to be found in Sligo and there is a long established, and highly recommended, summer school celebrating the poet's work.

That said, there is much more to Sligo and it's surroundings to be discovered and explored. The town is delightful and it's surrounding landscape different in character to any other Irish town. It has an abundance of good restaurants and a strong presence for the arts led by the

important Model Arts and Niland Gallery, home of the Niland Collection, one of Ireland's leading contemporary arts centres as well as the Hawk's Well Theatre.

But it's the surrounding landscape that will stay in your mind long after your visit is over. From the marvellous beaches to mysterious Knocknaree and most of all, to the brooding presence of Ben Bulben, towering over its surroundings in its own unique way. Sligo deserves to be properly explored, so plan to spend at least several days there. You'll be glad you did!

SLIGO TOWN
A busy, vibrant town, Sligo offers good shopping and many interesting attractions. As well as the Niland Art Gallery and the Hawk's Well Theatre mentioned separately, the Yeats Memorial Building and Art Gallery is somewhere I recommend visiting and not surprisingly, more

Yeats memorabilia can be found at the Sligo County Museum where a copy of his 1923 Nobel Prize award medal is on display, as well as a fine collection of paintings by Irish artists, including Sean Keating, George Russel and Jack B Yeats, brother of WB Yeats.

NILAND ART GALLERY AND HAWK'S WELL THEATRE

The Model, home of The Niland Collection, is one of Ireland's leading contemporary arts centres. Built in 1862 as the Model School, the present building has been extended on several occasions, increasing its size by a third to create a world-class visitor centre. The building boasts a restaurant and coffee dock, a bookshop, a fine gallery circuit, a purpose built performance space, and a suite of impressive artist studios on the top floor with superb views of Sligo town and county.

This award-winning building is home to the impressive Niland Collection of Art, one of the most notable collections in Ireland and featuring works by John and Jack B. Yeats, Estella Solomons, Paul Henry and Louis Le Brocquy among others.

The fast-flowing Garavogue River flows through the centre of Sligo town.

Creevkeel-Court Tomb, one of the finest examples of a court tomb anywhere in Ireland.

The Hawk's Well is a 340 seat theatre hosting a diverse programme of arts and entertainments including comedy, professional and amateur drama, a wide range of music from traditional and jazz to opera, together with dance, pantomime and children's theatre.

DRUMCLIFFE

Drumcliffe is a small village on the northern outskirts of Sligo town. Dramatically set between the striking backdrop of Ben

Bulben and the sea, it is famous as the location of the grave of the poet, WB Yeats, and draws thousands of visitors each year to the small Chirch of Ireland parish church and graveyard. The grave, with its enigmatic self-penned inscription:

'cast a cold eye on life, on death, horseman, pass by'

is close to the church.

The graveyard also contains a high cross and there are the ruins of a 6th century Columbian monastry nearby. In the adjoining car park is a fine sculpture recalling some of Yeats' best-known words – be sure not to miss seeing it. Also adjoining the Church and its grounds is a very pleasant Tea and Craft Shop, although it does tend to get very busy during the tourist season.

BEN BULBEN

No guide to Sligo would be complete without mention of Ben Bulben (sometimes spelt 'Benbulbin'), as its towering presence is visible from almost everywhere in Sligo. It is part of the Dartry

Ben Bulben dominates the Sligo skyline.
(Inset) the grave of WB Yeats at Drumcliffe churchyard with its enigmatic inscription.

Glencar Lake in the beautiful valley of Glencar.

Mountains, and was formed during the time when glaciers covered Ireland. Not surprisingly, it features in several Irish legends, most notably as one of the hunting grounds of the legendary Fianna, the band of warriors who may have existed in the 3rd century. Ben Bulben is also said to be the resting place of Diarmuid and Gráinne, the doomed lovers of Irish legend.

GLENCAR

Glencar is a small valley bordered on its northern side by the slopes of Ben Bulben and on its southern side by Glencar Lake. It's a beauiful place and there is a dramatic waterfall cascading from the heights of the mountain. The waterfall is well sign-posted and the valley provides a very plesant walk of about two hours along the generally quiet road that passes through the valley. As with so much in the locality of Sligo, the waterfall was immortalised by the poet WB Yeats in his poem 'The Stolen Child',

'Where the wandering water gushes, from the hills above Glencar'.

LISSADELL HOUSE

Lissadell House is a neo-classical Greek revivalist style county house located to the northwest of Sligo town, and has been the subject of a magnificent restoration project by the current owners, Edward Walsh and Constance Cassidy, who live there with their seven children.

Lissadell House is famous as the child-

hood home of Constance Markievicz and Eva Gore-Booth and her brother Josslyn Gore-Booth. Constance was one of the leaders of the 1916 Rising and was the first woman to be elected to Dáil Eireann (the Irish parliament) and was also the first woman to be elected to the British House of Parliament, although she declined to take her seat there. In Dáil Eireann she served as Minister for Labour thus becoming the first woman to sit in cabinet in a Western European democracy.

Lissadell House, the magnificent neo-classical county house a short distance from Sligo town.

WB Yeats knew both sisters and stayed at Lissadell in 1892 and 1893. His words immortalised Lisadell and the two Gore-Booth sisters.

The light of evening, Lissadell

Great windows open to the south

Two girls in silk kimonos, both

Beautiful, one a gazelle.

The cairn atop Knocknarea is said to be the resting place of Maeve, Queen of Connacht.

Many a time I think to seek

One or the other out and speak

Of that old Georgian mansion, mix

Pictures of the mind, recall

That table and the talk of youth.

Two girls in silk kimonos, both

Beautiful, one a gazelle.

The house and gardens are open to the public during the season and a visit is highly recommended.

KNOCKNAREA

Knocknarea dominates the skyline to the west of Sligo town. It is topped by a flat-topped cairn that is believed to be the resting place of the legendary Queen Maeve of Connacht. It is actually a Neolithic passage tomb and apart from the tombs in the Boyne Valley, is the largest in Ireland. The climb to the top of Knocknarea is not too difficult and once accomplished, provides spectatular views in all directions including to the Ox Mountains, Lough Gill, Slieve Leigue in west Donegal and even as far as Croagh Patrick on a clear day.

MULLAGHMORE

The Mullaghmore Peninsula, with its fine beach, is a favourite holiday destination close to Sligo town. The peninsula is dominated by the heights of Ben Bulben rising in the background and the gothic Classiebawn Castle that was a favoured holiday retreat of Lord Louis Mountbatten and it was just off the Mullaghmore coast that he, together with the Dowager Baroness Brabourne and teenager Paul Maxwell, were killed by a bomb planted by the Provisional IRA in August 1979.

Mullaghmore is also a centre for big-wave surfing and provides some of the most challenging surfing conditions along the west coast of Ireland.

GLENIFF HORSESHOE

Driving north from Sligo town along the N15 one comes to the village of Cliffoney. From there continue until the first crossroads where you should turn right towards the mountains. The road winds its way under Benwiskin Mountain to the base of Truskmore Mountain, the highest peak in the mountain range. It's a short drive made memorable by the spectacular scenery. High up on the mountain slopes is clearly visable the cave that is said to be the final hiding place of Diarmuid and Grainne, the doomed lovers of Irish legend.

Classiebawn Castle on the Mullaghmore Peninsula was once the holiday retreat of Lord Mountbatten.

ENNISCRONE

Enniscrone describes itself as one of Ireland's most popular family holiday seaside resorts, and who am I to argue. Certainly its 5 km beach surrounded by dunes offers magnificent views in all directions. As befits a holiday seaside town there are lots of activities to tempt the visitor including fishing, horseback riding, golf, kitesurfing, seaweed baths and surfing, not to mention a good selection of bars and restaurants.

CREEVYKEEL COURT TOMB

Creevykell Court Tomb is one of the best examples of a court tomb anywhere in Ireland and is located on the foothills of Tievebaun Mountain close to the sea near Mullaghmore. The tomb dates from the Neolithic period (c.4,000-2500 BC) and is a wedge shaped cairn around 50 metres long with an oval-shaped court at its eastern end. The tomb was excavated in 1935 when four cremation burials were unvcovered, along with Neolithic pottery, polished stone axes, flint knives, scrapers and two clay balls. Very impressive and recommended..

The beach at Mullaghmore.

PARKE'S CASTLE AND LOUGH GILL

Perched on the northern shore of beautiful Lough Gill on the Sligo to Dromahair road (R286) just a few short kilometres from Sligo town is the restored 17th century plantation Parke's Castle. In the tower house that forms part of the castle, Francisco de Cuellar, the shipwrecked Spanish Armada officer, was entertained by Sir Brian O'Rourke. De Cuellar was to write in later years: 'Although this chief is a savage, he is a good Christian and an enemy of the heretics and is always at war with them.' O'Rourke was executed for treason in London in 1591 and the castle was acquired by the Parke's. Guided tours are available and there are also cruises on Lough Gill that leave from beside the Castle. The restoration of the castle is excellent and gives one a real sense of what life in this 17th century stronghold must have been like.

Parke's Castle looks out over the waters of Lough Gill.

Strandhill beach.

William Butler Yeats:
Ireland's National Poet

William Butler Yeats (1865-1939) was born in Dublin. His father was a lawyer and a well-known portrait painter. Yeats was educated in London and in Dublin, but he spent his summers in the west of Ireland in the family's summer house in Connaught. The young Yeats was very much part of the *fin de siècle* in London; at the same time he was active in societies that attempted an Irish literary revival. His first volume of verse appeared in 1887, but in his earlier period his dramatic production outweighed his poetry both in bulk and in import. Together with Lady Gregory he founded the Irish Theatre, which was to become the Abbey Theatre, and served as its chief playwright until the movement was joined by John Synge. His plays are usually based on Irish legends; they also reflect his fascination with mysticism and spiritualism. *The Countess Cathleen* (1892), *The Land of Heart's Desire* (1894), *Cathleen ni Houlihan* (1902), *The King's Threshold* (1904), and *Deirdre* (1907) are among the best known.

After 1910, Yeats's dramatic art took a sharp turn toward a highly poetical, static, and esoteric style. His later plays were written for small audiences; they experiment with masks, dance, and music, and were profoundly influenced by the Japanese Noh plays. Although a convinced patriot, Yeats deplored the hatred and the bigotry of the Nationalist movement, and his poetry is full of moving protests against it. He was appointed to the Irish Senate in 1922. Yeats is one of the few writers whose greatest

The statue of WB Yeats in Sligo.

works were written after the award of the Nobel Prize. Whereas he received the Prize chiefly for his dramatic works, his significance today rests on his lyric achievement. His poetry, especially the volumes *The Wild Swans at Coole* (1919), *Michael Robartes* and *The Dancer* (1921), *The Tower* (1928), *The Winding Stair and Other Poems* (1933), and *Last Poems and Plays* (1940), made him one of the outstanding and most influential twentieth-century poets writing in English. His recurrent themes are the contrast of art and life, masks, cyclical theories of life (the symbol of the winding stairs), and the ideal of beauty and ceremony contrasting with the hubbub of modern life.

WB Yeats died on 28th January 1939 in France.

From *Nobel Lectures, Literature 1901-1967*, Editor Horst Frenz, Elsevier Publishing Company, Amsterdam, 1969

Useful web addresses

THE MODEL AND NILAND GALLERY	www.themodel.ie
THE HAWK'S WELL THEATRE	www.hawkswell.com
DRUMCLIFFE TEA HOUSE & CRAFT SHOP	www.drumcliffeteahouse.ie
SLIGO FOLK PARK	www.sligofolkpark.com
YEATS MEMORIAL BUILDING AND ART GALLERY	www.yeats=sligo.com
IRISH RAPTOR RESEARCH SANCTURY	www.eaglesflying.com
LISADELL HOUSE AND GARDENS	www.lissadellhouse.com
KNOCKNAREA	www.sligotown.net/knocknarea.shtml
SURFING AT MULLAGHMORE	www.offshore.ie/surf-mullaghmore/

PARKE'S CASTLE
www.heritageireland.ie/en/north-west/parkescastle/

LOUGH GILL BOAT TOURS	www.roseofinisfree.com

CREEVYKELL COURT TOMB   www.discoverireland.ie/arts-culture-
heritage/creevkeel-court-tomb/50210

ENNISCRONE	www.enniscrone.ie

Useful Maps Ordnance Survey Sheets 16 and 25

Surfing at Strandhill

Downpatrick Head, near to Ballycastle, on the North Mayo coast.

Ballina, situated on the River Moy, on the northern coast of Mayo, is the counties largest town.

NORTH MAYO AND ACHILL - THE LAND OF GRANUAILLE

For many years it has been my belief that Mayo is the most underated county in Ireland. I have many reasons for this belief, it's a big county with a natural beauty that is sometimes breath-taking and a diversity of landscape and history not matched elsewhere. Perhaps most of all, its because Mayo feels largly undiscovered and there is much to be explored by the traveller not wishing to drive in the wheel-tracks of the mass of visitors. But even the places that are well-known visitor attractions, such as Achill, Westport or Killary, are unspoilt and welcoming places.

Then there's Mayo's history, be it the incredible landscape of the Ceide Fields, the associations of towns like Killala and this whole coastline with the French invaders of the 18th century, tales of Captain Boycott or the romantic tales of pirate Queen Granuaille, the landscape bears witness to moments of triumph and tragedy in Ireland's history. Wherever you find yourself in Mayo you can be sure that you're walking hand in hand with history.

To explore Mayo properly you need a car and a car will open up the possibilities for you of discovering your own deserted beach or finding a forgotten valley, deserted, of course, in the beautiful Nephin Mountains. Take your time and allow plenty of it to properly discover this beguiling county and its varied landscape. If you do, I'll bet that you'll want to come back again and again.

BALLINA
Ballina, on the northern coast of Mayo, is situated on the famous River Moy, close to Killala Bay. The River Moy is internationally acknowledged as an exceptional salmon fishery, producing several thousand salmon to the rod annually.
The famous Ridge Pool, the salmon anglers paradise, is located in the heart of the town. Ballina is Mayo's largest town and there are a rich variety of pubs and restaurants in the town.

There are several visitor attractions including the ruins of Moyne Abbey, and of

The Round Tower at Killala is one of the best surviving examples of these landmark buildings.

Rosserk Friary dating back to the 15th century and the impressive St Muredach's Cathedral that stands imposingly on the banks of the River Moy. Ballina is, of course, the home of the former President of Ireland, Mrs. Mary Robinson, and the favourite fishing retreat of Ireland's favourite Englishman, the Republic of Ireland's ex-Soccer Manager, Jack Charlton.

The Dolmen of the Four Maols is located on 'Primrose Hill' behind Ballina's Railway Station. The dolmen dates from 2,000 BC, and is sometimes called locally the 'Table of the Giants'. Legend has it that the dolmen is the burial place of the four Maols. The four Maols murdered Ceallach, a 7th century Bishop of Kilmoremoy and were quartered at Ardnaree - the Hill of Executions. Tradition says that their bodies were buried under the dolmen.

Ballina played a role in the failed rebellion of 1798 and the Centenary memorial (the Humbert Monument) on Humbert Street in the town, was dedicated in 1898 to commemorate the 100th anniversary of the French landing at Killala in support of the rebellion. The monument was originally sculpted by a Dublin Craftsman but in recent years it has been restored locally. The figure on the monument is not Humbert as some believe, but Mother Ireland. Maud Gonne unveiled the monument, and at the unveiling event famously poured water over another speaker's head. The monument was moved to its current location on Humbert Street in 1987, where it was re-dedicated by Maud Gonne's son, Seán MacBride.

North Mayo's coastline is spectacular.

Fishing boats nestle against the pier in Killala Bay.

The Ceide Feilds Visitor Center near Ballycastle tells the story of the oldest known field systems in the world.

As befits its importance as a salmon fishing centre, the Ballina Salmon Festival is held annually in July in the town. The festival includes Heritage Day, where most of the centre of the town is closed to traffic and the streets are filled with arts and craft stalls and demonstrations of transport from days gone by. The festival finale is a Mardi Gras followed by a monster fireworks display

KILLALA

Killala is a picturesque village located to the north-west of Ballina, and is famous in Irish history for the part it played in the 1798 rebellion. In August of 1798, the French General Humbert arrived into Kilcummin pier from France and combined with the Irish forces against the English forces in the area. This year is chronicled in Irish history as the Year of the French and an excellent book and television history of the same name celebrate what was a unique event in Irish history. Killala's skyline is dominated by a round tower, dating to the 12th century, a testament to the historic roots of the village as an ecclesiastical centre. The Killala round tower was most likely used as a belfry and is one of the best examples of round towers in Mayo. In the centre of Killala is a Church of Ireland cathedral, built in 1670 over the remains of a ruined Catholic cathedral that had stood on the same site. The adjoining graveyard has a 9th century souterrain with numerous chambers.
There are beautiful, un-spoilt beaches in

the region, including nearby Ross - a Blue Flag beach, excellent for swimming and other water sports.

CÉIDE FIELDS

The Céide Fields, a short distance from the town of Ballycastle, are the oldest known field systems in the world, over five and a half millennia old. Theirs is a unique Neolithic landscape of world importance, the study of which has changed our perception of our Stone Age ancestors. The remains of stone field walls, houses and megalithic tombs are preserved beneath a blanket of peat over several square miles. They tell a story of the everyday lives of a farming people, their organized society, their highly developed spiritual beliefs, and their struggle against a changing environment that was beyond their control.

A visit to the multi-award winning Visitor Centre, which has exhibitions and an audio-visual show is highly recommended. You can also take a guided tour and discover a buried wall for yourself using a centuries old method of probing. Discover also the unique ecology of the bogland, with it's mosses, sedges, lichens, heathers, flowers and insect-eating sundews while listening to the abundant bird life. Highly recommended.

BELMULLET

Mullet is a peninsula on the north-west coast of Mayo. It's a Gaeltacht area where the Irish language is spoken but don't let

Impressive sea stack at Downpatrick Head, near Ballycastle.

not completed until 1851. During the Relief work for the Distress (in the middle of the Great Famine) in 1846 and 1847, the footpaths were formed and flagged. Another development during the 1840s was the development of a fishing station to exploit the coast's natural resources. It was opened in 1847 to wash and cure fish, with boats being built there too, but the station was forced to close due to local fishermen who were imprisoned for the theft of flour from a passing ship. Many people in Belmullet starved to death while soldiers guarded tons of meal, most of it being shipped to England.

A workhouse was erected on the site of the current hospital, and the infamous Head of the Treasury, Charles Trevelyan, notoriously decreed that relief was only to be given to workhouse people. Starving people crowded to the workhouse and at one stage at the height of the Famine, some 3,000 people were recorded as being in Belmullet workhouse.

THE MULLET PENINSULA

The Mullet Peninsula is one of Ireland's great unspoilt places with many empty sandy beaches waiting to be discovered and wonderful views in all directions. It's about 33 kms in length and about 12 km wide at its widest point, narrowing to just 400 metres in the region of Elly Bay. The Mullet Peninsula has much to offer in the way of interesting historical artefacts, and particularly notable is the parish of Kilcommon that lies to the northeast of the Mullet and has prehistoric megalithic tombs.

There are also several small islands lying off the coast of the Mullet peninsula including the Inishkea Islands, Inishglora and Duvillaun. There are lighthouses on other small islands off the coast at Blackrock and Eagle Island. The Saint Deirbhle heritage centre based at Aughleam near the southern end of the peninsula has a fine collection of books and historical information on the area. Highly recommended.

BLACKSOD BAY LIGHTHOUSE

If you visit the Mullet Peninsula then you

that put you off for English is spoken by everyone there as well. The town of Belmullet lies at the neck of the peninsula and has Broadhead Bay to the east of the town and Blacksod Bay to the south, linked by the short Carter's Canal that runs through the town.

Although there are records indicating the origins of the town going back to 1715, it wasn't until the establishment of the headquarters of the commander of the coastguard here that the town began to flourish, aided also by the building of a new road to Castlebar completed in 1824.

Because of the Famine, the canal was

Mayo's northern coastline is rugged and unspoilt.

are likely to visit Blacksod Bay and to hear there the story of its most westerly lighthouse and the part it played in the great events that led to the D-Day invasion of Europe in June 1944. When Irish Coastguard and lighthouse keeper Ted Sweeney sent his daily weather report. As he watched the barometer fall he had no idea that the lives of more than 150,000 Allied troops would hang on his words.

Blacksod's importance was due to the fact that it was the first land-based weather observation station in Europe where weather readings could be professionally taken on the prevailing European Atlantic westerly weather systems. The report from the Blacksod station convinced General Dwight D Eisenhower, Commander of the Allied Forces, to delay the D-Day invasion for 24 hours – a decision which averted a military catastrophe and changed the course of the Second World War.

The stone circle, known as 'Deirbie's Twist at Fallmore, Belmullet.

ACHILL ISLAND

If Mayo is the great un-discovered county of Ireland then Achill Island is the gem at its heart. There are many reasons to holiday in Achill and some of the most popular follow. The Atlantic Drive must not be missed and is best taken clockwise from Achill Sound around the islands soaring cliffs and into the village of Keel. Do pause along the way at Cloughmore to look back east across Clew Bay's alleged 365 islands towards Westport and south to Clare Island.

If you're looking for a fine beach then on Achill you'll be spoilt for choice as there are no fewer than five Blue Flag beaches as well as many more small and unspoilt beaches in the more remote parts of the island. For me the horseshoe Keem Beach on Keem Bay is the star, and is approached by a wonderful coast road. It even has a legend that St. Patrick blessed it and said than no one would ever come to harm there! The other main beaches are: Trawmore Strand (Keel); Dooega; Dolden Strand (Dugort) and Dugort.

On the south-eastern shore of Achill Is-

Located at the head of Elly Bay is the attractive Elly Beach, south of Belmullet on the Mullet Peninsula.

Tower. Here also are the ruins of an ancient church but it is the tower that has our

Kildavnet Tower is a 15th century Irish Tower House that ws once the home of the legendary pirate Queen, Grace O'Malley (Granuaille).

The western coast of Achill Island along the Atlantic Drive is spectacular.

attention as it is a fine example of a 15th Century Irish tower house. However, it is as the home of the legendary pirate Queen Granuaille (Grace O'Malley, 1530-1603) that it is best known. The Tower stands at a strategically important spot, guarding the waters of Achill Sound that link Clew Bay to the south with Blacksod Bay to the north. During the time of Granuaille it was one of several such strongholds that she controlled, including one at Clare Island, that allowed her to control the waters of Clew Bay as well as the seas off the west coast of Mayo.

Like all of the west of Ireland, Achill Island suffered much from emigration down the centuries and a poignant reminder of those times is the deserted village at Slievemore. Here are the remains of almost one hundred traditional stone cottages. The village was established some time in the 12th century and there is a megalithic tomb nearby, indicating dwellers in the area some 5,000 years earlier.

I must also mention Annagh, one of the most remote, and dramatic, places on Achill Island. Annagh is located on the northern coastline of Achill, and is a steep sided valley with a spectacular corrie lake and a small, sandy beach that are only accessible by foot over hills or by boat. The corrie lake at the heart of Annagh - Lough Nakeeroge East - is just 16m above sea level and is the lowest corrie

The Lighthouse at Blacksod Bay provided the important weather reports that determined the fate of the D-Day invasion of Europe in 1944.

The sparsely populated landscape that this drive through the Nephin Beg Range reveals.

lake in Ireland. A fine example of a glacial corrie lake, its moraine separates this freshwater lake from the seawater of Blacksod Bay to the north of Achill. Annagh has a long history, and a megalithic tomb discovered in the area suggests habitation up to 5000 years ago. Very highly recommended, like the rest of Achill Island.

NEPHIN BEG DRIVE

On the road (N59) between Achill Sound and Newport just a few kilometres before you enter Newport are signs for Furnace Lough and Lough Feeagh. Taking the road that leads up the eastern shore of Lough Feeagh will bring you into a wonderful, sparsely populated landscape and through the Nephin Beg Mountain range. I love this road and the landscape that unfolds and which will eventually emerge on the Mayo Plain on the R31, which in turn, leads into Newport. As you descend towards the R31 there are what appear to be small islands of cultivated green set amongst the rough moorland of the plain. Very highly recommended.

'Small islands in the Mayo Plain'.

A poignant inscription along the road recalls how immigration affected this area so deeply.

coṁóraṅ aṅ ḟoraoıs seo ṁırċıġ as éırınn a ċuır go mór le leas muıntır maheırıceá ı gcoıtınne agas muıntır nua-eaṫraċ go háırıṫe

This area of forest commemorates Irish emigrants who contributed so significantly to the welfare of the United States of America in general and of New York in particular

NEWPORT

Our final stop before heading into South Mayo, is the picturesque town of Newport, nestling on the shore of Clew Bay. The Black Oak River flows through the town. There is a very pleasant disused railway viaduct crossing the river and this, together with the Catholic Church on top of the hill, dominate the town. St. Patrick's Church was built in 1914 and is notable for having the last stained glass window completed by Harry Clarke in 1930. Another of Grace O'Malley's fortresses, Rockfleet Castle, is located to the west of the town.

Useful web addresses

BALLINA
www.mayo-ireland.ie/en/towns-villages/ballina/ballina.html

KILLALA
www.mayo-ireland.ie/en/towns-villages/killala/killala.html

CÉIDE FIELDS   www.museumsofmayo.com/ceide.html

BELMULLET
www.mayo-ireland.ie/en/towns-villages/belmullet/belmullet.html

THE MULLET PENINSULA
www.discoverireland.ie/Activities-Adventure/the-mullet-peninsula/12306

BLACKSOD BAY LIGHTHOUSE
www.independent.ie/irish-news/how-blacksod-lighthouse-changed-the-course-of-the-second-world-war-30319681.html

ACHILL ISLAND   www.achilltourism.com

                     www.visitachill.com/en/index.html

NEWPORT   www.newportmayo.ie

Useful Maps Ordnance Survey Discovery Series Sheets 22, 23, 24, 30 and 31

The beautiful Keem Bay and Beach is just one of many spectacular beaches on Achill Island.

The town clock in Westport's attractive square.

SOUTH MAYO -
A PARADISE FOR LOVERS OF ADVENTURE SPORTS

South Mayo is dominated by three mountain ranges: the Mweelrea Mountains in the east; the Sheefrey Hills and to the south east and bordering Lough Mask, the Partry Mountains. These mountains dictate the character of South Mayo and together with emigration from famine and poor farming land, are responsible for it being so sparsely populated. Only along its coastline stretching from Westport on Clew Bay to Leenaun at the head of Killary Fjord are there pockets of habitation. All of this makes South Mayo a paradise for lovers of adventure sports and indeed, there are many organised options for those who wish to pursue such activities.

But above all else, South Mayo is a place of great wild beauty. Over the years I've been drawn back there again and again, seeking out its special places, of which there are many. Base yourself in busy Westport or at Delphi and take the time to explore and discover why this part of ireland is so special.

WESTPORT

Westport is the third largest town in Mayo, and there is evidence of habitation in the area some 5,000 years ago as evidenced by the many megalithic monuments that are found on the Clew Bay Archeological Trail. In the 16th century Westport, or *Cathair na Mart* as it is known in Gaelic, was an important stronghold for the O'Malley Clan. The Pirate Queen, Grace O'Malley, held control of the fortress in Westport as well as many other strongholds along the shores of Clew Bay.

In the 17th century the Browne Family moved to Westport and built a home on the site of the O'Malley Fortress. In 1730 they employed a famous German architect, Richard Cassels, to design the magnificent Westport House, Interestingly the dungeons of the old O'Malley fortress can still be seen on a visit to Westport House, which is open to the public.

The village of Westport originally comprised thatched cabins that were situated on the front lawn of Westport House with a street and little alleyways leading down to the Carrowbeg River. In the mid 18th century Sir John Browne relocated the village to its current position and contracted the architect William Leeson to plan the town. Subsequently, a proposal announcing the new town of Westport appeared in the Dublin Journal in March 1767. In 1800, the current Mall was developed on both sides of the Carrowbeg River, consisting of 400 m of tree-lined boulevards, with two cascades and three crossings by stone arched bridges. The buildings on both sides of the Mall were built in the Georgian style and many remain intact to this day, creating a wonderful core to the modern town. Highly recommended.

WESTPORT HOUSE

Westport House has a fine history, as already detailed, and today is a major visitor attraction. There are many family activities available there including a Pirate Adventure Park with a Pirate Ship ride. Fiitingly, given her strong associations with the area around Clew Bay and with Westport itself, there is a statue of the Pirate Queen Grace O'Malley by the artist Michael Cooper situated in the extensive grounds of the house. From some 5,000 visitors in 1960 when the house was first

Traditional music is an important part of life in Westport.'

Westport House and its grounds contain several visitor attractions and are one of the west of Ireland's most popular places to visit.

opened to the public, some four million visitors have been welcomed there. Recommended.

LOUISBURG

The town of Louisburg is situated on the coast some 21 km west of Westport. It was established on the Bunowen River in 1795 by Lord Altamont of Westport House as a refuge for Catholics fleeing religious conflict in Ulster. It's a beautifully situated town set against the backdrop of Ireland's holy mountain, Croagh Patrick.

So much of this part of Mayo recalls Grace O'Malley, the famous Pirate Queen, and in Louisburg is the Granuaile Centre telling of her life and exploits. Its open from June to September daily from 10.00 am to 6.00 pm. To check that it is open call +353 98 66341.

A donkey keeps watch at Glen Keen Farm.

CROAGH PATRICK

Croagh Patrick, overlooking Clew Bay, is Ireland's holy mountain. There is a tradition of pilgrimage to the mountain stretching back, it is claimed, over 5,000 years from the Stone Age to the present day without interruption. Its religious significance dates back to the time of the pagans, when it is believed that people gathered there to celebrate the beginning of the harvest season. It was on the summit of the mountain that Saint Patrick

fasted for forty days in 441 AD and the custom has been faithfully handed down from generation to generation and is recalled today by an annual pilgrimage.

Each year, The Reek, as it is known to one and all, attracts about 1 million pilgrims. On 'Reek Sunday', the last Sunday in July, over 25,000 pilgrims visit the Reek. At the top, there is a modern chapel where mass is celebrated and confessions are heard. Individuals and groups come from all over the world and include pilgrims, climbers, historians, archaeologists and nature lovers.

Croagh Patrick is 5 miles from Westport and its conical shape soars high above the surrounding countryside. Croagh Patrick rises some 750 metres making it one of the highest mountains in the west of Ireland, and providing magnificent views of Clew Bay and the surrounding south Mayo countryside for those who acomplish the ascent.

SPANISH ARMADA VIEWPOINT, CORRAUN PENINSULA

The Spanish Armada Viewpoint offers exceptional views across Clew Bay and

Surfing at Louisburg.

southwest to Clare Island. It's no more than a small gravel surfaced lay-by adjacent to the Clew Bay coastal road with the backdrop of Corraun Hill (524 m), but is well worth the stop. The Spanish Armada, intent on attacking the south coast of England, was dispersed by a great storm and five of its ships floundered off the Mayo coast in 1588. These include; the *San Nicolas Prodaneli* and *El Gran Grin,* both of which sank at the mouth of Clew Bay with great loss of life.

CLARE ISLAND

Clare Island is a large mountainous island standing guard at the entrance to Clew Bay in County Mayo. It was once the home of the Pirate Queen, Grace O'Malley, and today approximately 160 people live there. It's a beautiful island and is the perfect place to visit if you want to 'get away from it all'. For almost two centuries, the island's Lighthouse has been a nautical landmark perched high on the cliffs. Today, this heritage property offers sanctuary of a different kind, and the architecturally listed building has been lovingly transformed into fully catered, luxury accommodation, complimented by magnificent sea views and an inspiring, natural environment. Highly recommended.

Clare Island is accessible by daily ferry services from Roonagh Pier near Louisburgh. The return trip costs €15 and a map of the island is provided with the ticket. The island also has a hostel, some Bed and Breakfasts and a yoga and meditation centre. The island is particularly suitable for exploration by bicycle, and they can be rented in Glen (beside the pier) for €10 for the day. A visit to the beguiling Clare Island is highly recommended.

DOO LOUGH

The road south from Louisburg to Leenaun takes one through the Doo Lough Pass. It's a place of wild beauty making it hard to imagine the terrible tragedy that took place here during the great irish Famine. On Friday 30th March 1849 two officials of the Westport Poor Law Union arrived in Louisburgh to inspect those people in receipt of relief monies to verify if they should continue to receive them. For some reason the inspection did not take place and the officials went on to Delphi Lodge – then a hunting lodge – 19 km south of Louisburgh. The people who had gathered for the inspection were then instructed to appear at Delphi Lodge at 7:00 am the following morning if they wished to continue receiving relief. For much of the night and day that followed it appears that hundreds of destitute and starving people had to undertake what for them, given their existing state of debilitation, was an near impossible journey, in very bad weather conditions. It was reported shortly afterwards that the bodies of seven people, including women and children, were subsequently discovered on

Croagh Patrick, Ireland's holy mountain, rises majesticaally to overlook Clew Bay.

Grace O'Malley, Ireland's pirate queen.

Grace O'Malley – Pirate Queen

In the early 14th century the Clan O'Malley controlled the southern shore of Clew Bay and most of the barony of Murrisk. Ruthless pirates, they terrorised the ships traveling into and out of Galway town, forcing all those who fished off the Connemara coast to pay them a tax. In addition they traded with the coastal areas of France and Spain and built a row of castles around Clew Bay to protect their territory.

Grace O'Malley was born around 1530 at Belcare Castle near Westport. She is best known by her Irish nickname *Granuaile* or *Gráinne ni Mhaille*. As a child she lived at her family's castles at Belclare and Clare Island. She was well educated and is said to have spoken Latin. Upon the death of her father, she inherited his large fleet of ships and became Queen of Umaill, chieftain of the Ó Máille clan.

She married twice, her first husband dying in battle. In 1580, after 15 years of battles and negotiations, Iron Dick Burke, Grace's second husband, was granted a knighthood by the English governor of Connacht, Sir Nicholas Malby. He was also given the highest title in Connacht, the McWilliam title. When he died, the new governor, Sir Richard Bingham, and his men campaigned against Grace and her followers. She made a dangerous and historic journey sailing up the Thames seeking an audience with Queen Elisabeth I. It is said, that when they met at Greenwich Palace, Grace refused to bow before Queen Elizabeth because she was herself a Queen, and not a subject of the Queen of England. The two women spoke in Latin and evidently had respect for each other leading them to come to an agreement. Queen Elisabeth I released her sons Tibbot Burke and Murrough O'Flaherty, and her half-brother, Dónal na Píopa, who had been held as hostages, while Grace brought to an end her piracy against England.

Grace lived to an old age, dying in 1603 at Rockfleet Castle and was buried in the Cistercian Abbey on Clare Island.

The Lighthouse on Clare Island offers the ultimate 'hideaway' accommodation.

the roadside between Delphi and Louisburgh overlooking the shores of Doo Lough lake and that nine more never reached their homes. Local folklore maintains the number that perished because of the ordeals they had to endure was far higher.

A cross and an annual Famine Walk between Louisburgh and Doo Lough commemorates this terrible event. The monument in Doo Lough valley at the northern end of the lough has an inscription from Mahatma Gandhi:

'How can men feel themselves honoured by the humiliation of their fellow beings?'

SILVER STRAND

Silver Strand is a remote and unspoiled beach located approximately 25 km south of Louisburgh. Its a fine sandy beach that is open to the west and looks towards the islands of Inishturk and Inishbofin. The beach is located in an ecologically impor-

The rugged Clare Island lies a short distance off the South Mayo coast.

The remote, beautiful and utterly unspoilt Silver Strand Beach.

tant area and was awarded the Green Coast Award for 2016. Personally, for me, this is one of my favourite places in Ireland and to my mind, easily the most beautiful beach on the entire west coast. Go there on a good day and you'll be pretty close to Heaven. Very highly recommended.

The area close to Silver Strand has also a rich archaeological heritage with over 700 known archaeological monuments, and 20 areas of scientific interest. There are court-tombs at Furmoyle and Aillemore, a megalithic wedge-tomb at Srahwee, a clapperbridge (stone bridge with 37 arches) at Killeen, and numerous other monuments, especially around Killadoon.

THE SHEEFFREY MOUNTAINS DRIVE
At the southern end of Doo Lough is a small road signposted for Drummin. This road is a wonderful drive through some very remote areas and from Drummin one can choose either to return to Louisburg or continue on and join the N59 that will take you northeast to Westport or south west to Leenaun. Recommended.

The view along Lough Doo.

Delphi Resort enjoys an unrivalled location between Doo Lough and Leenaun.

Excellent cuisine is available at Delphi Resort.

DELPHI

In the midst of all this wild countryside is Delphi, an oasis with a Greek name. It owes its name to the Marquis of Sligo, who built a famous hunting lodge here. It is located on the Owengarr River that connects Fin Lough to Doo Lough, between the fjord of Killary Harbour to the south and the Sheeffry Hills to the north, in a valley surrounded by the Mweelrea Mountains and the neighbouring peaks of Ben Creggan and Ben Gorm creating a beautiful hideaway.

There are two hotels here: Delphi Lodge based in the hunting lodge built by Lord Sligo and the Delphi Resort Adventure Centre. Both are recommended and the location cannot be bettered.

KILLARY FJORD

Killary Harbour is Ireland's only true fjord and extends some 16 km in from the Atlantic to its head at Aasleagh, just below Aasleagh falls. It also forms the border between counties Mayo and Galway. Killary Harbour is also extremely deep, over 45 m at its centre, and this offers a very safe, sheltered anchorage, as a result of the depth and the mountains to the south and north. Its a centre for shellfish farming, and strings of ropes used to grow mussels are visible for much of its length.

To the north lies Mweelrea, the highest mountain in Connacht and County Mayo, while to the south are the Twelve Bens and the Maumturk Mountains of Connemara. Near the head of the fjord is Leenaun, a picturesque village in County Galway.

The wild beauty of Doo Lough was the scene of a terrible tragedy in Famine times.

A group of adventurers enjoy the many outdoor possibilities along the coast of South Mayo.

The winding road from the southern end of Doo Lough to Drummin passes through a remote and sparsely populated landscape.

Useful web addresses

WESTPORT	www.westporttourism.com
	www.destinationwestport.com
WESTPORT HOUSE	www.westporthouse.ie
CROAGH PATRICK	www.croagh-patrick.com

SPANISH ARMADA VIEWPOINT
www.discoverireland.ie/Arts-Culture-Heritage/spanish-armada-viewpoint/91831

CLARE ISLAND   www.clareisland.ie
www.greatlighthouses.com/lighthouses/clare-island-lighthouse/
      www.clareislandlighthouse.com
      www.clareislandferry.com

SILVER STRAND
www.mayo-ireland.ie/en/wild-atlantic-way/silver-strand.html

DELPHI	www.delphioadventureresort.com
	www.delphilodge.ie

KILLARY FIORD
www.destinationwestport.com/places-to-visit/natural-beauty/killary-harbour-fjord/

**Useful maps: Ordnance Survey Diswcovery Series – Sheets 30, 31§, 37 and 38
Fir Tree Aerial Map of Connemara, West Galway & South Mayo**

Killary Harbour is Ireland's only fjord and forms the border between Counties Mayo and Galway.

Against a background of the Twelve Bens, Clifden nestles on the very edge of Europe.

CLIFDEN TO ROUNDSTONE - PERFECT BEACHES AND WONDERFUL SEAFOOD

Between the towns of Clifden and Roundstone lie some of the best and most easily accessible beaches in Ireland, so good that on a day when the sun shines, you could be forgiven for thinking you've been transported to a South Seas island with its white beaches and shining blue waters. But there is more to this corner of Connemara than beautiful undisturbed beaches; there's a wealth of interesting history surrounding the town of Clifden and the bars and restaurants of the harbour village of Roundstone will delight even the most particular visitor.

CLIFDEN

I've always regarded Clifden as the capital of Connemara, a title this delightful town surely deserves. Situated on the very edge of Europe, it's a surprisingly cosmopolitan town situated between the spectacular Twelve Bens and the Atlantic Ocean, attracting thousands of tourists each year. The town was founded at the start of the 19th century by John D'Arcy who lived in the now ruined Clifden Castle west of the town.

Clifden gained prominence after 1905 when Guglielmo Marconi decided to build his first high power transatlantic long wave wireless telegraphy station 6 kms south of the town so as to minimize the distance to its sister station in Glace Bay, Nova Scotia. The first point-to-point fixed wireless service connecting Europe with North America opened for public service with the transmission of 10,000 words on 17 October 1907. At peak times, up to 200 people were employed by the Clifden

On the Sky Road north of Clifden.

The monument recalling the pioneering work of the Marconi Station south of the town of Clifden.

wireless station and among them was Jack Phillips, who later perished as Chief Radio Operator on the Titanic.

DERRYGIMLAGH BOG

On 15 June 1919 the first non-stop transatlantic flight by Alcock and Brown crash-landed in Derrygimlagh bog, close to Marconi's transatlantic wireless station. When Captain Alcock spotted the green bog he thought it was a meadow where he could safely land their Vickers Vimy bi-plane but the plane's landing gear sank into the soft bog and collapsed. Alcock and Brown had to walk into town with minor injuries. When they later returned it was to discover that the locals had helped themselves to parts of the plane as souvenirs. Both the Marconi station and the landing site are today marked by monuments.

BALLYCONNEELY

From Clifden take the R341 towards Ballyconneely. A left turn at Ballinaboy Bridge will take you over the bog road that crosses the famous Roundstone Bog copnservation area. However, unless you want to explore the Roundstone Blanket Bog, continue on to the village of Bally-conneely, the entry point to the Errismore Peninsula and the ideal place from which to explore the many superb beaches in the area, especially along nearby Mannin Bay where there are several beaches

Alcock and Brown

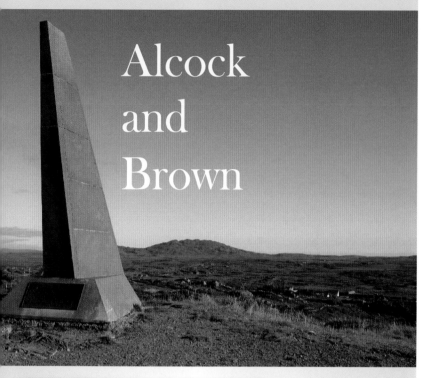

Top: The monument to the pioneering transatlantic flight of Alcock and Brown close to where they larrived at Derrygimlagh Bog.

Left: How the New York Times broke the news that the Atlantic Ocean had been conquered by air to its readers.

Captain John Alcock and Lieutenant Arthur Whitten Brown, in a modified Vickers Vimy IV, made the first non-stop crossing of the Atlantic in a heavier-than-air machine. The two RAF pilots took off from Lester's Field, near St. Johns, Newfoundland, on June 14, 1919, and landed June 15, 1919, at Derrygimlagh Bog near to Clifden in Ireland. The time for the crossing was sixteen hours, twenty-seven minutes.

The news of the adventure spread like wildfire and the two men were received as heroes in Dublin and London. For their accomplishment, they were presented with Lord Northcliffe's *Daily Mail* prize of £10,000 by Winston Churchill, who was then Britain's Secretary of State. A few days later, both men were knighted at Buckingham Palace by King George V, for recognition of their pioneering achievment.

including a coral beach, and to the south, Ballyconneely Bay.

In the recent past, evidence of early coastal settlement over 5,000 years old, has been discovered, including middens of burnt stone, charcoal, shells and stone blades.

ROUNDSTONE

Having explored the beaches in the area around Ballyconneely, continue along the R341 coast road to the harbour village of Roundstone. But before you come to Roundstone, watch out for the sign directing you to Dog's Bay, a personal favourite of mine and one of the most perfect beaches you will find in Ireland. Actually, its two beaches back-to-back,

Gurteen Bay being its mirror image. This is somewhere to linger over before continuing on into the village of Roundstone.

The backdrop to Roundstone is the rugged mountain of Errisbeg, and the village was built in the 1820s by the Scottish engineer, Alexander Nimmo, who had settled in Connemara.

It's a village of great bars and restaurants, many of which have outdoor dining areas to add to the wonderful atmosphere. In truth, where ever you eat, the food, especially the seafood, will be good, but mention should be made of O'Dowd's Restaurant and Bar, and Eldon's and Vaughan's Restaurants. All recommended.

The fabulous shining blue waters and white sands of Bunowen Bay southwest of the village of Ballyconneely.

Dog's Bay - as perfect a beach as you will ever find in Ireland.

The harbour village of Roundstone is particularly noted for its many fine seafood bars and restaurants.

Useful web addresses

CLIFDEN   http://www.connemara.net/clifden/

ROUNDSTONE   http://www.connemara.net/roundstown-village/

VAUGHAN'S RESTAURANT (ROUNDSTONE HOUSE HOTEL)
                     http://www.roundstonehousehotel.com/restaurant/

ELDON'S HOTEL, ROUNDSTONE   www.eldonshotel.com

BALLYCONNEELY   http://www.connemaraireland.com/ballyconneelly/

O'DOWD'S RESTAURANT AND BAR, ROUNDSTONE
                     http://www.odowdsseafoodbar.com/

Useful maps: Ordnance Survey Discovery Series – Sheets 37 and 44

The blanket bog of Derrygimlagh where Alcock and Brown made a landing after their epic Atlantic flight.

Galway City is a lively and exuberant city with a young population.

GALWAY AND CONNEMARA - THE CITY OF THE TRIBES

Galway City is the gateway to Connemara and is a lively city with the exuberance that goes with it's young population and its renowned university. It's a great place to visit and is the ideal base from which to explore Connemara. The city is full of history and its sometimes narrow streets evoke its medieval past. It's a busy place during summer with visitors drawn from all over the world and its shops and restaurants reflect that. Its also somewhere that you'll be bound to encounter some lively traditional Irish music and the craic, as they say, is mightly!

GALWAY CITY
At the heart of Galway City is Eyre Square. The square was presented to the city in 1710 by Mayor Edward Eyre, from whom it took its name. In 1965, the square was officially renamed 'Kennedy Memorial Park in honour of US President John F. Kennedy, who visited here during his 1963 visit to Ireland shortly before his assassination in November of that year.

Another notable feature in Eyre Square is the Browne doorway that was originally the doorway of the Browne families home at Lower Abbeygate Street from where it was moved in 1905 to Eyre Square.

St. Nicholas is the largest medieval parish church in Ireland in continuous use as a place of worship and is at the heart of Galway's life. The oldest sections of the church date from 1320, although it is possible that St. Nicholas was built upon the ruins of an earlier structure, and part of the chancel's south wall may incorporate some of this earlier material. Local tradition says that Christopher Columbus prayed here in 1477 before sailing on one of his attempts to reach the New World.

Another landmark building in the city is Lynch's Castle, once owned by one of the fourteen tribes that ruled Galway city in centuries gone past. The interior of Lynch's Castle is still very impressive with coats of arms, stone fireplaces and a separate exhibition. The Lynches were a wealthy family, several of whom served as Galway mayor. One of the mayors, James Lynch Fitzstephen, found his own son guilty of the murder of a Spanish sailor who became involved with a female family member in 1493. Lynch hanged his son Walter himself when everyone else refused to participate. The term 'Lynch Law' arose from this unfortunate episode. The old prison on Market Street in

sea can be found Galway's famous Spanish Arch. The Spanish Arch was originally a 16th century bastion, which was added to Galway's town walls to protect merchant ships from looting. At this time, it was known as *Ceann an Bhalla*, meaning 'Head of the Wall'. Its current name, Spanish Arch, refers to a time when Spanish galleons regularly docked here. In 1755, the arches were partially destroyed by the

Galway Harbour at night.

Galway City displays a black marble plaque marking the actual spot of the execution.

The name of the Claddagh area comes from the Irish word *'cladach'*, meaning a stony beach. The people of the Claddagh area have been fishing from here for millennia, and its existence has been recorded since the arrival of Christianity in the 5th century. Throughout the centuries, the Claddagh people kept Galway City supplied with fish, which they sold on the square in front of the Spanish Arch. Today the area is best known for its traditional jewellery, the Claddagh Ring, which is worn by people all over the world.
Where Galway's River Corrib meets the

tidal wave generated by the 1755 Lisbon earthquake. In recent times part of the Arch has been converted into the Galway City Museum.

Situated behind the famous Spanish Arch, Galway City Museum houses exhibitions which explore aspects of the history and heritage of Galway City, focusing on the medieval town, the Claddagh village and Galway, 1800-1950. In addition, the Museum mounts temporary exhibitions and hosts a variety of exhibits from other museums, galleries and special interest groups. The building itself affords spectacular views of the Claddagh, the Spanish Arch, the River Corrib and Galway Bay.
Kirwan's Lane is one of the finest medieval

Street art in one of Galway's narrow streets.

The Twelve Bens are at the very heart of Connemara.

laneways in Galway, and is located in what is now referred to as the Latin Quarter of Galway. It contains many relics of 16th and 17th century architecture and is at the centre of an area that was originally within the city walls. It is named after one of Galway's fourteen tribes - the families who ruled the town for several centuries. The area has been significantly restored over the years and has rejuvenated the heart of Galway's historical town centre. It is now home to many bohemian style cafes, restaurants, bars and craft-shops.

The annual Galway Races at Ballybrit are the highlight of Galway's busy social scene.

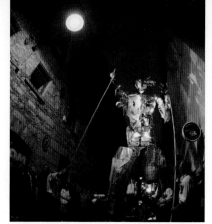
Galway's famous Macnas group tell wonderful stories using giant figures.

TWELVE BENS

The Twelve Bens, or Twelve Pins is a range of sharp-peaked quartzite mountains located northeast of Roundstone in the very heart of Connemara. Wherever you find yourself in Connemara, the Twelve Bens will form an imposing backdrop. It is said that dedicated climbers can hike all twelve peaks in a single day. Frequent rainfall and steep-sided mountains produce an abundance of small trickles and streams which descend into wide-bottomed valleys below the Twelve Pins to join larger streams and pools. The highest peak in the Twelve Bens is Benbaun at 729 metres.

RENVYLE

Although this section of the guide does not cover the area from Clifden to Roundstone – covered already – there is one part of the western coast of Connemara that must be mentioned here. The Renvyle peninsula is home to some of Connemara's most spectacular scenery, with dramatic sweeping beaches and fabulous mountain views. Local activity is centered on the lively villages of Tullycross and Tully, both of which offer warm and welcoming pubs, restaurants and accommodation.

Pony trekking is a popular activity, as are many water sports, which take place at the beaches of Glassilaun, White Strand, Lettergesh and Tully. Don't overlook Derryinver Quay and Ballinakill Harbour that are also well worth a visit.

The traditional music scene is vibrant in

Macnas are an essential part of the magic of Galway.

Young swimmers enjoying the sea at Salthill.

Renvyle and regular musical concerts and dancing take place at the *Teach Ceol* in Tully. The Connemara Mussel Festival takes place on the May Bank Holiday annually showcasing the locally produced seafood dishes in a festival atmosphere. Recommended.

CONG

Cong is situated on an island formed by a number of streams that surround it on all sides. Cong is located on the isthmus connecting Loughs Corrib and Mask, near the towns of Headford and Ballinrobe and the villages of Clonbur, the Neale and Cross.

Cong was the location for John Ford's 195 Oscar-winning film, *The Quiet Man,* featurin John Wayne, Maureen O'Hara and Barry Fitzgerald. Much of the film was filmed on t grounds of Ashford Castle. The town and castle area remain little changed since 195 and Cong's connection with the movie mak it a tourist attraction. The film is still celebrated by the local 'Quiet Man Fan Club'.

Cong is the home of Ashford Castle, a luxu hotel, which was converted from a Victorian faux lakeside castle, built by the Guinness family. Ashford Castle is a tourist attraction its own right. Cong also features a ruined

The beautiful Derryclare Lough nestles amongst the Twelve Bens.

Ross Errily Friary near Headford is one of the best preserved monuments of the period anywhere in Ireland.

medieval abbey, Cong Abbey, where Rory O'Connor, the last High King of Ireland, spent his last years. It also gave its name to a piece of Celtic art in the form of a metal cross shrine called the Cross of Cong. The 'Cross of Cong' is now held in the National Museum of Ireland, Dublin. There is also a High Cross in the village.

OUGHTERARD

Oughterard is an attractive village nestled beside Lough Corrib (the largest lake in the Republic), at the start of the Connemara Mountain Range and only 17km from Galway City.

A traditional music session in full swing in Galway.

The beautiful Renvyle Beach paradise on a sunny day.

An upturned currach on a deserted beach - the perfect place for conversation!

Traditional Galway Hookers sailing in Betraboy Bay.

Useful web addresses

ARRAN ISLAND FERRIES	www.aranislandferries.com
AER ARANN	www.aerarranislands.ie
LETTERFRACK WATERTOURS	www.letterfrackwatertours.com
GALWAY CITY	www.galway-ireland.ie/

www.galwaytourism.ie/pgalway-city-landmarks.html

GALWAY ATLANTAQUARIA	www.nationalaquarium.ie
GALWAY CITY MUSEUM	www.galwaycitymuseum.ie

SPANISH ARCH
www.galwaytourism.ie/pThe-Spanish-Arch.html

DELPHI ADVENTURE RESORT	www.delphi.ie
CORRIB CRUISES	www.corribprincess.ie
ATHENRY HERITAGE CENTRE	www.athenryheritagecentre.com
CLADDAGH VISITOR CENTRE	www,thecladdagh.com
GLENGOWLA MINES	www.glengowlamines.ie
MOYCULLENRIDING CENTRE	www.moycullenriding.com
GLENOSH COTTAGES, MAAM VALLEY	www.glenlosh.com

THE TWELVE BENS
www.connemara.galway-ireland.ie/twelve-bens.htm

MAAM	www.connemaraireland.com/maam/
RENVYLE	www.connemara.ie/en/connemara/renvyle/
CONG	www.congtourism.com
THE QUIET MAN MUSEUM, CONG	www.quietman-cong.com
OUGHTERARD	www.oughterardtourism.com/index.html

ROSS ERRILY FRIARY
www.megalithicireland.com/Ross%20Errilly%20Friary,%20Galway.html

MACNAS	www.macnas.com

Useful Maps: Ordnance Survey Discovery Series sheets 37, 38, 39, 44, 45 and 46.

Munster

Coast road on the Dingle Peninsula.

Exposed limestone covers the north west of County Clare creating the region known as The Burren.

THE BURREN -
AN OTHER WORLDLY LIMESTONE LANDSCAPE

The Burren is a very special place. And one of my favourites. It's an area of exposed limestone that covers the north west of County Clare. It's a landscape like no other, other worldly, and at first sight bleak and barren. But the reality is very different, for this unique landscape with it's limestone pavements is world famous for the unusual blending of Arctic-Alpine and Mediterranean species of flowers that bloom in its cracks (known as 'grikes') during the summer months. Summer is the ideal time to visit the Burren when the limestone landscape is everywhere dotted with thousands of colourful wildflowers.

But it's not just the geology and botany of the Burren that will surprise and delight – it's archaeology is simply amazing with monuments from 6,000 years of Ireland's past all over the landscape. Truly, the Burren is somewhere to linger and to savour the uniqueness of the place ranging from the world famous Cliffs of Moher on it's southern limit to places like the Ailwee Caves or the famous Poulnabrone Dolmen on Ballyalban Hill. For those with an interest in motorsport, the Burren was also the site of two famous hillclimbs. The first was on the aforementioned Ballyalban Hill and ran from just past the turn to the Ailwee Caves to a couple of hundred yards past the Poulnabrone Dolmen. Drive this road and you'll realise what a challenge this hill was. Indeed, it was the longest and fastest hillclimb ever used in Ireland or Britain. I loved competing on it but like every hillclimb, it was one to be respected.

Across the valley was the other hill, aptly named Corkscrew Hill and completely different in character to Ballyalban. Together these two hills provided a unique weekend in the Irish motorsport calender.

KINVARA

Kinvara is like the northern gateway to the Burren region. First sight for most visitors is the romantically positioned 16th century Dunguaire Castle just to the northeast of the village. It's renowned for its medieval banquets and is open to the public from April to October.

The village of Kinvara has plenty of shops and pubs including good places to eat, and is well worth taking the time to explore. Also just north of Kinvara is the beach at Traught, also well worth a visit

'Green' paths in The Burren.

A Burnet Rose on Black Head - this unique landscape is world-famous for the rare flowers that bloom there in Summer.

Black Head and beyond it Galway Bay.

either to swim of just to walk. Don't leave the area of Kinvara without visiting the Burren Nature Sanctuary at Cloonasee – particularly recommended for young visitors and adults alike. There you can arm yourself with the knowledge of the Burren and its history that will make your visit all the more memorable.

BALLYVAUGHAN
Ballyvaughan is a small harbour village on the southern shore of Galway Bay and, despite other contenders for the title, I've always regarded it as the 'capital' of the Burren. By the way, don't be put off by the confusion of signs with completely different spellings of the name of the village. Someone had the bad idea of reviving an ancient name for the village and this spelling appears on a lot of the newer signposts. It's a silly idea and one that only causes unnecessary confusion to visitors. It's Ballyvaughan to the vast majority of visitors and always will be. Speaking of signs there are two signposts side-by-side in the village festooned with signs that make a very popular photograph for visitors. I bet you take a photograph too.

AILLWEE CAVE AND BIRDS OF PREY
A couple of kilometres south of Bally-

vaughan (and well sign-posted) are the joint attractions of Aillwee Cave and the Bird's of Prey and Education Centre. The cave opened in 1976 and I remember being very impressed when I visited it soon afterwards. In the forty years since the facilities and the journey into the cave have been admirably developed and it is now a major attraction in the area. I revisited it again recently and was fascinated, as before, but I have to say I would have welcomed better lighting throughout.

Of much more interest personally was the Birds of Prey Centre, which is a much more recent addition and is claimed to be the largest selection of birds of prey in the country. I don't doubt the claim and spectacular flying displays are scheduled throughout the day. If you're visiting, and I strongly recommend you do, check the times of the flying displays as they are something not to be missed and will stay in your memory for ever.

This crowded sign post in Ballyvaughan is a photo favourite with visitors.

The Birds of Prey Centre adjacent to the Ailwee Cave makes for a memorable visit.

The Poulnabrone Dolmen, a Neolithic portal tomb built before 2,900 BC.

POULNABRONE DOLMEN

One of the most photographed portal tombs in Ireland, Poulnabrone Dolmen dates back to the Neolithic period and was built sometime between 4,200 and 2,900 BC. IN 1985 a crack was discovered in the eastern portal stone. Following the resulting collapse, the dolmen was dismantled, and the cracked stone was replaced. Excavations conducted during that time found that between 16 and 22 adults and six children were buried under the monument. Personal items buried with the dead included a polished stone axe, a bone pendant, quartz crystals, weapons and pottery. These items are now at the Clare Museum at Ennis.

DOOLIN

Doolin is a coastal village with a split personality. On the coastline where the Atlantic waves provide surfers with plenty of action, the ferries leave for the Aran Islands of *Inis Mor, Inis Meáin* and *Inis Oírr.* It's also possible to cruise from Doolin along the nearby Cliffs of Moher. The cruise takes about one hour and includes entry into the Cliffs of Moher Visitor Centre. I haven't taken this cruise but it seems to me an excellent and different way to view the grandure of the cliffs and should be a memorable experience.

A short distance inland from the coast is the tiny village of Doolin. It's a good spot to stop for a meal and I recommend Gus O'Connor's pub on the aptly named Fisher Street, which as you would expect, has an excellent fish menu.

Also close by is *Pol an Ionáin* – Doolin Cave – that features what is claimed to be the largest free hanging stalactite anywhere in the world.

Saker Falcon - just one of the birds that can be viewed at the Birds of Prey Centre.

CLIFFS OF MOHER

What can one say about the Cliffs of Moher – one of Ireland's most popular visitor attractions and a must-see for most people. The Cliffs stretch for 8 kilometres and rise to an impressive 214 metres above the Atlantic Ocean. They are also home to Ireland's largest seabird colony with up to 30,000 breeding pairs. An eco-friendly visitor centre was opened here in 2007 and is set into the hill-side providing an all-weather experience. When it comes to photographs of the Cliffs, there is an excellent panoramic viewing area on the top floor of O'Brien's Tower.

THE BURREN CENTRE

Finally, on the southern tip of the Burren is the village of Kilfenora. The Burren Centre located there is open from mid-March to the end of October and provides a detailed explanation of how the Burren was created and its many unique features. Adjacent to the Burren Centre is St.Fachtnan's 12th century Cathedral and medieval high crosses.

O'Brien's Tower at the Cliffs of Moher, offers an excellent platform for photographs of the Cliffs.

The west facing Cliffs of Moher bathed in sunset's light.

Useful web addresses

DUNGUAIRE CASTLE, KINVARA	www.shannonheritage.com
BURREN NATURE SANCTURY, CLOONASEE	www.bns.ie
AILWEE CAVE AND BIRDS OF PREY	www.aillweecave.ie
CLIFFS OF MOHER	www.cliffsofmoher.ie
DOOLIN, O'CONNOR'S PUB & RESTAURANT	www.gusoconnorspubdoolin.net
DOOLIN, ARAN ISLANDS FERRY	www.doolinferry.com
DOOLIN, DOOLIN CAVE	www.doolincave.ie
THE BURREN CENTRE, KILFENORA	www.theburrencentre.ie
GREGAN'S CASTLE HOTEL, CORKSCREW HILL	www.gregans.ie
POULNABRONE DOLMEN	www.megalithicireland.com/poulnabrone.htm

Useful maps: Ordnance Survey Discovery Series – Sheets 51 and 52

Doolin's waves provide good surfing conditions.

The Loop Head Peninsula juts out into the Atlantic and forms the northern coast of the Shannon Estuary.

LOOP HEAD - RUGGED CLIFFS AND EMPTY ROADS

Loop Head is perhaps one of the least discovered parts of Ireland but it is well worth taking the time to explore and to sample its varied attractions. Loop Head comprises the southwestern promontory of County Clare bordered in the south by the Shannon Estuary and to its west by the Atlantic Ocean. It's Atlantic coastline has remained unspoilt and its cliffs stretch from the seaside resort of Kilkee through Castle Point and the Bridges of Ross to Loop Head itself, crowned by a lighthouse that is open to the public.

The peninsula is almost completely surrounded by Special Areas of Conservation and Natural Habitat Areas, and is famous for its wildlife, beaches, cliffs, caves and sea stacks.

KILKEE

Kilkee is the main town of the peninsula and a popular seaside resort. Now I have to say that I'm not a fan of seaside resorts but Kilkee is my exception. It's built around a semi-circular bay with a one kilometre long sandy beach. A reef – Duggerna Reef – stretches across its mouth and so it is naturally protected

from the fury of the Atlantic seas. There are high cliffs on either side of the bay that was visited in the past by Lord Alfred Tennyson and Sir Aubrey de Vere. In more recent times the Cuban revolutionary, Che Guevara, visited the town in 1961 and stayed at The Strand Guesthouse where his signature can be viewed in the visitor's book. A letter (source: http://irelandsown.net/Che.html) he wrote to his father reads:

Dear Dad:

With the anchor dropped and the boat at a standstill, I am in this green Ireland of your ancestors. When they found out, the [Irish] television came to ask me about the Lynch genealogy, but in case they were horse thieves or something like that I didn't say much.

Happy holidays,

We're waiting for you

Ernesto

Tortoiseshell Butterfly on Loop Head.

Kilkee is built around a semi-circular bay and sandy beach.

The Strand Seafood Bistro and Guesthouse run by Johnny and Caroline Redmond and their family is still in business today and it is well worth dining there. Another place I recommend in which to dine in Kilkee is the award winning Murphy Blacks Restaurant

CASTLEPOINT
The coast road from Kilkee to Castle Point winds its way past spectacular sea cliffs and sea stacks. There is a mighty sea cave situated below the car park but this is only visible from below.

KILKEE CIVIC TRUST

Ché Guevara
(1928 - 1967)

**Cuban Revolutionary
stayed in this Hotel in
1961**

The Cuban revolutionary, Che Guevara, made a brief visit to Kilkee in 1961.

THE BRIDGES OF ROSS

The Bridges of Ross were so named for a trio of spectacular natural sea arches. However, two of them fell into the sea, and today, even though only one 'bridge' remains, the name persists in the plural. The surviving Bridge of Ross lies on the western side of the natural harbour that is Ross Bay, looking north to the Atlantic Ocean, near the village of Kilbaha.

The area is regarded as one of the best birdwatching sites in Europe. In late summer and autumn, it becomes a birder's paradise as thousands of rare seabirds pass close to shore on their southbound migration.

LOOP HEAD LIGHTHOUSE

The first lighthouse on Loop Head was a stone vaulted building constructed in 1670. The current structure is 23 metres high and dates from 1854 and was converted to automatic operation in 1991. In recent years it has been opened to the public and makes for an unusual attraction, well worth visiting.

Loop Head Lighthouse

The Bridges at Ross - now just one 'bridge', the other two having collapsed in recent years.

Spectacular sea-stacks line the cliffs between Kilkee and Ross.

CARRIGHOLT

I rather like Carrigaholt, sandwiched between two harbours and with its 15th century castle. Its also got cosy pubs and seafood restaurants where you can enjoy the local catch. And of course, there are the highly recommended dolphin watching boat trips that set out from here

KILRUSH

You could perhaps argue that Kilrush is not on the Loop Head peninsula but any visitor to the area will visit it so I'm including it here. Kilrush is bigger than Kilkee and has a fine selection of shops as well as several pubs that are good to eat in. I'd recommend Crotty's Pub on Market Square that also offers accomodation. If you've the time I suggest picking up

the leaflet from the Tourist Office for the Kilrush Historic Town Trail that actually offers two trails – one a 1.5 km. route taking about 20 minutes and the longer being 6 kms. And taking about an hour. As well as the historic and interesting buildings along the way the longer route includes the Vandeleur Demesne with its walled garden of tropical plants.

DOLPHIN WATCHING

The Shannon Esturary is home to over 120 bottlenose dolphins as well as other wildlife including grey seals, gannets. guillemots and razorbills. Boat trips leave Carrigaholt and Kilrush and take about two hours. Be sure to dress in warm clothes. Highly recommended.

Over 120 Bottlenose dolphins have made the Shannon Esturary their home.

Useful web addresses

CROTTY'S PUB AND ACCOMODATION   www.crottyspubkilrush.com
DOLPHIN SIGHTSEEING   www.discoverdolphins.ie
    www.dolphinwatch.ie
THE STRAND SEAFOOD BISTRO AND GUESTHOUSE
    Tel: 065 905 6177   www.thestrandkilkee.com
KILKEE   www.kilkee.ie
KILRUSH   www.kilrush.ie
LOOP HEAD LIGHTHOUSE   www.loophead.ie
MURPHY BLACKS RESTAURANT
    Tel: 065 905 6854   www.murphyblacks.ie

Useful maps: Ordnance Survey Discovery Series – Sheets 57 and 63

Loop Head Cliffs

King John's Castle is an impressive sight across the River Shannon.

IN AND AROUND LIMERICK CITY - FLYING BOATS AND CASTLES

My guess is that you will be keen to reach the west coast but there are several attractions in and around Limerick city that are just too good to miss. Limerick city itself is an attractive city with a rich and varied history nestling along the banks of the mighty River Shannon. All of the places I'm recommending are either on the outskirts of the city or within a short drive, with the exception of the Hunt Museum and King John's Castle that are centrally located in the city but easy to access.

KING JOHN'S CASTLE

King John's Castle stands in the heart of Limerick city, something it has done for over 800 years. The Castle is situated on 'King's Island' in the heart of medieval Limerick City and overlooks the majestic river Shannon. It was built between 1200 and 1210 and has since been repaired and extended many times and now houses an interpretative centre containing a particularly imaginative historical exhibition, telling the story of the Castle.

The walls of the castle were severely damaged in the 1642 Siege of Limerick, the first of five sieges of the city in the 17th century. In 1642, the castle was occupied by Protestants fleeing the Irish Rebellion of 1641 and was besieged by an Irish Confederate force under Garret Barry. Barry had no siege artillery so he undermined the walls of King John's Cas-

tle by digging away their foundations. Those inside surrendered just before Barry collapsed the walls. However, such was the damage done to the wall's foundations that a section of them had to be pulled down afterwards.

The courtyard and the Castle display some of the trades and traditions of the 16th Century and visitors can enjoy panoramic views of Limerick City and the surrounding countryside from atop it's walls and towers. Particularly interesting are the archaeological excavations that have revealed pre-Norman settlements and evidence from the traumatic siege of 1642. These can be viewed in a unique underground display. Indeed, it would be hard to imagine how the exhibition and its imaginative displays could be bettered. I thoroughly recommend visiting the castle and also its excellent café and shop.

BUNRATTY CASTLE

There was a time when Bunratty was one of the corner-stones of tourism in Ireland. Since then there has been a revolution in tourism and the nature of attractions worth seeing on this island. The castle, which is only one part of the attraction, the balance being an extensive folk park, is a formidable affair. Built in 1425, it is claimed to be the most complete and authentic medieval fortress in Ireland and contains furnishings, tapestries and works of art from that period.

Foynes was the centre of the aviation world between 1937 and 1945. The story of the flying boats is told in this award winning museum...

FOYNES
FLYING BOAT
& MARITIME
MUSEUM

★ Board the World's only replica of the B314 Flying Boat

★ 3D hologram show of the night Irish Coffee was invented here in 1943

- Aviation Museum
- Maritime Museum
- Control Tower
- Irish Coffee Story
- War Years Display
- New Flight Simulators
- 1940s Style Restaurant
- Gift Shop

Foynes, Co. Limerick
- Tel: +353 (0)69 65416
GPS: 52.6115, -9.1082
- info@flyingboatmuseum.com
- www.flyingboatmuseum.com
Open Daily: Mid March - Mid-Nov

WILD ATLANTIC WAY
SLÍ AN ATLANTAIGH FHIÁIN

Limerick City Gallery of Art.

There has been a castle on the site of Bunratty Castle since 1425 AD.

The Bunratty Collection features over 450 items of medieval furniture and artefacts, all housed in the castle. However, most people will know the castle for the famous medieval banquets which operate there at night throughout the year.

The castle is the latest of a series of castles built on the site since 1425 AD. A stronghold of the O'Briens – the kings and later earls of Thomond or North Munster, the castle has three floors, each with a great hall. The four towers are each six stories high. Recommended.

Bunratty Folk Park, set on 26 acres, is a fascinating recreation of 19th Century Ireland and features various types of farmhouses, a church, a magical walled garden and village street complete with pub, post office and various shops.

THE HUNT MUSEUM
The Hunt Museum exhibits one of Ireland's greatest private collections of art and antiquities, dating from the Neolithic to the 20th Century, including works by Renoir, Picasso and Yeats. It reflects the diverse tastes and interests of the two people who formed it, John and Gertrude

Medieval banquets are staged regularly in Bunratty Castle.

Hunt. There is also an important collection of Irish archaeological material ranging from Neolithic flints and Bronze Age material, including a Bronze Age shield and cauldron, to later Christian objects such as the unique 9th century Antrim Cross. Artists' works in the collection include Pablo Picasso, Pierre Auguste Renoir, Roderic O'Conor, Jack B. Yeats, Robert Fagan and Henry Moore.

The museum is housed in the former custom house at Rutland Street, Limerick and if museums are your thing, a visit is highly recommended.

The Folk Park adjoining Bunratty Castle has many interesting examples of Irish cottages and farm buildings.

The Keep of St. John's Castle.

The thirteen-arch bridge that joins the villages of Ballina (on the east side of the Shannon) and Killaloe on the western side.

KILLALOE AND BALLINA

Situated on the banks of the River Shannon, Killaloe is perhaps best-known as the birthplace of Brian Boru (c. 941 - 1014 AD), and High King of Ireland, (1002 - 1014 AD). While Brian was High King, he ruled from Killaloe. Brian Boru was to fall in his moment of triumph while winning a great victory over the Vikings at the Battle of Clontarf (1014 AD) in the process ending Viking influence in Ireland. The towns of Killaloe and Ballina are amongst Ireland's most picturesque attractions and are joined by a 13 arch bridge, which links not only the two towns, but also the counties of Clare and Tipperary.

St. Flannan's Cathedral, unique for its stone carving inscriptions is in Killaloe, while both villages host restaurants, galleries, pubs, and shops as well as a Sunday Farmers Market. Recommended.

FOYNES FLYING BOAT AND MARITIME MUSEUM

The award winning Museum at Foynes is the world's only Flying Boat Museum and is to my mind one of the top attractions that simply must be visited while in Ireland. It is so unique that time spent here will certainly be a highlight of any exploration of the west of Ireland.

Foynes played a key role in the establishment of passenger flights across the Atlantic both before and during the Second World War. The famous Flying Boats operated by Imperial Airways and Pan American Airways were frequent visitors to Foynes on the Shannon Estuary and the era is recalled in the museum with excellent displays of memorabilia, all housed in the original terminal building. But the star of the show is a full-scale mock-up of the fuselage of a Boeing B314 Flying Boat. It's a revelation to step inside and see the facilities it offered to its small number of passengers. Indeed, the Boeing had more in common with a luxury ocean liner and provided a dining room for the 14 passangers, a honeymoon suite and sleeping berths for all of the passengers and crew.

The Museum also has a Maritime Exhibition portraying the history and personality of the River Shannon from Limerick City to Loop Head. Don't miss the 3D

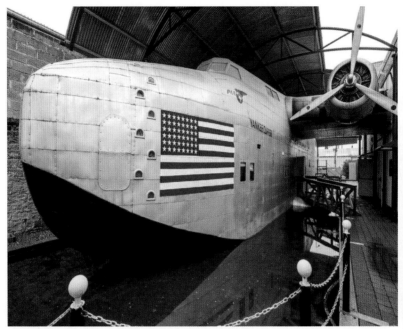

The highlight of the highly recommended Foynes Flying Boat Museum is this full size replica of one of the Boeing flying boats that crossed the Atlantic from Foynes.

hologram re-enacting how Irish Coffee was devised in Foynes one cold wet night in 1943 by Chef Joe Sheridan to rejuvenate tired passengers after a long and weary journey across the Atlantic. The museum also has a restaurant, named in honour of Shannon pioneer, Brendan O'Regan, where you can enjoy lunch or an afternoon tea. All highly recommended, and a different experience that will be long remembered.

LOUGH GUR

Lough Gur is a lake in south County Limerick, between the towns of Herbertstown and Bruff. The lake takes the form of a horseshoe at the base of Knockadoon Hill and some rugged elevated countryside. The signifigance of Lough Gur is its location at the heart of a remarkable archaeological landscape featuring sites that represent every major period of human history in Ireland.

Local artist Vincent Killowry's fine painting of a PAA Clipper at Foynes.

Physical evidence of occupation from the Neolithic, Bronze Age, Iron Age, Early Christian, Medieval, Early Modern and Modern eras have all been found in the immediate vicinity of Lough Gur and visitors to the Heritage Centre located there can learn about the rich heritage of the site by viewing the interactive multi-media exhibition that brings to life over 6,000 years of archaeology and history. The exhibition has something for all ages and brings the visitor on a journey through the history of Lough Gur starting during the Mesolithic Era, and progressing until the 19th century.

Visitors also have an opportunity to actively engage with the exhibition, and can have a role in forming individual experiences at the centre by choosing which interactive elements to investigate.

The interpretive centre at Lough Gur is modelled on a 5,000 year old Neolithic dwelling.

Useful web addresses

FOYNES FLYING BOAT MUSEUM AND MARITIME MUSEUM

    www.flyingboatmuseum.com

BUNRATTY CASTLE AND FOLK PARK   www.shannonheritage.com

KING JOHN'S CASTLE   www.shannonheritage.com

THE HUNT MUSEUM   www.huntmuseum.com

KILLALOE   www.discoverkillaloe.ie

LOUGH GUR   www.loughgur.com

Useful maps: Ordnance Survey Discovery Series – Sheets 58, 64 and 65

Dingle's most famous resident - Fungi the Bottlenose Dolphin that has been enjoying human company since he first arrived in 1983.

THE DINGLE PENINSULA - THE MAGIC PENINSULA

For many visitors, the Dingle Peninsula is 'Kerry'. It represents all of the best of Kerry and provides an experience that they will remember long after they have left. Of course, such a view does not do justice to the rest of Kerry which has so much to recommend it, but the Dingle Peninsula does seem to have a magic all its own.

Everything there radiates from the town of Dingle and it's the centre of all activity on the peninsula and the best place to base yourself if you intend to spend time there. But do take the time to explore some of the places that are not so obvious. In particular head out to Brandon Point, in the shadow of Mount Brandon, at 950 m the highest mountain on the Dingle Peninsual and the ninth highest peak in Ireland. (Interestingly, it's the highest peak outside the Macgillycuddy's Reeks). Slea Head is truly beautiful and so too is the area around Smerwick Harbour and Ballydavid Head, to its northeast. And don't neglect to visit Inch Strand, captured in so many Hollywood films or the South Pole Inn of the remarkable Tom Crean, at Annascaul, or to cross the Conor Pass between the north and south of Dingle Peninsula.

What I'm really saying is that there is so much to see on this peninsula, make sure you give yourself sufficient time to properly explore it. It weaves a magic few escape.

DINGLE
The charming town of Dingle is the only town on the northernmost peninsula of County Kerry. Its about 50 km from Tralee

Dingle is a pretty fishing and tourist town with pubs and restaurants to suit all tastes.

Don't miss the Dingle Oceanworld Aquarium with its great marine displays.

so there's always lots going on and there are boat trips out into the bay to see Fungie between April and October. An annual event that must be mentioned is 'Other Voices', in which an array of artists from across the musical spectrum perform at this intimate musical event held in St. James' Church in Dingle and which is transmitted worldwide online and as a television series. Past performers have included Ellie Goulding, Amy Winehouse, Elbow, The National, Damien Rice, Snowpatrol, Ryan Adams and many, many others.

and about 70 km from Killarney. Its particularly noted for the adult Bottlenose Dolphin that has been enjoying human contact in Dingle Bay since 1983. Christened 'Fungie', the Dolphin is easily the towns most famous inhabitant.

Be sure also not to miss the Dingle Oceanworld Aquarium. The Aquarium offers some excellent underwater displays featuring deadly Piranha, Catfish and Pacu as well as many tropical fresh water

Trips into Dingle Bay to see Fungi are immensely popular with visitors.

Dingle is a delightful place to visit and has a host of pubs and restaurants that are good places to eat. It's a busy fishing port

species. There is a state of the art Shark Tank, as well as a new Polar Penguin exhibition. Recommended.

The beautiful Coumeenoole Beach on Slea Head. Dingle is full of beaches like this waiting to be discovered.

BLENNERVILLE

The village of Blennerville was at one time the main port of emigration from County Kerry during the years of the Great Famine (1845 to 1848). It was also, during those years, the home port of the famous emigrant barque 'Jeanie Johnston'. At the Blennerville Visitor Centre you will find the working windmill that stands out as the dominant landmark in Tralee Bay, where the town of Tralee meets the Dingle Peninsula, as well as a fascinating display on Irish emigration including models of the infamous coffin ships.

In addition to the exhibition gallery, craft shop and restaurant, the Visitor Centre includes an audio visual presentation, an emigration display and a bird watching platform with telescope overlooking 'Slí na nÉan' ('the Way of the Birds').

Visitors can experience the scale and complexity of the Windmill machinery and can climb to the top of the windmill. Recommended.

TRALEE BAY NATURE RESERVE

If you've an interest in wildlife, especially in bird-watching, then a visit to the Tralee Bay Nature Reserve will be a must for you, to see where migratory pale-bellied Brent Geese spend from October to April feeding on the eelgrass and green seaweeds on the mudflats and grazing in nearby fields and salt-marshes when this food is scarce. Birds of the bay include turnstone, ringed plover, dunlin, redshank, bar-tailed godwit, golden plover and curlew.

INCH STRAND

Inch, they say, is famous for being the place where an inch is actually three miles long! Its beach has been chosen several times as a film location for Hollywood movies that are familiar household names including *Ryan's Daughter* and *Playboy of the Western World*. Its a fabulous place and its easy to see why this

Dingle is one of the seafood capitals of Ireland.

dramatic setting has been picked time and time again.

A popular attraction for bird-watchers is the nature reserve behind the banks of sand dunes along the strand. These wetlands are important wintering grounds for many ducks and waders. A visit is recommended.

stone building remains waterproof. The visitor's centre offers you the opportunity to explore the site, as well as providing an audio video display featuring the history of Gallarus and other archaeological sites nearby. Recommended.

THE BLASKET ISLANDS
Located off the coast of Dun Chaoin,

The Slea Head Drive is one of the most memorable you will undertake anywhere in Ireland.

SLEA HEAD DRIVE
The Slea Head Drive is a circular route beginning and ending in Dingle town. Its one of the great Irish drives and provides stunning views of the western tip of the Dingle Peninsula as well as the Blasket Islands. Its best to drive the route in a clockwise direction as this is the direction tour buses use and thus avoid eating them head-on along the narrow road. Very highly recommended.

GALLARUS ORATORY
Located on the Slea Head Drive overlooking Smerwick Harbour on the Dingle Peninsula about 10km from Dingle, Gallarus Oratory is the best-preserved early Christian church in Ireland, and was built in the 7th or 8th century, Despite it having been exposed to the winds and harsh Atlantic weather for over 1200 years, the

Dingle, the Blasket Islands are the most westerly land area of Europe and were inhabited for thousands of years before they were abandoned in 1953. The islands feature some beautiful and unspoilt beaches, extraordinary bird life and a peaceful and relaxing atmosphere. Boat trips to the Islands are available, weather permitting, from Dunquin. Highly recommended.

DUNBEG FORT
Dunbeg Fort is an archaeological site and audio-visual centre, located on the Slea Head Drive, at Fahan, and was built in the Iron Age. Its an elaborate example of a promontory fort, and was built on a sheer cliff which projects South into Dingle Bay, at the base of Mount Eagle on the Slea Head Road.
Impressive and highly recommended.

Looking towards the Blasket Islands from Slea Head.

THE CELTIC AND PREHISTORIC MUSEUM, VENTRY

Located in Ventry, the Celtic and Prehistoric Museum has a fossil room, floors of 300 million year old sea worms, a large nest of 70 million year old dinosaur eggs, and an ancient Egyptian mummy case and much else besides. Visitors can actually handle authentic tools used by our European cousins Homo Erectus, Neanderthal and Cromagnon man in the cave room where the walls are covered with reproductions of some of the oldest cave paintings in the world. Well worth a look. Recommended.

BALLYFERRITER

The village of Ballyferriter is the only substantial village west of Dingle town, and nestles in a beautiful green valley between the hill of Croaghmarhin to the south and a ridge of jagged peaks to the north - Sybil Head and the Three Sisters. To the east of Ballyferriter, Smerwick Harbour has a two-mile long stretch of white sandy beach called *Béal Bán*, while to the west, the Atlantic is faced by high rocky cliffs.

THE CONOR PASS

The Conor Pass has the distinction of being the highest mountain pass in Ireland, and provides the most dramatic and scenic way of entering or leaving Dingle. The views from the top are stunning but are often masked by low clouds. This narrow, twisting road runs between the town of Dingle and Kilmore Cross on the north side of the peninsula, where roads fork to Cloghane/Brandon or Castlegregory. Perhaps not for the feint-hearted. Otherwise, worth a look.

The rugged coastline of the Dingle Peninsula faces the mighty Atlantic Ocean.

The Gallarus Oratory was built in the 7th or 8th century and is the best preserved early Christian church in Ireland.

TOM CREAN – HERO EXTRAODINARY

Born in Annascaul, Tom Crean took part in three of the four major British expeditions to the Antarctic in the early part of the last century and spent more time there than either of the more celebrated figures of Sir Ernest Shackleton or Captain Robert Scott.

Tom Crean first went south in 1901 with Scott's Discovery expedition, on which he served his polar apprenticeship and learned the skills needed to survive in the most inhospitable place on earth. A decade later he returned to the Antarctic when Scott made his ill-fated attempt to reach the South Pole in 1911. Tom was a key figure on that expedition, dragging a sledge to within 150 miles of the South Pole before being ordered to return to base camp. He was among the last three men to see Scott alive within reach of his goal, and only a few months later he went back to the ice to find and bury Scott's frozen body.

It was during the return to base camp that Tom performed what many regard as the greatest single-handed act of bravery in the history of Antarctic exploration. When one of his companions, Lt. Evans, collapsed 35 miles from safety, Tom volunteered to go for help. It was an impossible journey across treacherous terrain in sub-zero temperatures, and his only food consisted of two sticks of chocolate and three biscuits. He had no sleeping bag or tent and was already physically exhausted, having been on the march for three months and having by then covered around 1,500 miles. His solitary trek lasted eighteen hours and earned him the Albert Medal, then the highest award for gallantry.

Soon after, Crean played a central role in the dramatic Endurance expedition with Shackleton. When the ship was crushed in the ice of the Weddell Sea, Crean helped to sail the tiny *James Caird* lifeboat across the Southern Ocean, the most dangerous seas on earth. He then walked 40 miles across the forbidding mountains and glaciers of South Georgia with Shackleton and another companion to bring rescuers to his twenty-two comrades left stranded on Elephant Island.

Following a lifetime of adventure, Tom returned to his native Annascaul where he opened the South Pole Inn. It is only in recent times that this modest unsung hero's exploits have been given the recognition they deserved.

The famous beach at Inch, the backdrop for several Hollywood films.

ANNASCAUL

Annascaul will forever be associated with the Antarctic explorer Tom Crean who accompanied Shackleton on his famous open boat journey across the Southern Ocean to bring help to his crewmates. Crean was a member of three major expeditions to Antarctica during the Heroic Age of Antarctic Exploration, including Captain Scott's 1911–13 Terra Nova Expedition. This saw the race to reach the South Pole lost to Roald Amundsen and ended in the deaths of Scott and his polar party. During this expedition, Crean's 35 statute miles (56 km) solo walk across the Ross Ice Shelf to save the life of Edward Evans led to him receiving the Albert Medal for Lifesaving. Tom Crean retired to his birthplace Annascaul, and opened the South Pole Inn, still there today. Recommended.

The spectacular Conor Pass - perhaps not for the faint-hearted!

Useful web addresses

BLENNERVILLE
www.discoverireland.ie/Arts-Culture-Heritage/blennerville-windmill/15650

TRALEE BAY NATURE RESERVE
www.npws.ie/nature-reserves/kerry/tralee-bay-nature-reserve

CASTLEGREGORY   www.castlegregorykerry.com

DINGLE   www.dingle-insight.com

FUNGIE   www.dingledolphin.com/fungie/

OTHER VOICES   www.othervoices.ie

THE BLASKET ISLANDS   www.greatblasketisland.net/boat-trips/

BALLYFERRITER   www.dingle-peninsula.ie/ballyferriter.html

INCH BEACH   www.inchbeach.com/attractions.htm

ANNASCAUL   www.annascaul.ie

TOM CREAN   www.tomcreandiscovery.com

**Useful Maps: Ordnance Survey Discovery Series sheets 70 and 71
Fir Tree Series of Aerial Maps: Iveragh & Dingle Peninsulas**

Traditional shop front in Dingle town.

One of the landmarks on the Killarney to Moll's Gap Road is this short tunnel dating from the construction of the road in the 1820's.

BALLAGHBEEMA -
A DRIVE INTO THE WILD HEART OF KERRY

I'd like to share one of Ireland's best kept secrets with you. No doubt well known to readers from Kerry, this route will almost certainly be new to those from outside 'The Kingdom', as Kerry is known to Irish natives. It's a personal favourite of mine and I first discovered it about fifteen years ago. What brought it to my attention was a photograph of a group of cyclists going through Ballaghbeema Pass in 1899. I was struck by the wildness of the place and determined to find and visit it. But I'm jumping ahead. For this drive started from Killarney's Lake Hotel with it's magnificent views of the mountains and lakes where they have been welcoming touring motorists since the beginning of the last century. Its an excellent base for exploring Kerry and I thoroughly recommend this hotel.

MUCKROSS HOUSE
Taking the Kenmare Road out of the hotel, one soon comes to Muckross House. Set in the Killarney National Park,

this 19th century Victorian mansion is located on the small Muckross Peninsula between Muckross Lake and Lough Leane, two of the lakes of Killarney. The house, its gardens and traditional farm are Kerry's premier visitor attraction.

The house was built for Henry Arthur Herbert and his wife, the water-colourist Mary Balfour Herbert, between 1839 and 1843. Its appearance is reminiscent of several large houses in Scotland something that is not surprising as it was designed by the famous Scottish architect William Burn. Queen Victoria enjoyed the house and its gardens when she visited in 1861. I recommend a visit to the house but do make sure you plan to allow time to explore some of the National Park (Ireland's oldest) in which it is situated. The views are simply stunning.

MOLL'S GAP
Continuing from Muckross House on the Kenmare Road, you climb up along the

Derrynane House at Caherdaniel, the home of the 'Liberator', Daniel O'Connell, and now a museum recalling his achievements.

An unusual sign at Lady's View near to Moll's Gap.

classic Circuit of Ireland rally stage eventually reaching Moll's Gap. The Gap is so named for Moll Kissanne, who ran a small pub (a *'sheebeen'*) at this place during the construction of the Killarney to Kenmare Road in the 1820's. Much of the attraction of Moll's *sheebeen* was the poitin, or illicit home-made whiskey, that she sold there. Today there is a thriving souvenir shop on the site and there are fine views towards the Macgillycuddy's Reeks mountains.

KENMARE

From Moll's Gap it's a gentle drive to the bustling town of Kenmare. The town is one of the jewels of Kerry, with lots of good shops, restaurants and coffee shops centered around the triangle of streets that form the heart of Kenmare. It's at the gateway to the popular Ring of Kerry and also, to the south of the town, the Ring of Beara, so it's a busy cross-roads. From Kenmare the road heads beside the coast to Blackwater Bridge, Tahilla, Parknasilla and into Sneem – all the while travelling the Ring of Kerry route.

STAIGUE FORT

Between Sneem and Caherdaniel watch for the signpost to the historic Staigue Fort. Although a couple of miles off our route a diversion to see this circular stone fort is one well-worth taking. This is one of the best surviving stone forts in Irland and it stands on a low hill, surrounded on three sides by mountains, and commanding a fine view of Kenmare Bay. Its very impressive with its four metre thick walls and outer wall some 5.5 metres high and is thought to have been built in the late Iron Age between 300 and 400 AD.

WATERVILLE

From Caherdaniel the road winds around Cahernageeha Mountain before dropping

The road from Killarney to Moll's Gap travels over the classic Circuit of Ireland Rally stage.

Staigue Fort is an excellent sample of a circular stone fort, and well worth exploring.

down to Waterville and lovely Ballinskellis Bay. This is a good place to stop for lunch in one of the many cosy pubs in this seaside town beloved by 'The Little Tramp', Charlie Chaplin, and his family who holidayed here year after year.

Up to this point we've followed the Ring of Kerry but now the route really becomes interesting. Leaving Waterville continue until the junction with several roads at the church on the outskirts of the town, taking the road signposted for Glencar.

BALLAGHOISIN PASS

For a while this road slowly climbs up the center of the Iveragh Peninsula and at first has little to recommend it other than a lack of other traffic but as one crests the Ballaghoisin Pass everything changes and a magnificent vista stretching to the mighty Macgillycuddy's Reeks stretches ahead of you – Ireland's highest mountain, Carrauntoohil - being easy to pick out among them.

Continue on towards the mountains until the staggered crossroads at Bealalaw Bridge where the signpost to the south-east points to Ballaghbeema Pass.

The statue of Charlie Chaplin in Waterville, where he and his family spent their holidays for many years.

BALLAGHBEEMA PASS – IREL:AND'S WILDEST PLACE

The road now climbs easily towards the Pass and although narrow, this is not a concern as you are unlikely to meet traffic, and in any case there are numerous places to pull over. Reaching the Pass, the rocks tower above the road and the views in every direction reveal why this spot has rightly been called 'the wildest place in Ireland'. Wild it may be but it is a landscape of extrodinary beauty and will remain long in your memory. Do stop,walk about and savour the remoteness of this place, the like of which becomes harder to find with each passing year.

From Ballaghbeema it's a gentle drive down to the main road near Dereendarragh and then on to Moll's Gap before returning back down the road to Killarney that we climbed at the start of our journey.the many magnificent views you will encounter along its route.

The road through Ballaghbeema winds it's way through this rugged and remote pass.

The view from Ballaghoisin Pass towards the Macgillycuddy Reeks is one of the finest on this island.

The author's Daimler SP250 crests the top of the wild Ballaghbeema Pass.

Useful web addresses

THE LAKE HOTEL, KILLARNEY	www.lakehotelkillarney.ie
MUCKROSS HOUSE AND GARDENS	www.muckross -house.ie
KENMARE	www.kenmare.ie
STAIGUE STONE FORT	www.theringofkerry.com/staigue-fort/
WATERVILLE	www.visitwaterville.IE
BALLAGHBEEMA	www.gokerry.ie/locations/ballagh-beama/

Useful maps: Ordnance Survey Discovery Series – Sheets 78 and 83

The southern end of Caragh Lake is framed by high ground.

CARAGH LAKE - UNDER THE SHADOW OF THE MACGILLICUDDY'S REEKS

Over the many years that I've been exploring Ireland's scenic routes, I've come to the realisation that this part of Kerry, bounded in the north by the Macgillicuddy's Reeks, to the west by Caragh Lake, to the east by the Ballaghbeama Pass and to the south by the Ballaghisheen Pass is amongst the most beautiful places anywhere on this island.

Caragh Lake forms its western boundary and is a wonderful introduction to the charms of this area. For the sake of this exploration I suggest travelling southwest on the N70 road from the pretty town of Killorglin. Turn off the N70 at the sign for Caragh Lake near the Kerry Bog Village. At every point on my journey the Macgillicuddy's Reeks formed an ever-changing backdrop of brown and blue in the distance, like sentinels presaging something special. And so Caragh Lough proves to be. Once the road has joined the western edge of the lake, a series of mountain vistas open up across the lake. On the western side of the lake rises Seefin (493 m) followed in a southerly line

by Beenreagh (495m) and Macklaun (607 m).

The eastern shore of Caragh Lake is not as high but nevertheless, the land rises up in several promontories – most notably Gortnagan Mor (246 m) and Gortnagan Beg (298 m) – to create a very attractive view across the lake. At its southern end the lake narrows and once again the views are outstanding with the ever-present Macgillacuddy's Reeks forming a wonderful backdrop.

All too soon the road moves away from the southern end of the lake, heading first southwest and then swinging around to the southeast. Here, the nature of the landscape changes and is covered by an ancient wood with several small bridges before coming to Blackstone bridge over the River Caragh that feeds into the lake. Here, near Blackstone Bridge, there was once a village of Welsh miners who mined pig iron to be made into cannonballs.

From the pretty Blackstone Bridge, con-

The Lake Hotel
·KILLARNEY·
★ ★ ★ ★

Relax in a one of the elegant, lakeside lounges and experience a truly breath-taking setting.
An essential stop when touring the South West.

A warm welcome awaits you at
The Lake Hotel, Killarney.

the difference...*family run*

www.lakehotel.com
info@lakehotel.com : Reservations +353 (0) 64 66 31035
The Lake Hotel : Lake Shore : Muckross Road : Killarney : Co. Kerry : Ireland

The majesty of the Macgillicuddy's Reeks viewed from across the Kenmare River.

tinue on to the junction with the road to Waterville via the Ballaghisheen Pass. Swing right along this road and you'll soon come to the area known as Glencar and to The Climber's Inn, an ancient hostelry well-known to those who climb the nearby Macgillacuddy's Reeks. There's much to explore here: turning left at the junction with the Waterville Road will bring you in a short distance to the edge of Lough Acoose while the Ballagh-beama Pass is also close-by, as is the picturesque sheet of water which is Cloon Lake to the south.

However, to complete your circumnavigation of Caragh Lake, at the crossroads from Blackstone bridge leading to Caragh, swing left and left again just before Caragh Lake Forest so that you return to the lakeshore, continuing until you return to the N70 to Killorglin.

Finally, a word about the Macgillicuddy's Reeks (*Na Cruacha Dubha* – The Black Peaks) which dominate the landscape around this drive. Ireland's most magnificent mountains, they contain our highest summits, Carrantuohill (1039 m),

At the point where one first meets the western end of Caragh Lake, coming from the N70.

Having briefly left the lakeside, one enters a wooded area with several bridges.

Beenkeragh (1010 m) and Caher (975 m). There are several deep corrie lakes amongst the mountains, including lonely Coomloughra Lough and another known as "The Devil's Looking-glass'. It was in the Reeks that Ireland's last wolves were killed in the 18th century.

This is a region of endless fascination with so much to be explored. The drive along the edge of Caragh Lough provides an excellent starting point and is the entrance into a wonderful landscape.

Useful web addresses

CARAGH LAKE	www.caraghlake.typepad.com
CARRIG COUNTRY HOUSE	www.carrighouse.com

MACGILLYCUDDY'S REEKS
www.activeme.ie/guides/walks/macgillycuddys-reeks-carrauntoohil-entire-mountain-range-walk-kerry-ireland/

KILLORGLIN	www.killorglinringofkerry.com
THE BOG VILLAGE	www.kerrybogvillage.ie

Useful maps: Ordnance Survey Discovery Series Sheet 78
Fir Tree Aerial Maps – Iveragh & Dingle Peninsula

Blackstone Bridge over the River Caragh near where in the past Welsh miners mined pig iron for the manufacture of cannonballs.

Caragh Lough pictured from its southern end where the lake narrows considerably.

The rugged Atlantic coastline at Allihies.

The colourful houses of the pretty village of Allihies, the most westerly on the Beara Peninsula.

THE BEARA PENINSULA - THE ROAD LESS TRAVELLED...

The northern coastline of Bantry Bay is formed by the peninsula known as Beara, dominated by the Slieve Miskish Mountains and capped by Dursey Island at its most westerly point. Along the peninsula's southern shore is Bear Island which forms a natural anchorage at the town of Castletown Bearhaven, more commonly known as Castletownbear. It's a rugged landscape as evidenced by the relatively few roads that penetrate its interior and has always conveyed to me the impression, rightly or wrongly, as the least-travelled of the Cork and Kerry peninsulas.

I particularly recommend exploring the loop from the small town of Eyeries on it's northern coast along Coulagh Bay travelling anti-clockwise around the wildest part of the peninsula on the R575. With Miskish Mountain (386 m) at first to the south, the road winds its way parallel to the coastline. For those with an interest in such things, there is ample evidence of ancient habitation of this area with numerous standing stones, cairns and boulder burial sites close by the road. At Caherkeen the road rises quickly to cross a ridge providing the first of many fine views back towards Kenmare and onward towards Cod's Head. The R575 soon turns

south – Cod's Head being all but inaccessible to road traffic – and from here to the town of Allihies twists and turns in spectacular fashion around Knocknagallaun (376 m) through some of the most wonderful scenery along this route. This whole area was once noted for it's copper mines and here and there evidence of this long-ceased activity is still visible.

The R575 runs south-west out of Allihies before turning south over the Bealbarnish Gap. Shortly after crossing the Gap you will meet the R572 which runs along the rest of our route to Castletown BearHaven and also west the short distance to Ballaghboy from where one can cross by cable car to Dursey Island. Once again, as along this entire route, the number of early archeological sites is very striking. The R572 then runs south until it reaches the southern coastline of the Beara Peninsula before turning first east and then north-east and on to Castletown Bearhaven.

Along the way it once again provides spectacular views of Bantry Bay and south towards the Sheep's Head Peninsula. On a beautiful Summer's day there can be few places more beautiful that the Cork and Kerry peninsulas, as you travel the remaining kilometres into the town along the O'Sullivan Beara Way. It is this blend of history and the natural beauty of the place that make the Beara Peninsula so special and worthy of exploration.

CASTLETOWN BEAR

Castletownbear – literally 'The Town of the Castle of Bear' is a pretty town with a varied history. The nearby ruins of Dunboy Castle attest to the part it played after the Battle of Kinsale in 1601, when the followers of O'Sullivan Bear held the fortress against a vastly superior force of some 4,000 men until all its walls had been shattered and the surviving defenders slaughtered. Before this, O'Sullivan Bear himself had already taken the majority of his followers north to another of his castles, Ardea, on the northern coast of the Beara Peninsula.

It was following the fall of Dunboy Castle that O'Sullivan, faced with overwhelming odds, set out on his epic march to join his northern allies. Of the more than 1,000 who set out on the march, just 35 remained when they gained refuge at the O'Rourke Castle in Leitrim.

GLENGARRIFF

Glengarriff takes its name from the Irish 'Gleann Garbh' meaning 'Rough Glen'. The surrounding scenery is certainly rough and rocky and changes dramatically depending on the season, but the area is famous for its lush vegetation that is a result of its uniquely temperate microclimate.

The Village is best described as a small traditional Irish village and has a variety of pubs and restaurants, shops and art galleries and is a great place to visit. The nearby Italian Gardens on Garnish Island attract large numbers of visitors each year.

GARNISH ISLAND

Garnish Island is situated in the sheltered harbour of Glengarriff on Bantry Bay. Garnish is world renowned for its gardens that are laid out in walks and it is famous for many specimen plants that are rare in the Irish climate. A ferry runs to the island from Glengarriff Pier and includes a visit to seal island where there is a very tame seal colony.

The Gardens were the result of a creative partnership between Annan Bryce and

Castletown Bear's tranquil harbour serves a town with a varied history.

Garnish Island is famous for its gardens containing many specimen plants that are rare in the Irish climate.

Harold Peto, architect and garden designer. In 1953 the island was bequeathed to the Irish state, and was subsequently entrusted to the care of the Commissioners of Public Works.

The Island also has a Martello tower on its southern shores that has been restored by the OPW. There are fine views of the bay from the battlements of the tower.

Colourful shops in the attractive village of Glengarriff.

ADRIOGLE

Adriogle is situated on the north-western shore of Bantry Bay. The location of the village is dominated by Hungry Hill (685 m), the highest of the Caha range that form the spine of the Beara Peninsula. Hungry Hill gave its name to Daphne du Maurier's famous novel about the local copper-mining barons of the 19th century. The beautiful Caha mountains offer excellent hill-walking opportunities at all grades. Climb Hungry Hill and you'll discover the hidden lakes of Coomarkane and Coomadavallig, and see the Mares Tail Waterfall, said by some to be the highest in Ireland.

HEALY PASS

The Healy Pass takes you between two of the highest summits in the Caha mountain range and rises to 334 m above sea level. It was created in 1847 during the

The serpentine road on the southern side of the Healy Pass.

The ruins of the Man Engine House that served the copper mines at Allihies.

famine years in order to help prevent starvation. It is named after Tim Michael Healy, a politician from Cork who served as the first governor general of the Irish Free State. Upon his retirement, Healy asked that the bridleway winding through the pass be upgraded and improved. This was done and the road became an important driving route and today attracts enthusiastic drivers for its Alpine-like twists and turns.

ARDGROOM

Ardgroom is a small village on the northern side of the Beara Peninsula. Its name refers to two gravelly hills deposited by a glacier, Dromárd and Drombeg.

Near the village lie a number of megalithic monuments. Signposted is the stone circle to be found a short distance to the east of the village, just off the old Kenmare road. Its name is 'Canfea' but it is usually called the Ardgroom Stone Circle. To the north-east lie the remains of another stone circle. The Canfea circle consists of 11 stones, 9 of which are still upright with one alignment stone outside the circle. It is unusual for a stone circle in that its stones tend to taper toward points. Also in the vicinity are the remains of at least two ring forts, as well as a number of standing stones and stone rows.

EYERIES

Eyeries is a village that lies at the base of Maulin, which, at 623 m, is the highest peak in the Slieve Miskish mountain range. Eyeries has been the location for a number of films including *The Purple Taxi* (1977) starring Fred Astaire, Peter Ustinov, and Charlotte Rampling, and also the 1998 TV series *Falling for a Dancer*, a film about life and love in 1930s Ireland based on the novel by Deirdre Purcell.

Nearby is the fascinating Ballycrovane Ogham stone, which at 5.3 m high is the tallest known. It bears the inscription 'MAQI DECCEDDAS AVI TURANIAS' which translates as *'Mac Deich Uí Turainn'* or 'son of Deich the descendant of Turainn'. Neither of these two people are known to Irish history.

ALLIHIES

The name Allihies comes from the Irish *Na hAilichí* meaning 'the cliff fields'. The village is the last on the west of the Beara Peninsula and there are fine views from the Barnes Gap. The village itself is notably colourful and across the fields can be seen the Man Engine House of the Copper Mines.

Since the Bronze age the area abound Allihies had been the site of extensive copper-mining. In 1812 John Lavallin

The nature of the terrain provides few opportunities for cultivation like this field near Cod's Head.

Puxley (1772-1856) established a company to operate the Berehaven copper mines at Allihies, and during the following century, between 1812 and 1912, some 297,000 tons of ore were recorded as passing through Swansea from the mines at Allihies. An attempt was made to restart mining in the late 1950s by a Canadian mining company, but was not successful.

Daphne du Maurier's novel *Hungry Hill* is a fictionalized saga of several generations of a mine-owning dynasty and is based loosely on the history of the Puxley family.

Do pay a visit to the Allihies Copper Mine Museum where you will also find an art gallery and café. It tells a fascinating story and is highly recommended.

DURSEY ISLAND

Dursey Island is another place in Ireland that takes its name from its Viking past, in Irish being *Oileán Baoi* which derives from Island of the Bull in Viking Norse. It is one of the few inhabited islands that lie off the southwest coast of Ireland and is situated at the western tip of the Beara Peninsula. The Island is 6.5 km long and 1.5 km wide, and is separated from the mainland by a narrow stretch of water called the Dursey Sound that has a very strong tidal race, and with a reef of rocks in the centre of the channel that are submerged at high tides. This peaceful island, with only a handful of semi-permanent residents, is connected to the mainland by Ireland's only cable car.

Dolphins and whales can regularly be seen in the rich waters that surround Dursey, in addition to a wide range of different types of seabirds and butterflies.

Near Cod's Head the road winds its way between mountains and scattered homes.

Coastline near to Cod's Head.

Useful web addresses

GLENGARRIFF www.glengarriff.ie

www.glengarriff.org

GARNISH ISLAND www.garnishisland.com

www.harbourqueenferry.com

ADRIGOLE
www.explorewestcork.ie/villages/adriogle/

ARDGROOM www.bearatourism.com/ardnews.html

EYERIES www.eyeries.ie

ALLIHIES www.bearatourism.com/infoallihies.html

ALLIHIES COPPER MINE MUSEUM www.acmm.ie

DURSEY ISLAND www.durseyisland.ie
www.durseyisland.ie/cabele-car-timetable.html

Useful maps: Ordnance Survey Discovery Series Sheets 84 and 85

The Fir Tree Series of Aerial Maps – The Beara Peninsula and South
West Cork

Mizen Head, Ireland's most south-westerly point.

The quiet roads of the Sheep's Head Peninsula travel an unspoilt and beautiful landscape.

SHEEP'S HEAD AND KILMORE PENINSULAS - UNSPOILT AND UNCROWDED

The Sheep's Head peninsula has been designated as a European Destination of Excellence in recognition of the sustainable tourism on offer in this most unspoilt part of Ireland. It's an empty landscape compared to the other Cork and Kerry peninsulas and because of this offers a different experience. The Sheep's Head Way is a walking and cycling route that provides the adventurous with the perfect way to explore the stunning natural landscape of this West Cork peninsula. You'll find Sheep's Head Way maps and directions, and places to stay in Bantry and on the Sheep's Head Way website. So, if you've got the time and the inclination this is the perfect place to abandon your car for a day or two and explore this most unspoilt part of Ireland at a more leisurely pace. Unforgettable.

BANTRY

Bantry, at the head of Bantry Bay is the natural base from which to explore the Sheep's Head and Kilmore Peninsulas. Now Bantry Bay is one of the finest and safest harbours in Europe and is situated in a strategic position on the edge of the Atlantic Ocean. Being very deep with no dangerous rocks or sand banks and shel-

tered from most winds by the mountains that surround it, from earliest times it has been used as a haven by fishermen and merchant ships. Its history is fascinating.

In times gone by, the fleets of the English, Spanish, French and Dutch fished in the bay, paying taxes to the O'Sullivan Clan who controlled the bay. And it was from Bantry that ships sailed loaded with young Irishmen, recruited for the French, Spanish, Austrian and Dutch armies.

In March 1689 a French fleet sailed into the bay with 7000 soldiers, arms, ammunition and money for James II in support of his war against William of Orange. In the subsequent battles of Derry and the Boyne many of these soldiers were to die. In due course the survivors embarked at Bantry and as they sailed down Bantry Bay to return to France, an English fleet, under Admiral Herbert, entered the bay searching for them. In the battle that followed the French out-witted the English and made their escape. Many ships were badly damaged and there were casualties on both sides. Both sides managed to claim victory!

Just eight years later in the year 1697 it was the turn of William of Orange's troops to land at Bantry. While on15th December 1796, Bantry was once again the destination of a French Fleet, some 43 ships and 15,000 men having set sail from Brest in support of the Irish patriot, Wolfe Tone and the United Irishmen. Tone, a founder member of the United Irishmen, was determined to establish an Irish Republic by armed rebellion, but easterly storms off the Irish coast dispersed the fleet and while some succeeded in making anchor in Bantry Bay, most of the French fleet were scattered in the Atlantic. At the end of January 1797, the order was given to abandon the attempted invasion and the few remaining ships in the bay that were capable of doing so set sail for France.

Bantry today is the focal point for visitors to not only the Sheep's Head and Kilmore Peninsulas but also to the western part of Cork County. It's an attractive town, dominated by tourism and fishing and wears its history well.

BANTRY HOUSE AND GARDEN

Bantry House and Garden is a stately home situated overlooking Bantry Bay. It today houses an important private collection of furniture and objects of art. It was home to Captain Richard White and the White family for many centuries before the house was opened to the public in 1946. In 1987 the East Wing of the house was restored to be used as a Bed and Breakfast. The original design of the garden dates back to the second Earl of Bantry's European travels. He transformed the house and garden into a 'Palazzo' like those he had seen on the continent. Recommended.

CARRIGANASS CASTLE

Located about fifteen minutes drive to the north-east from Bantry is Carriganass Castle, recently restored and worth taking the time to explore. The tower-house is the best preserved part of the structure today and once rose five stories above an outcrop of rock on which it is built on the north bank of the Ouvane River that flows into Bantry Bay at Balluylickey, about 6 km away.

The castle's most famous occupants were Sir Owen O'Sullivan, who was knighted by Queen Elizabeth I, and Donal Cam O'Sullivan who commanded the

Bantry House contains an important private collection of furniture and art. It's gardens follow the Italian style.

A moments pause on the Sheep's Head coastline.

Munster forces at the Battle of Kinsale in 1601. After the fall of Dunboy Castle, Donal Cam led a famous retreat march with 1000 followers from Glengarriff to Leitrim. The retreating troop made their way along the foothills immediately north of the castle where there is a *leacht* or memorial cairn marking the death of one of the group. Made in the depths of winter, the majority of those who made the march perished along the route.

KEALKILL STONE CIRCLE

Within walking distance of Carriganass Castle is another historic monument, one that existed long before Donal Cam O'Sullivan set out on his fateful march to Leitrim. Kealkill's stone circle is one of the most striking examples of megalithic architecture in Ireland. It consists of a circle of five axial stones, with a further two stones nearby, the tallest of which is over 4 m high. There is also a small cairn that is also located close to the circle itself.

Sheep's Head Lighthouse.

The sundial and memorial garden at Ahakista remember those who died in the Air India bombing of 1985.

The walk from Carriganass Castle through the village and on up to the circle is not an easy walk, the views from there, across Bantry Bay towards Beara, and out towards West Cork's highest peak, Knockboy (Cnoc Baoi), are simply breathtaking and make the effort expended very worthwhile..

AHAKISTA

At Ahakista on the southern side of the Sheep's Head Peninsula is a poignant reminder of the perilous times in which we live. A memorial garden and sundial has been created there to honour the memory of the victims of the 1985 Air India disaster.

Air India Flight 182 was an Air India flight operating on the Montreal – London – Delhi route. On the 23 June 1985, the aircraft operating on the route, a Boeing 747-237B, was destroyed by a bomb at an altitude of 9,400 m and crashed into the Atlantic Ocean while in Irish airspace. A total of 329 people were killed, including 280 Canadians, 27 British citizens and 22 Indians. The incident was the largest mass murder in modern Canadian history.

The sundial was sculpted by Cork sculptor Ken Thompson and was donated by the people of Canada, India and Ireland.

The Sheep's Head Way is a walking route of unparalleled beauty .

314

The tiny Mizen Head village is a safe haven for sailors and fishermen.

It's a place to stop and pause and contemplate those who died in the disaster and who are remembered on this most beautiful of places on Irish soil.

KILMORE PENINSULA

Kilmore, also known as the Mizen Peninsula, is the bigger of these two peninsulas and is quite different in character to Sheep's Head. It's also more developed and by that I mean that the roads are better and there are more villages along the way as well as bigger towns like Crookhaven, Schull and Ballydehob. If you really want to get away from it all, then Sheep's Head is the place for you, but Kilmore has many attractions worth seeking out.

MIZEN HEAD

The Mizen Head Signal Station, built at Ireland's most south-westerly point, five miles from Goleen, is open to the public and is a ten minute walk from the car park,
along the path, down 99 steps and across the spectacular arched Bridge, Mizen Head is famous for its wildflowers and wildlife including dolphins, whales, seals, gannets, kittiwakes and choughs. In fact, the bird migration north-south flight path is just a mile off shore. To the south-east of Mizen Head lies the famous Fastnet Rock Lighthouse. Mizen Signal

Station had the first Radio Beacon in Ireland, and was in use as a lighthouse until 1993 when the last of the Irish Lights Keepers finally left the Mizen. The wild beauty of the place is astounding. Highly recommended.

BARLEY COVE

Barleycove is a Blue Flag beach a short distance from Mizen Head on the southern coast of the Kilmore Peninsula. The beach backed by sand dunes, and what is really interesting about the place is that the sand dunes were thrown up in the tidal wave which swept Europe after the earthquake in Lisbon in 1755.
Today the dunes have been partially eroded but are protected like much of the coastal area here as European designated Special Areas of Conservation. The road

Something different spotted at Kilchronane.

315

The pedestrian bridge on the path to the Mizen Head Signal Station.

goes to the east of the beach across a causeway bisecting Lissagriffin Lakes and at the T-junction turning right will take you to Crookhaven and Goleen..

CROOKHAVEN

The tiny village of Crookhaven lies tucked snugly on the sheltered side of a narrow neck of land which creates a deep inlet - the 'crooked haven' which gave this little settlement its name.

SCHULL

The name, Schull or Skull, derives from a medieval monastic school, of which no trace remains. Located on the southwest coast of the Kilmore Peninsula, the village enjoys a scenic location, dominated by Mount Gabriel (407 m). It has a sheltered harbour, popular for recreational boating. The town's secondary school, Schull Community College, houses one of the only planetariums in Ireland along with a sailing school, and each year Schull harbour hosts the Fastnet International Schools Regatta.

SCHULL PLANETARIUM

An unexpected discovery in Schull is that of a planetarium attached to the local community college. Built in Schull by the late Herr Josef Menke, a German industrialist who had a keen interest in astronomy, it's a 70 seat planetarium with an eight metre dome and can project the night sky from anywhere in the northern hemisphere. The planetarium was opened by the then President of Ireland, Dr. Patrick Hillary in 1989 and today offers a different experience to visitors to this part of west Cork. Highly recommended.

BALLYDEHOB

The village of Ballydehob is dominated by the magnificent 12-arched railway viaduct that is now a walkway. The village is pretty and there is good fishing available from boats including several types of shark. There's also a monument to Ballydehob's most famous son, the world wrestling champion Danno O'Mahony, who famously wresled in Madison Square Gardens in the 1930s.

Cape Clear on Clear Island to the south of Kilmore Peninsula.

The Blue Flag Beach at Barley Cove.

Useful web addresses

BANTRY	www.bantry.ie
BANTRY HOUSE AND GARDEN	www.bantryhouse.com
THE SHEEP'S HEAD WAY	www.livingthesheepsheadway.com

AIR INDIA MEMORIAL
www.livingthesheepsheadway.com/air-india-disaster-memorial/

CARRIGANASS CASTLE	www.carriganasscastle.com

KEALKILL STONE CIRCLE
www.carriganasscastle.com/kealkill-stone-circle/

DURRUS	www.explorewestcork.ie/villages/durrus/
MIZEN HEAD	www.mizenhead.ie
BARLEYCOVE	www.schull.ie/where-to-go/barleycove/
CROOKHAVEN	www.crookhaven.ie

SKULL
www.discoveringcork.ie/cork/cork-towns/schull/

SKULL PLANETARIUM	www.westcorkweb.ie/planetarium/

BALLYDEHOB
www.explorewestcork.ie/villages/ballydehob/

Useful maps: Ordnance Survey Discovery Series Sheet 88
Fir Tree Series of Aerial Maps – The Beara Peninsula & South West Cork

The Rock of Cashel and the ancient buildings on it are one of the most impressive sites in Ireland.

CASHEL AND ITS SURROUNDINGS - CASHEL OF THE KINGS

If you're touring in Ireland then it's likely that the Rock of Cashel features on your itinerary. It's Ireland's most dramatic ancient site and the first glimpse of the buildings atop the Rock is sure to makes your senses tingle. Impressive as that first sight of the Rock of Cashel can be, up close its even more impressive and leaves a lasting impression on visitors. Given its importance I thought it would be worthwhile in the paragraphs that follow delving a little deeper detail into its history in the hope that a little knowledge will enhance your visit there.

But of course, Cashel is not the only place that cries out to be visited in this area. Especially, don't miss Cahir Castle, the unique Swiss Cottage nearby or the beautiful Glen of Aherlow. As always in Ireland, there's so much there just waiting to be discovered by you.

ROCK OF CASHEL

The Rock of Cashel was the traditional seat of the kings of Munster for several hundred years prior to the Norman invasion. The impressive complex on the Rock has a character all it's own and is one of the most remarkable collections of Celtic art and medieval architecture to be found anywhere in Europe. Only a few remnants of the early structures survive and the majority of the current buildings date from the 12th and 13th centuries. The oldest of the buildings is the well-preserved round tower (28 m high), built around 1100 AD. Its entrance is 3.7 m from the ground, and the tower was built

A carved coat-of-arms within the Rock of Cashel.

The oldest of the buildings at Cashel is the well-preserved Round Tower.

Regensburg, Dirmicius of Regensburg, sent two of his carpenters to help in the work and the twin towers on either side of the junction of the nave and chancel are strongly suggestive of their Germanic influence, as this feature is otherwise unknown in Ireland. Other notable features of the building include interior and exterior arcading, a barrel-vaulted roof, a carved tympanum over both doorways, the magnificent north doorway and chancel arch. In addition, the chapel contains one of the best-preserved Irish frescoes from this period.

The Cathedral, built between 1235 and 1270 AD, is built to a cruciform plan, with a central tower and terminating westwards in a massive residential castle. The Hall of the Vicars Choral was built in the

The town of Cashel is attractive and worthy of exploration in its own right.

using the dry stone method.

Cormac's Chapel, the chapel of King Cormac Mac Carthaigh, was begun in 1127 AD and consecrated in 1134 AD. It is a sophisticated and impressive structure, with vaulted ceilings and wide arches that draws on contemporary European architecture combined with uniquely Irish elements. The Irish Abbot of

15th century. In 1647 Cashel was sacked by English Parliamentarian troops under Murrough O'Brien, 1st Earl of Inchiquin. The Irish Confederate troops there were massacred, as were the Roman Catholic clergy. Inchiquin's troops also looted or destroyed many important religious artefacts. The entire plateau on which the buildings and graveyard lie is walled, and in the grounds around the buildings an

An aerial view of the Rock of Cashel that gives an idea of the complexity of the building.

The statue of Christ the King in the Glen of Aherlow.

extensive graveyard includes a number of high crosses

Queen Elizabeth II visited the Rock of Cashel during her visit to Ireland in 2011. Highly recommended.

.

CASHEL

Perhaps, overshadowed by the glories of the Rock of Cashal, the pretty town of Cashel adjacent to the monument is worthy of exploration. Cashel was once the seat of the Kings of Munster. The town lies in the center of Tipperary's fertile Golden Vale. There's a Heritage Centre and Tourist Information office, located on Main Street that includes a model of Cashel in the 1640's. The Centre also has a multi-media presentation in several languages, and the historic charters of Charles II (1663) and James II (1687) are on display there. You should also seek out the Georgian St. John's Cathedral, The Bolton library and The City Walls.

CAHIR

Once the stronghold of the powerful Butler family, the imposing Cahir Castle was built in 1142 AD by Conor O'Brien, Prince of Thomond, and retains its impressive keep, tower and much of its original

Cahir Castle, built in 1142 AD is one of the largest and best preserved castles in Ireland.

defensive structure. It is one of Ireland's largest and best-preserved castles and is situated on a rocky island on the River Suir. Within the castle there is an excellent audio-visual show about the castle and its history

In recent times the castle was used for a battle scene in John Borman's film Excalibur and also as a location for the ac-claimed television series The Tudors. Highly recommended.

SWISS COTTAGE
Just 2 km south of Cahir town off the R670 is Swiss Cottage, a delightful 'cottage orné' built in the early 1800s by Richard Butler, 1st Earl of Glengall to a design by the famous Regency architect John Nash. Its interior contains a graceful

Swiss Cottage, near Cahir, is a delightful 'cottage omé'.

The 'Vee' is a dramatic pass between Waterford and Tipperary with outstanding views of the surrounding counties.

spiral staircase and some elegantly decorated rooms. The wallpaper in the Salon was manufactured by the Dufour factory and is one of the first commercially produced Parisian wallpapers.

Different and unusual, a visit to Swiss Cottage is highly recommended.

GLEN OF AHERLOW

The Glen of Aherlow is a lush valley where the River Aherlow runs between the Galtee Mountains and the wooded ridge of Slievenamuck. Bounded by the rural villages of Bansha and Galbally, the Glen was historically an important pass between Limerick and Tipperary.

Within the Glen is the Statue of Christ the King. Erected in 1950, Christ the King, overlooks the valley at its most scenic viewpoint with hand raised in 'blessing the Glen and all who pass by', and attracts many visitors each year. The entrance to the Glen of Aherlow Nature Park is adjacent to Christ the King. The Nature Park is a series of loop walking trails, suitable for families, with information panels on the flora and fauna of the area and picnic tables.

Within the valley there are a variety of prehistoric and early Christian sites including St Pecaun's Holy Well, St Berrihert's Well and Kyle and St Sedna's Well in Clonbeg Churchyard.

FETHARD

The town of Fethard is remarkable for having been heavily fortified and completely surrounded by town walls as part of the policy of Edward I of establishing fortified market towns. The town walls rise to a height of 7.6 m and can still be seen today. Most of the circuit survives, making Fethard the most complete medieval circuit in Ireland. Knockelly Castle, a well-fortified tower house, is one of

The Glen of Aherlow is a lush valley between the Galtee Mountains and the wooded ridge of Slievenamuck.

many historical buildings in the area. Recommended.

THE VEE

'The Vee' is a V-shaped turn on the road leading to a gap in the Knockmealdown Mountains. The Vee itself is on the Sugar Loaf, but the pass from Tipperary to Waterford lies between Knockaunabulloga and the Sugar Loaf. What makes the Vee noteworthy and worth visiting are the breathtaking panoramic views visible from the pass. The pass rises to 610m above sea level above Bay Lough, and as it does so it gives wonderful views of a portion of the famous 'Golden Vale' between the Knockmealdown and Galtee Mountain Ranges. Recommended.

Geese pictured in the grounds of Cahir Castle.

Useful web addresses

ROCK OF CASHEL
www.heritageireland.ie/en/south-east/rockofcashel/

CASHEL TOWN   www.heritagetowns.com/cashel.shtml

CAHIR CASTLE   www.heritageireland.ie/en/south-east/cahircastle/

THE SWISS COTTAGE
http://www.heritageireland.ie/en/south-east/swisscottage/

GLEN OF AHERLOW   www.aherlow.com

FETHARD
www.discoverireland.ie/Activities-Adventure/fethard-historic-town-walk/85440

THE VEE   www.clogheen.net/see-do/the-vee/

Useful maps: Ordnance Survey Discovery Series Sheets 66 and 67.

Kinsale, the gourmet capital of Ireland, is one of the brightest jewels on the southern coast.

KINSALE AND THE CORK COAST - HISTORY AND GREAT BEACHES

KINSALE

Kinsale is a historic port and fishing town some 29 km south from Cork city, near to the Old Head of Kinsale. It's a very pretty town that wears its history well, full of narrow streets and with an unparalleled reputation for good food. Its a place that captivates visitors by its beautiful setting, with the long waterfront, narrow winding streets and Compass Hill rising sharply behind the town. There's a large yachting marina and its summer population is swelled by tourists and yacht enthusiasts. There's also a 'Gourmet Festival' and nearby Charles Fort in Summercove is a partially restored star fort built in 1677.

The Old Head of Kinsale was the site of some of the earliest settlements in Ireland, and a number of Christian settlements were later established in the countryside surrounding the site of the present town. The old fortifications of Charles Fort and James Fort guard the narrow entrance to Kinsale from the sea. The town also has poignant memories of the sinking of the liner *'Lusitania'* in 1915, off the Old Head of Kinsale, and it was in the courthouse in the town that the inquest into the tragedy took place.

The star-shaped military fortress called Charles Fort, was constructed between 1677 and 1682, during the reign of King Charles II, to protect the strategically important town and harbour of Kinsale. William Robinson, who was also the architect of the magnificent Royal Hospital in Kilmainham, Dublin, and Superintendent of Fortifications, was the designer of the fort. One of the largest military forts in

Explore Kinsale's charming ancient and narrow streets.

Ireland, Charles Fort has been associated with several of the most momentous events in Irish history, including the Williamite War in 1690 and the Irish Civil War of 1922 - 23. After the establishment of the Irish Free State, Charles Fort remained garrisoned by the British army until 1922. Highly recommended.

Directly across the harbour and opposite Charles Fort, is James Fort. The commanding position of both forts superbly guard Kinsale's small harbour. James Fort was built in 1607 and was captured in 1690 by Williamite forces. The fort is a most interesting example of 17th century military architecture and offers wonderful views of the town, river, and across the harbour to Charles Fort. Recommended.

Another interesting building is the Court-

function having been that of a market house. The elegant facade was added in 1703 and is very clearly Northern European in style. The museum houses a large number of local artifacts relating to Kinsale's maritime past as well as from the Battle of Kinsale and the famous Kinsale Giant. Recommended.

Very close to the regional Museum is St Multose Church. St Multose founded a monastery here in the 6th century AD and this church is named for him. Built in 1190 AD, it is the oldest building in Kinsale. It is an interesting example of Norman architecture and has remained in continuous use to the present day with but minor alterations. It was in this church that Prince Rupert was proclaimed King Charles II upon hearing the news that King Charles I had been executed in London.

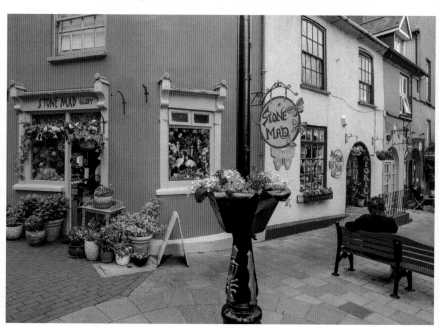

Kinsale's streets are colourful and filled with interesting shops to linger over.

house and Regional Museum which was built about 1600. The courthouse was used for the inquest into the sinking of the liner *Lusitania* in 1915. The main structure of this building dates back as far as the 1590's, town records showing its primary

Prince Rupert's fleet was at anchor in Kinsale harbour at the time. Recommended.

Kinsale is somewhere to linger, explore its ancient narrow streets, eat in its excellent restaurants, learn its fascinating history

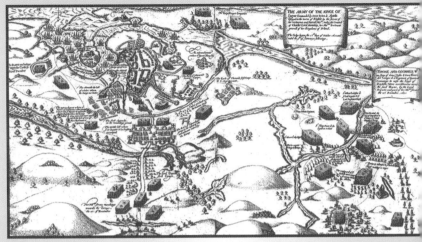

A map of the siege and Battle of Kinsale in 1601.

THE BATTLE OF KINSALE

The Battle of Kinsale was one of the most important battles fought in Irish history. It was fought on Christmas Eve morning 1601, in the small port of Kinsale on the southern coast of Ireland. Two of the most important Gaelic leaders in Ulster, Hugh O'Neill and Hugh Roe O'Donnell, led the Irish side, while facing them was the Lord Deputy Mountjoy, and his English Army.

O'Neill had previously persuaded the Spanish King, Phillip III, to send 6,000 soldiers to help the Irish cause, but only 4,000 Spanish soldiers actually made it to Kinsale. A siege of the port was mounted by the English forces for over two months, until O'Neill arrived with his army in mid-November. O'Neill's army had walked over 300 miles in freezing weather conditions, and by the time they reached Kinsale, they were in no condition to fight.

Due to a lack of communication between the Irish and Spanish forces, the Spanish Army retreated when they should have been charging towards the enemy. As a result the Irish were outnumbered and the Spanish surrendered. On the Irish side some 1,200 fell in the Battle of Kinsale and almost 800 were wounded, of whom many died later. Devastating also to the Irish cause was the great loss of weaponry in the battle. O'Neill and his army were forced to retreat back to Ulster but only a few years later, he and other clan leaders left Ireland forever in what came to be called 'The Flight of the Earls' in 1607. Spain, who had been at war with England since 1585, signed a peace treaty with England after Kinsale, thus ending any lingering hope the Irish might have had of help from there. By then, largely as a result of the defeat at the Battle of Kinsale, the whole of Ireland was under English rule for the first time.

Chairs for sale on a shop front in Clonakilty.

and relax. This town, the gourmet capital of Ireland, is one of the brightest jewels on Ireland's coastline, and will be one of your best memories of Ireland.

CLONAKILTY

Clonakilty is a pretty town in the very heartland of West Cork. It's pedestrian-friendly streets, cobbled paving and leafy trees are joined by colourful and carefully maintained traditional shop, restaurants and pub facades and during the summer

months there are colourful displays of flowers at every turn. Close by is spectacular scenery and some excellent Blue Flag beaches and a number of interesting attractions including the West Cork Model Railway Village and the Michael Collins House in Emmet Square where 'The Big Fellow', Clonakilty's most famous son, spent his youth.

SKIBBEREEN

Skibbereen is one of West Cork's most picturesque towns, and has a fine Heritage Centre located in the award winning, beautifully restored, Old Gasworks Building. The main exhibition in the Heritage Centre commemorates the tragic events in the 1840s that are known in Irish History as the Great Hunger. Skibbereen, along with many areas of the west, was very badly affected and lost up to a third of its population to hunger, disease and emigration.
The Lough Hyne Visitor Centre is another attraction worth visiting and explores the unique nature of this salt-water marine lake that is Ireland's first Marine Nature Reserve.

COURTMACSHERRY

Courtmacsherry is primarily a seaside village and has a variety of safe and sheltered sailing areas. Its also an important

The statue of Clonakilty's most famous son, Michael Collins, at Emmet Square.

RNLI Lifeboat station where the fastest lifeboat vessels are stationed. The first lifeboat station was established here as long ago as 1825 – one of the first in Ireland. When word reached Courtmacsherry of the sinking of the *Lusitania*, the RNLI Lifeboat *Kweiza Gwilt* put to sea and its crew rowed for three hours to the scene of the sinking some eighteen kilometres off the Old Head of Kinsale only to find bodies rather than survivours in the water.

BALTIMORE

The fishing village of Baltimore serves the nearby islands of Cape Clear, Sherkin and Heir, all reacable by ferry from its pier. Baltimore's history is dominated by the sea and in 1631 an event occurred there – known as the Sack of Baltimore - that was unique in Irish history, when the entire population of the town was carried off by pirates. The fort of *Dún na Séad* (Fort of the Jewels) was also sacked by sea-borne raiders more than once in its history.

Surfing at Garretstown Beach, Kinsale.

TIMOLEAGUE

Timoleague is yet another picturesque village, perched on the edge of a long sea inlet and dominated by the ruins of a 13th century abbey. Founded by the Francisicans in 1240 AD on the site of a 6th century monastic settlement founded by St. Molaga, from whom the town derives its name, being the Irish for 'House of Mologa' or *Tigh Molaga*.

ROSSCARBERY

Dominated by the historic St. Fachtma's Cathedral, Rosscarbery is built around an attractive central square. The town is busy in summertime when the nearby beaches of Owenahincha and The Warren are very popular with holidaymakers.

The imposing Cork and Ross Church, Clonakilty.

bookstór

New & Vintage Books

Somewhere to linger... a bookshop in Kinsale.

Near Rosscarbery is the delightful Owenahincha Beach.

Inchydoney Beach on the Haven Coast near Clonakilty.

Useful web addresses

KINSALE	www.visitcorkcounty.com/place/kinsale/
KINSALE RESTAURANTS	www.kinsalerestaurants.com

CHARLES FORT, KINSALE
www.discoverireland.ie/Arts-Culture-Heritage/charles-fort/370

JAMES FORT, KINSALE
www.discoverireland.ie/Arts-Culture-Heritage/james-fort-kinsale/49739

REGIONAL MUSEUM, KINSALE
www.kinsale.ie/2010/06/11/regional-museum/

ST. MULTOSE CHURCH, KINSALE
www.discoveringcork.ie/st-multose-church/

CLONAKILTY	www.clonakilty.ieInch
INCHYDONEY ISLAND LODGE & SPA	www.inchydoneyisland.com
COURTMACSHERRY HOTEL	www.courtmacsherryhotel.ie

MICHAEL COLLINS HOUSE, CLONAKILTY
www.michaelcollinshouse.ie

SKIBBEREEN HERITAGE CENTRE	www.skibberitage.com

Maps: Ordnance Survey discovery Series Sheet 86, 87 and 89

Traditional boats sailing at the Baltimore Wooden Boats Festival.

The English Market is a 'must-see' on any visit to Cork City.

The centre of Cork city is dominated by the River Lee.

IN AND AROUND CORK - THE REBEL COUNTY

Cork City is located in the province of Munster, and is the second largest city in the Irish Republic and the third most populous on the island of Ireland. In 2005, the city was selected as the European Capital of Culture.

The city is situated along the River Lee that splits into two channels at the western end of the city; the city centre is divided by these channels, making the geography of the city somewhat confusing to visitors. The channels re-converge at the eastern end where the quays and docks along the river banks lead towards Lough Mahon and Cork Harbour, one of the world's largest natural harbours. The city's nick-name of 'the rebel city' originates, not in the Irish Civil War as many believe, but in its support for the Yorkist cause during the English 15th century War of the Roses. Corkonians, as the natives of the city are called, often refer to the city as 'the real capital' in reference to its role as the centre of anti-treaty forces during the Irish Civil War.

Cork is a special place to visit. The friendly nature of Cork people is a delight as is their helpfulness to visitors. They are justifiably proud of their city and maintain a friendly rivalry with Dubliners regarding the relative merits of the two cities. In truth, the two cities are chalk and cheese.

Cork retains a human scale and has much that is unique to it. There is plenty to do and see and the history of the cities attractions is different to other locations in Ireland.

In addition there are the satellite towns of Cork which themselves have much to offer, in particular the harbour town of Cobh on Little Island with its many links with the sea and with the doomed maiden voyage of the RMS Titanic. Take the time to explore Cork and its surroundings properly – it will reward you with many pleasures along the way.

THE ENGLISH MARKET

There are many surprises to be found in Cork and one of the very best is the English Market . Located just off Grand Partade, the English Market is a covered market and is a Victorian wonderland of local food produce and food items imported from all over the world. The origins of the market can be traced back to King James I in the year 1610, and the market has been supplying the city of Cork since 1788. In 1980 a diastrous fire destroyed it and Cork Corporation refurbished it to an award-winning design by the Cork city architect TF MacNamara. As well as the stallholders selling food of all kinds, there are restaurants and cafés to enjoy.

people such as Crubeens (pigs' feet) and Tripe and Drisheen. The main entrance to the English Market is from Grand Parade but there are also entrances from Princes Street, New Market Lane or the wonderfully named Mutton Lane. The English Market is open from 8.00 am to 6.00 pm from Monday to Saturday and a visit is very highly recommended.

SHANDON BELLS AND TOWER

Without a doubt the most iconic symbol of Cork City is Shandon Bells and the Tower at St. Anne's Church. As they say, it's easy to find, just'look for the gold fish in the sky', a reference to the weather-vane atop the tower high above the surrounding buildings. It's also very unusual in that the north and east facings of the tower are finished in red sandstone while the south and west facings are in white ashlar limestone. This red and white effect is said to be from where the sporting colours of Cork are derived.

The tower of St. Anne's Church at Shandon is an iconic symbol of Cork.

This is one of the world's great food markets and no other market in Ireland or Britain comes close. As well as all the more usual foods you'll also find several of the foods that are favourites of Cork

St. Anne's Church is one of the oldest churches in the city having been built in 1722. In it you can climb 132 steps to gain a spectacular view over the city in every direction. (The tower is 36.65m/120ft high). Along the way you can view the internal workings of the famous clocks, the 'Four Faced Liar'

One of the most memorable aspects of Her Majesty Queen Elizabeth's Irish visit was her tour of the English Market.

and also the 18th century bells in the belfry whose sound is so famous. The bells weigh a total over six tonnes and were first cast by Abel Rudhall of Gloucester in 1750. They bear two inscriptions:

'When us you ring we'll sweetly sing'

and

'Since generosity has opened our mouths our tongues shall sing aloud its praise'.

Incidiently, the four sided clocks gained their name 'The Four Faced Liar' when true to Cork wit, locals noticed that they rarely all showed the same time. Recommended.

ELIZABETH FORT

Elizabeth Fort is located on Barrack Street on the south side of the city. Only recently opened as a visitor attraction, Elizabeth Fort was originally built as a fortress in 1601 during the reign of Elizabeth I on high ground outside the city. walls. The original fortress was built of timber and earth and was twice demolished before the basic structure of the current fort was built between 1624 and 1626 and in works under Cromwell in 1649.

In subsequent years its importance as a defensive structure declined and it be-

The Cork Jazz Festival attracts world-class performers from all over the world - in this case the great Jimmy Scott.

came a barracks. In 1817, it was turned into a prison and was used to hold prisoners awaiting deportation. In the late 19th century it was returned to military use once more and during the Irish War of Independence it was used as a base by the infamous 'Black and Tans'. During the succeeding Irish Civil War the fort was burned by anti-treaty forces in August 1922.

Rebuilt, the fort became a Garda station in the 1920s and continued in this role until 2013. In 2014 it was refurbished and opened to the public. It's a fascinating place with a colourful history and is well worth a visit. There are superb views over the city and a visit is recommended.

Street art abounds in Cork City, like this striking example.

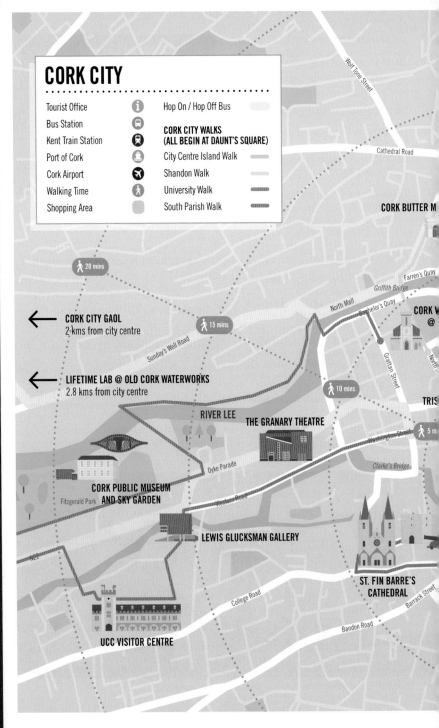

CORK CITY

Tourist Office	🛈	Hop On / Hop Off Bus	
Bus Station	🚌	**CORK CITY WALKS**	
Kent Train Station	🚆	**(ALL BEGIN AT DAUNT'S SQUARE)**	
Port of Cork	⚓	City Centre Island Walk	
Cork Airport	✈	Shandon Walk	
Walking Time	🚶	University Walk	
Shopping Area		South Parish Walk	

Wolf Tone Street

Cathedral Road

CORK BUTTER M

Farren's Quay

Griffith Bridge

North Mall

Bachelor's Quay

CORK W @

🚶 20 mins

← **CORK CITY GAOL**
2 kms from city centre

🚶 15 mins

Sunday's Well Road

Gratton Street

North

← **LIFETIME LAB @ OLD CORK WATERWORKS**
2.8 kms from city centre

🚶 10 mins

TRIS

RIVER LEE

THE GRANARY THEATRE

Washington Street

🚶 5 m

Clarke's Bridge

Dyke Parade

**CORK PUBLIC MUSEUM
AND SKY GARDEN**

Fitzgerald Park

Western Road

LEWIS GLUCKSMAN GALLERY

N22

N71

**ST. FIN BARRE'S
CATHEDRAL**

Barrack Street

College Road

UCC VISITOR CENTRE

Bandon Road

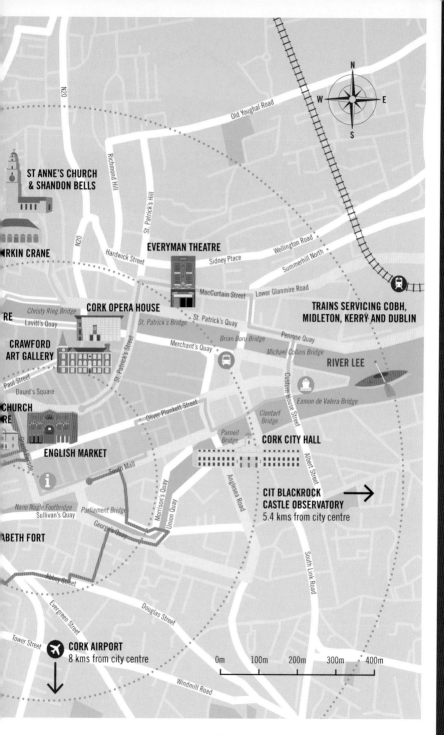

ST ANNE'S CHURCH & SHANDON BELLS

RKIN CRANE

EVERYMAN THEATRE

Richmond Hill

St. Patrick's Hill

N20

Hardwick Street

Sidney Place

Wellington Road

Summerhill North

MacCurtain Street

Lower Glanmire Road

Old Youghal Road

TRAINS SERVICING COBH, MIDLETON, KERRY AND DUBLIN

CORK OPERA HOUSE

Christy Ring Bridge

Lavitt's Quay

St. Patrick's Quay

St. Patrick's Bridge

St. Patrick's Street

Merchant's Quay

Brian Boru Bridge

Penrose Quay

Michael Collins Bridge

RIVER LEE

CRAWFORD ART GALLERY

Paul Street

Daunt's Square

CHURCH RE

ENGLISH MARKET

Oliver Plunkett Street

Custom House Street

Eamon de Valera Bridge

Clontarf Bridge

Parnell Bridge

CORK CITY HALL

Albert Street

South Mall

Morrison's Quay

Union Quay

Anglesea Road

CIT BLACKROCK CASTLE OBSERVATORY
5.4 kms from city centre

Nano Nagle Footbridge
Sullivan's Quay

Parliament Bridge

Georges Quay

ABETH FORT

Abbey Street

Evergreen Street

Douglas Street

South Link Road

Tower Street

CORK AIRPORT
8 kms from city centre

Windmill Road

0m   100m   200m   300m   400m

Greenm Parade

N20

Smith-Barry, about to test a captured German Albatros V at Gosport in 1917.

Robert Smith-Barry

Smith-Barry – the Man who taught the World to Fly

Robert Smith-Barry was born in 1886 and was directly descended from the fourth Earl of Barrymore of County Cork. He grew up on the Fota Estate and after a somewhat 'difficult' education he started to take flying lessons at Larkhill, the birthplace of the Royal Flying Corps (RFC), in 1911. Smith-Barry made rapid progress and flew solo for the first time on October 14th 1911.

With the outbreak of World War I Smith-Barry went to France but was severly injured in a flying accident in which his passenger was killed. After a spell as an instructor in Norfolk he returned to France and took part in the Battle of the Somme. Smith-Barry quickly rose to be squadron commander even if, as someone put it half-admiringly, 'he dosesn't care a damn for anyone'. That may have been so, but Smith-barry had become very concerned at what he considered the low standards of RFC training. In November 1916 he wrote a paper suggesting that training aircraft should have dual controls togather with a whole host of other far-sighted proposals. Hugh Trenchard, the head of the RFC, appointed Smith-Barry to command of No 1 Training Squadron at Gosport giving him a free hand to implement his ideas.

At Gosport, Smith-Barry introduced a systemized form of flying training, revolutionizing the training of RFC pilots. In time his methods were adopted by air forces and flying schools around the world and still form the basis of pilot training today. After the war, Smith-Barry standardized flight training across the Commonwealth before resigning in 1943 because of difficulties arising from his leg injury in the First World War. In 1949 he underwent an operation on his leg but failed to recover and died after suffering a relapse. Smith-Barry's copntribution to aviation was enormous, touching all those who fly, even those starting their flight training today.

CORK CITY GAOL

Cork City Gaol at Sunday's Well was built to replace the old gaol at Northgate Bridge in the heart of the city. It opened in 1824 and closed in 1923. On its opening

Fota Island Wildlife Park is a wonderland for young and old visitors alike.

it was praised as being 'the finest in the three kingdoms'. Perhaps the most famous of its prisoners was Countess Constance Markievicz, the first woman to be elected to the British Parliament in 1918 and later Minister for Labour in the first Dail in 1919.

The top floor of the Governors house was used as a radio broadcasting station (6CK) by the national radio station - Radio Eireann (now RTE) from 1927 until the 1950's. From 1923 to 1993, apart from the foregoing, and some storage use of the exterior ground by the Department of Posts & Telegraphs, the Cork City Gaol complex was allowed to become totally derelict until its innovative restoration and reopening to the public as a visitor attraction in 1993. Recommended.

FOTA ISLAND

Fota Island was originally the home of the Smith-Barry family for nearly 800 years before the sale of the estate to University College Cork in 1975. Fota House is now managed by the Irish Heritage Trust while the gardens and arboretum are cared for by the Trust and the Office of Public Works. The Wildlife Park came about from a suggestion made by Dr. Terry Murphy, the then Director of Dublin Zoo, that a Wildlife Park be established somewhere in Ireland. Eventually it was decided to base the new project at Fota Island and work began on the site in 1980, with the Park opening to the public in Summer 1983. Today some 450,000 visitors enjoy the Wildlife Park each year making it the biggest visitor attaction outside Leinster.

The Wildlife Park is a great experience imaginatively laid-out and is a wonderful place to bring young people to teach them about the animal world. Guided tours are available and if you've a little more time available to spend, why not take one of the special behind the scenes experience tours and let the wardens share their passion for animals with you. You'll feel your own love for animals grow along with your understanding of the human/animal connection. Spending a day participating in the care and feeding of some of the world's most endangered animals is an experience you'll long remember. Highly recommended.

BLACKROCK CASTLE OBSERVATORY

Blackrock Castle is a castellated fortification located at Blackrock, about 2 km from the centre of Cork city on the banks of the River Lee. Originally developed as a coastal defence fortification in the 16th century to protect upper Cork Harbour and port, the site now houses an observatory, visitor centre and restaurant.

I really cannot recommend a visit highly enough – Blackrock Castle Observatory provides a number of award winning exhibitions that explain the Universe, the Cosmos and life in Outer Space. There are also castle tours and other attractions changing from time to time. All in all a great place to bring any young person with even the slightest curiosity about the Universe in which we live and very highly recommended.

BLARNEY CASTLE

A Medieval fortress built on the River Martin, Blarney Castle is one of Ireland's oldest visitor attractions. The current building is the third to stand on the site, the first building – a wooden structure - having been erected in the tenth century. Sometime around 1210 AD this was replaced by a stone structure with its entrance some twenty feet above ground level. Eventually this building was demolished and its foundations used for foundations for the structure you see today. This fortress was built by Dermot Mc-Carthy, King of Munster in 1446 AD and today the castle you see is the keep of a much larger structure, now all but gone.

McCarthy supplied 4,000 soilders from Munster to join the forces of Robert the Bruce at the Battle of Bannockburn in 1314. In recognition for his support, Robert gave to McCarthy half of the Stone of Scone and it is this stone that is incorporated into the battlements of the castle, where visitors kiss it in the expectation of 'receiving the gift of Blarney'.

Personally, not having any liking for heights, I find the climb to the Blarney Stone difficult and not at all to my liking, although no doubt, giving the volume of visitors each year, I am most certainly in the minority.

The castle, however, is impressive and the castle gardens would be worth travelling to see even if the castle were not there. Recommended with the reservation that

Blarney Castle and Gardens is one of the longest established and most famous visitor attractions in Ireland.

Cobh is dominated by the Cathedral of St. Colman's overlooking the town.

COBH

Cobh is the jewel in Cork's crown. One of the finest natural harbours in the world, the tiny fishing village of Cove on the south side of Little Island was virtually unknown up until the early 1800s. During the French Revolutionary and Napoleonic Wars between 1792 and 1815, Cork harbour became a vital refuelling and assembly point for naval and commercial ships. It was said that at any one time there could be up to three hundred ships seen at anchor off Cove.

By the time of Queen Victoria's visit to Cove in 1849, the village had grown into a busy town. Victoria renamed the town Queenstown and it became an important stop-over on the trans-atlantic routes. Irish emigrants sailed from here to America while convicts were transported to the penal colonies in Australia. When the early transatlantic steamers began to ply their trade, Queenstown was their point-of-departure from Europe. Indeed, between 1848 and 1950 over six million adults and children emigrated from Ireland with some 2.5 million departing from Queenstown. When Ireland gained its in-

dependence from Britain the name of the town was changed back to a gaelic version of Cove, hence the name of Cobh today.

There's much to see and do in Cobh. The town is built on a hill and its skyline is dominated by the imposing St. Colman's Cathedral. Today, the town is best known for its associations with two great ships and their tragic fates. The first of these, of course, is the RMS Titanic. Queenstown was the final port of call for Titanic on its maiden voyage before she set out to cross the Atlantic. Some 123 passengers boarded the ship at Queenstown and only 44 of them survived the sinking.

Today their story, and that of Titanic, is told at the Titanic Experience, a permanent visitor attraction situated in the original White Star Ticket Office in the heart of Cobh. I found the Titanic Experience to be excellent, made all the more so by very friendly staff and by the more personal nature of it compared to the Titanic Belfast. There are a number of very clever touches about how you discover the story that are brilliant. The Titanic Experience has my highest possible recommendation. Not to be missed.

The Titanic Experience in Cobh is outstanding and tells the story of the 123 passangers who boarded the ill-fated liner at Cobh.

The other ship associated with Cobh is the Lusitania. The tragic sinking of the Lusitania on 7th May 1915 off the Old Head of Kinsale claimed the lives of 1,198 people while 700 were rescued. The bodies of over 100 of those who died are buried in the Old Church Cemetery just north of the town, and the Luisatinia Peace Memorial is located in Casement Square.

Incidiently, it's a little known fact that during World War I the United States Navy established the Queenstown Naval Air Station from where they operated flying boads along with a sister station at Ferrybank, Wexford.

Memorabilia of the White Star Line who operated the RMS Titanic is to be seen thorough out Cobh.

You can view the world's biggest copper pot still at the Jameson Distillery at Midleton.

MIDLETON

Finally, I want to make mention of the Jameson Distillery at Midleton. In 1975 Jameson moved from its original home on Bow Street, Dublin, to Midleton. Its possible to tour the buildings of the Old Midleton Distillery which date from 1825, and to view the original klins, grainstores, maturation warehouses and the stillhouse – home to the world's largest copper pot still.

The memorial to the victims of the Lusitania in Cobh.

Useful web addresses

THE ENGLISH MARKET	www.englishmarket.ie
SHANDON BELLS & TOWER	www.shandonbells.ie
ELIZABETH FORT	www.elizabethfort.ie
CORK CITY GAOL	www.corkcitygaol.com
FOTA WILDLIFE PARK	www.fotawildlife.ie
BLARNEY CASTLE AND GARDENS	www.blarneycastle.ie
THE QUEENSTOWN STORY	www.cobhheritage.com
TITANIC EXPERIENCE	www.titanicexperiencecobh.ie
LUSITANIA	www.oldheadofkinsale.com
	www.www.lusitaniacentenary.com
	www.cobhmuseum.com
JAMESON	www.jamesonwhiskey.com

INDEX

A page number in **_bold italic_** type indicates a photograph.

ACKNOWLEDGEMENTS

BOB MONTGOMERY: Front cover; page 2 & 3; 11; 16; 18; 30 top; 32 bottom; 35 bottom; 51 top & middle; 52 bottom; 54 middle; 55 top & middle; 73; 75 bottom; 76 bottom; 79, 80; 81; 82 top & bottom; 83 top and middle; 85, 86; 87; 90; 100; 101; 109 top; 115; 121 middle; 125; 134 top; 138 bottom; 140 bottom; 144 bottom; 146 bottom; 155 top & bottom; 156 top; 158; 159; 166 top & bottom; 175; 186; 187; 188; 190; 191; 203; 215; 217 top; 218 top; 221 top; 232 top; 233 all; 234; 241 top; 243 top & bottom; 248; 249 all; 265 all; 265; 266 bottom; 268; 270 all; 272 top; 273; 276 bottom; 278; 279; 281; 289; 291; 292; 293; 294 all; 295 all; 296; 297; 299; 300; 301 all; 306; 308 top; 311; 314 top; 315 bottom; 319 bottom; 320 top; 321; 322 bottom; 323; 324; 325; 345 top left.

A special thanks to Failte Ireland and the Northern Ireland Tourist Board who provide such a valuable photographic resource to those seeking to bring visitors to this beautiful island.

TOURISM IRELAND: 1; 12; 13; 14; 21; 22 all; 23 bottom; 24 bottom; 25; 26; 27; 28; 29 all; 30 bottom; 31; 32 top; 33 top; 34 all; 35 top; 36 all; 37; 38 top; 40 all; 41; 42 all; 44 all; 46 all; 47; 48 bottom; 49; 50 all; 57; 58; 59; 60; 61 all; 64 all; 65; 66; 67 all; 69; 70; 71; 74 all; 75 top; 76 top; 77 all; 88; 89; 92; 93 all; 94 all; 95; 96 all; 97; 98 all; 99 all; 100 top; 102; 103 all; 104 all; 105 all; 106; 107 all; 108; 109 bottom; 110; 111; 112; 113 all; 114 all; 117 all; 118; 119 all; 120 all; 122; 123 all; 124; 126; 127 all; 128; 129; 130; 131; 132 all; 133 bottom; 134 bottom; 135 all; 136; 137 all; 138 top; 139; 140 top; 141; 144 top; 146 top; 147; 148 all; 149; 150; 151 all; 152; 153; 154; 156 bottom; 157; 188; 189; 204/205 all; 206 all; 207 all; 208/209 all; 210; 211 all; 212; 213; 214; 216; 217 bottom; 218 bottom; 219; 220 all; 221 bottom; 222; 223; 224; 225; 226 all; 227; 228; 229; 230 all; 231 all; 232 bottom; 235; 236 all; 237 all; 238; 240; 241 bottom; 243 middle; 244; 245; 246 all; 247 top; 250; 251; 252; 253; 254 all; 255 all; 256/257 all; 258 all; 259 all; 261; 262; 263; 264 all; 265; 266 all; 270 top271 bottom; 272 bottom; 275; 276 all; 277; 280; 282 all; 283 all; 284; 286 all; 287; 289 top; 290; 292 top; 299 top; 302; 303; 304/305 all; 307; 308 all; 309; 310; 312; 313 all; 314 bottom; 315 top; 316; 317; 318; 319 top; 320 bottom; 321 top; 322 top; 326 all; 327; 329 all; 330; 331; 332; 333; 335; 334; 336 all; 337 all; 338/339; 341; 342; 343; 344 all; 345 top right,; OBC all.

TOURISM NI: 23 TOP; 24 top; 38 bottom; 39; 45; 160; 161; 162 all; 163; 164; 165; 167; 169; 170; 171; 172; 173; 174; 175 top; 176; 177; 178; 179; 180; 181 all; 183; 184 all; 185; 192; 193 all; 194; 195 all; 196; 197 all; 199 all; 200;

AER CORPS: 33; 133 top; 269; 285;

ANDREW POLLOCK: 52 middle

RAYMOND WALLS: 52 top left & right

AUTHOR'S COLLECTION: 8; 9; 51 bottom; 38 top; 54 bottom; 72; 141;143 top & bottom; 84 bottom; 201; 239; 247 bottom; 288; 340;

RIAC : 51 top left; 54 top; 68; 121; 142,

OPW: 48 top; 91;

VINCENT KILLOWREY: 198; 280 bottom.

ROBERT MONTGOMERY: 4

DELPHI RESORT: 242 all

The advertisers who have supported this first edition of DRIVE IRELAND.

Finally, a special thanks to Alan Pepper for his unfailing patience and committement during the design and make-up of DRIVE IRELAND.